COOKBOOK

NORRLANDs BAR & GRILL

MAT/food
JOHAN AHLSTEDT
NICLAS RYHNELL
SEVERIN SJÖSTEDT

FOTO/photo
PELLE BERGSTRÖM

STYLIST/style
MIKAEL BECKMAN

TEXTER/texts
ANNICA TRIBERG

KULNARISKA KOMMENTARER/culinary comments
BJÖRN HALLING

RECEPT/recipes
ANETTE DIENG

ÖVERSÄTTNING/translation
ELAINE LEMM

DRYCKER/beverages
ANDERS JANSSON

DRINKAR/drinks
NICLAES WALLMARK

GRAFISK FORM/graphic design
JENNY SJÖSTEDT

TRYCKT HOS/printed at
FÄLTH & HÄSSLER I VÄRNAMO 2000

UTGIVEN AV/published by
WAHLSTRÖM & WIDSTRAND

ISBN 91-46-18182-2

COOKBOOK

NORRLANDs BAR & GRILL

TRE ENKLA MÄN SOM
GÖR NÅGOT VI TYCKER ÄR BRA

Att den som gjort en resa ofta har mycket att berätta
är en gammal sanning. Och att skriva ner minnen
från sin resa blir då ett sätt att bevara något som är
förgängligt. Redan när du kommer hem är ju allt över.

Det vi gör på Norrlands Bar & Grill är förgängligt
på precis samma sätt som en resa. I samma sekund
du lämnar lokalen är vår prestation borta, uppäten.
Kvar är i bästa fall minnet av en god måltid.

Vissa kolleger brukar kalla matlagning den mest
förgängliga konstarten. Konst eller inte, att göra en
kokbok är i alla fall ett sätt för oss att få maten att
bestå lite längre. Medan andra kanske skulle välja
att skriva en mer neutral bok med längre hållbarhet
har vi medvetet valt att i stället göra ett tidsdoku-
ment. Precis den här maten lagar vi just nu, när det
nya årtusendet sakta börjar ta form.

Hade boken givits ut för några år sedan skulle
den troligen ha sett helt annorlunda ut, och om det
blir en uppföljare i framtiden hoppas vi att den ska
skilja sig från den här.

En av de värsta fallgroparna för en restaurang är
nämligen att bli statisk, att inte tillåta förändringar,

att inte våga – eller orka – vara nyfiken. Det är inte så många år sedan den nerkokta grädden var en trygg kamrat att luta sig mot. Nu är den till stor del utbytt mot betydligt modernare mixade buljonger som talar tidens språk. Fett är en smakförhöjare, inget man baserar en hel rätt på.

Ett annat belysande exempel är olivoljan. Alla kockar med några år i kockmössan kommer säkert ihåg plåtdunken med olja som stod på golvet i köket. Skulle det vara olja tog man en skvätt av den. Hur den smakade? Ja, vem vill minnas ... I dag har vi ett enormt utbud av oljor, inte minst olivoljor, och vi väljer med omsorg vilken sort vi vill ha. Likaså har vi fått helt nya smakkombinationer. Vi tänker i fett kontra syra, i sött kontra surt och så vidare. Men inte bara vår smak har förfinats, även råvarorna har blivit bättre. Där vi förr trånade över andra länders utbud, kan vi i dag konstatera att även Sverige ligger långt framme.

Att vara nyfiken är förstås inte detsamma som att vara dumdristig. Vår trygghet ligger i den fransk-italiensk-svenska matlagning som vi har gjort till vår bas. Den är en stabil grund att stå på, jämförd med de ganska bräckliga fundament många unga köks-chefer bygger höga hus på.

Vi kallar det gärna «gastronomisk mogenhet». Det betyder att vi naturligtvis tillåter oss att pröva den ena galna idén efter den andra, men att detta sker i köket, aldrig på matsedeln. Gästen ska inte behöva vara försökskanin när vi testar nya infall. Gästen betalar dyrt för vår kunskap, dumdristigheterna måste vara bortsållade långt innan tallriken går ut i matsalen.

Men även om vi vill undvika gastronomiska kullerbyttor, så tillåter vi oss gärna en och annan väl inövad frivolt då och då – allt för att hålla både vårt och gästens intresse vid liv.

När vi öppnade den 5 september 1995 lovade vi oss att aldrig stanna upp. Därför reser vi mycket för att söka inspiration. Paris, London och New York besöker vi flitigt, men av olika skäl. Är London en stor matstad eller bara bra på kroginredning? Har Paris somnat in eller finns alltjämt den bästa maten här? Är New York förtrollande fantastiskt eller bara stort och stökigt? Vi reser och diskuterar. Ofta slutar det med att vi går ut i köket och testar än det ena än det andra.

Om Italien är vi däremot ganska överens: det är ett matland som kanske inte leder den gastronomiska utvecklingen just nu, men dit man alltid kan åka för att luta sig tillbaka, hitta lugnet och tryggheten och finna att här är alla smakerna bevarade precis som vi minns dem.

Några av alla våra funderingar hoppas vi ska genomsyra denna bok, från bilder till recept. Somligt är enkelt att laga, annat kräver både kunskap och tid. Men en sak är gemensam: Det är rätter att minnas. Rätter som förtjänar om inte ett evigt liv, så i alla fall att bli ihågkomna en liten stund.

Med många hälsningar från tre män som gör något vi tycker är bra.

Severin Sjöstedt, Johan Ahlstedt och Niclas Ryhnell

THREE PLAIN MEN
DOING SOMETHING WE LIKE

Travel, they say, broadens the mind, but you'd better put everything down on paper when you get back home, or after a time it'll all be forgotten.

What we do at Norrlands Bar & Grill is as transient as any journey. So writing a cook book is for us a way of making the food keep a bit longer. We have deliberately made it a document of our time. This is exactly the food we are preparing right now, as the new millennium slowly takes shape.

If ever there is a sequel, we hope it will be something different.

Because one of the worst pitfalls a restaurant can tumble into is getting into a rut, avoiding change and losing the spirit of experiment and inquiry. Now of course, being experimental in the kitchen does not mean being foolhardy. Our security lies in the French-Italian-Swedish cooking on which we have based things. This is a firm foundation to build on. We like to call it «gastronomic maturity», which to us means: by all means take chances, but in the kitchen – not on the menu.

When we opened on 5th September 1995, we

promised ourselves never to stand still. Paris, London and New York are frequent ports of call. And we all agree about Italy as the place you can return to for that laid-back experience of tranquility and security, with all the flavours preserved exactly as we remember them.

We hope that some of our thinking will permeate this book. Some of the recipes are easy, others demand both time and knowledge. But they all have one thing in common: memorability. If they don't quite qualify for eternal life, they do at least deserve to be remembered for a little while.

Here they come, then, with best wishes from three plain men doing something we like.

Severin Sjöstedt, Johan Ahlstedt and Niclas Ryhnell

INNEHÅLL/contents

KALLA

cold

TONFISKTATAKI
tuna tataki

TONFISKTATAKI

Bryn tonfiskbiten hastigt i lite av olivoljan i en het
panna. Ta upp tonfisken ur pannan och pressa över
juice från en halv lime. Salta och peppra. Ställ fisken
kallt i 10 minuter.

Gör en vinägrett på resterande limejuice,
limeskal, olivolja och peppar. Vänd ner melon- och
gurktärningarna i vinägretten.

Skär tonfisken i tunna skivor med en vass kniv.
Fördela skivorna samt melon- och gurkblandningen
på tallrikarna. Garnera med koriander.

4 personer

200 g tonfiskfilé
1/2 dl förstapressad olivolja
1 lime, juice och rivet skal
salt och svartpeppar
50 g vattenmelon, tärnad
1/2 gurka, tärnad

GARNITYR
färsk koriander

TUNA TATAKI

serves 4

50 ml extra virgin olive oil
200 g tuna fillet
juice and grated rind of 1 lime
salt and black pepper
50 g water melon, diced
1/2 cucumber, diced

GARNISH
fresh coriander

Heat a little olive oil in a hot pan and brown the tuna quickly on both sides. Remove from the pan and squeeze over half of the lime juice. Season with salt and pepper. Leave in a cool place for 10 minutes.

Make a vinaigrette with the remaining lime juice, rind, olive oil and pepper. Mix the melon and cucumber together and stir in the vinaigrette.

With a sharp knife slice the tuna thinly, arrange the slices with the melon and cucumber mixture between four plates and garnish with coriander.

OLIVOLJA/olive oil

I jämförelse med de länder där man odlar oliver är vi svenskar nybörjare när det gäller olivolja. Så var lite nyfiken och prova dig fram! Vi steker alltid i en bra olivolja, kvaliteten ska vara hög men det behöver inte vara förstapressad olivolja (extra vergine). Ofta använder vi spansk olivolja till själva matlagningen. Till smaksättning och dressing, däremot, tar vi fram en riktigt fin italiensk olivolja. Just nu använder vi gärna en extra vergine från gården Terreno i Toscana.

Compared to the countries where they grow olives we are just beginners in the field. However, be curious, try different oils until you find the perfect match! We always fry in good quality olive oil, however it doesn't need to be extra virgin. We often use a Spanish olive oil for cooking and for seasoning and dressings we prefer a good Italian olive oil of the highest quality. At the moment we are using a virgin oil from the Terreno vineyard in Tuscany.

GAZPACHO
MED TOMATGRANITÉ OCH HAVSKRÄFTOR

4 personer

12 havskräftsstjärtar
2 msk olivolja
salt och vitpeppar

TOMATGRANITÉ
sockerlag av 1 1/2 dl vatten +
1 1/2 dl strösocker
1 kg tomater
1 msk olivolja
1 msk rödvinsvinäger
salt och svartpeppar
1 msk finhackad basilika
1 tsk finhackad dragon

GAZPACHO
1/2 röd paprika
1/4 gurka, skalad
3 tomater
2 msk finhackad schalottenlök
1 liten vitlöksklyfta
1 msk sherryvinäger
100 g finrivet vitt bröd
2 ägg
2 dl förstapressad olivolja
salt och vitpeppar

Koka upp vatten och socker till en sockerlag, låt svalna. Skålla, skala, klyfta och kärna ur tomaterna till granitén. Fräs tomatköttet i olivolja. Tillsätt vinäger och sockerlag. Låt koka i 20 minuter. Mixa och passera tomaterna genom en finmaskig sil. Smaksätt med salt, peppar och örter. Bred ut tomatblandningen tunt i en form. Frys och rör om med en visp då och då.

Skär grönsakerna till gazpachon i mindre bitar. Mixa dem med schalottenlök, vitlök och vinäger. Slå blandningen över brödet. Mixa brödblandningen och passera den genom en sil.

Vispa först i ägg och sedan olivolja droppvis. Smaksätt gazpachon med salt och peppar.

Fördela havskräftsstjärtarna på fyra spett och stek dem hastigt i olivolja i en het panna. Salta och peppra.

Häll soppan i kalla tallrikar och servera den med tomatgranité och havskräftsspett.

GAZPACHO WITH TOMATO GRANITÉ AND LANGOUSTINES

serves 4

12 langoustine tails
2 tbsp olive oil
salt and white pepper

TOMATO GRANITÉ
150 ml sugar + 150 ml water
1 kg tomatoes
1 tbsp olive oil
1 tbsp red wine vinegar
salt and black pepper
1 tbsp finely chopped basil
1 tsp finely chopped tarragon

GAZPACHO
1/2 red pepper
1/4 cucumber, peeled
3 tomatoes
2 tbsp finely chopped shallots
1 small clove of garlic
1 tbsp sherry vinegar
100 g finely shredded
white bread
2 eggs
200 ml extra virgin olive oil
salt and white pepper

Bring the sugar and water to the boil and leave to cool. Blanch the tomatoes for the granité, peel, cut into quarters and deseed. Sweat in olive oil. Add the vinegar and syrup and boil for 20 minutes. Blend in a food processor, then strain through a fine sieve. Season with salt, pepper and the herbs. Spread the tomato mixture thinly into a shallow dish. Freeze and from time to time stir with a whisk to break up the ice crystals.

Cut the vegetables for the gazpacho into small pieces, with the shallots, garlic and vinegar blend together in a food processor. Pour the mixture over the bread and return to the food processor blending again, strain through a sieve. Add the eggs and whisk in the olive oil little by little. Season the gazpacho with salt and pepper to taste.

Divide the langoustine tails between four skewers and fry quickly in olive oil in a hot pan. Season with salt and pepper.

Pour the soup into cold plates and serve with tomato granité and the cooked langoustines.

GAZPACHO /gazpacho

Ursprunget till denna kalla grönsakssoppa kommer från spanska Andalusien, där soppan har svalkat många under heta sommareftermiddagar. I Sverige har vi kanske mer sällan ett så direkt behov av svalka, däremot njuter vi gärna av den goda smaken. Vi har valt att ytterligare förstärka tomatsmaken genom att servera en tomatgranité till. Dessutom lyxar vi till soppan med havskräftor.

This cold vegetable soup originates from Andalusia in Spain where it has cooled many people during hot summer afternoons. In Sweden we may not need to be cooled that often, but that doesn't prevent us from enjoying the rich taste. To enhance the taste of tomatoes we serve the soup with a tomato granité. As a little added luxury we also serve it with langoustines.

ANKLEVERTERRIN MED LINSER OCH TRYFFELVINÄGRETT
foie gras with lentils and truffle vinaigrette

ANKLEVERTERRIN MED LINSER,
TRYFFELVINÄGRETT SAMT GRILLAD BRIOCHE

Plocka anklevern fri från blodådror. Lägg levern i en form. Blanda de torra ingredienserna till marinaden och strö dem över anklevern, stänk på portvin, täck formen med plastfilm och låt anklevern marinera i kylen i 12 timmar. Lägg anklevern på en plåt och ställ den i 120° ugn i 5–10 minuter. Låt levern svalna i kylen.

Lägg en bit plastfilm på arbetsbänken. Placera ankbröstskivorna omlott på plastfilmen. Forma anklevern till en sträng på skivornas mitt. Rulla ihop till en korv med hjälp av plasten. Låt den ligga i kyl i minst ett dygn.

Blanda tryffelvinägretten enligt receptet.

Lägg linserna i en kastrull. Täck dem ordentligt med vatten. Lägg i morot, purjolök, en hel schalottenlök, kryddor och bacon. Sjud linserna mjuka i 10–15 minuter. Sila och plocka bort grönsakerna, kryddorna och baconskivan. Smaksätt linserna med tryffelvinägrett och salt. Vänd ner en finhackad schalottenlök och fint strimlad tryffel.

Skiva ankleverterrinen och servera den rumstempererad med linser och grillade briocheskivor.

4 personer

1 kg anklever
200 g kallrökt ankbröst, tunt skivat

MARINAD
11 g salt
2 g salpeter
1 g strösocker
3 g nymalen vitpeppar
1/2 dl vitt portvin

LINSER
50 g små gröna linser
1/2 morot
en liten bit purjolök
2 schalottenlökar
1 timjankvist
1 lagerblad
1 skiva bacon
tryffelvinägrett, se recept s. 306
salt
1 liten svart tryffel

TILL SERVERING
brioche, se recept s. 317

FOIE GRAS TERRINE WITH LENTILS, TRUFFLE VINAIGRETTE AND BRIOCHE

serves 4

1 kg duck foie gras
200 g cold smoked duck breast, thinly sliced

MARINADE
11 g salt
2 g saltpetre
1 g caster sugar
3 g white pepper
50 ml white port

LENTILS
50 g small green lentils
1/2 carrot
a small piece of leek, white only
2 shallots
1 sprig of thyme
1 bay leaf
1 slice of bacon
truffle vinaigrette (p.318)
salt
1 small black truffle

SERVE WITH
brioche (p. 330)

De-vein the liver and place in a shallow dish. Mix the dry ingredients for the marinade and sprinkle over the liver, followed by a dash of port. Cover the dish with cling film and leave to marinate in the fridge for 12 hours. Heat the oven to 120°C, place the liver on a baking sheet and cook for 5–10 minutes, then cool in the fridge.

Place a piece of cling film on the work surface, lay the duck breast slices overlapping each other with the liver on top. Using the cling film, roll tightly to form a sausage. Chill in the fridge for 24 hours.

Make the truffle vinaigrette according to the recipe.

Place the lentils in a saucepan with the carrot, leek, one whole shallot, the spices and bacon, cover with plenty of cold water. Bring to the boil, then simmer until the lentils are soft, approximately 10–15 minutes. Strain and remove the vegetables, spices and bacon. Stir in the truffle vinaigrette, a finely chopped shallot, shredded fresh truffle and season with salt.

Slice the terrine and serve at room temperature with lentils and grilled slices of brioche.

BRIOCHEBRÖD
brioche

PATA NEGRA-SKINKA
MED FIKON OCH BALSAMVINÄGER

4 personer

1 dl balsamvinäger
8 tunna skivor pata negra-skinka
sallad
2 färska fikon, klyftade

Koka ihop balsamvinägern till en sirapsliknande konsistens.

Servera pata negra-skinkan med fikonklyftor, sallad och reducerad balsamvinäger.

PATA NEGRA-SKINKA MED FIKON OCH BALSAMVINÄGER
Pata negra ham with figs and balsamic vinegar

PATA NEGRA HAM
WITH FIGS AND BALSAMIC VINEGAR

serves 4

100 ml balsamic vinegar
8 thin slices of pata negra ham
salad
2 green figs, cut into wedges

Reduce the vinegar until thick.

Serve the pata negra slices with the figs, salad and reduced balsamic vinegar.

SALT / salt

Salt löser sig inte i olja. Till dressing blandar vi därför alltid salt och vinäger först. Därefter tillsätter vi oljan droppvis, (om dressingen delar sig, mixa med en matsked kokande vatten, så blir dressingen hel igen). Men allt salt smakar inte lika. Det godaste saltet är utan tvekan *fleur de sel*, det vill säga toppskiktet från saltbassängerna. Den milda sältan passar som bordssalt eller som smaksättning mot slutet av matlagningen. Salt är en perfekt souvenir från semesterresan. Den som åker till franska Bretagne kan till exempel köpa det gråa, nästan fuktiga, *sel de Guerand* och sedan njuta av den rika smaken hemma.

Salt doesn't dissolve in oil, therefore for dressings we always start by blending the salt and vinegar together, then adding the oil. If the dressing separates, add a tablespoon of boiling water and whisk. The best salt, without doubt, is *fleur de sel*, being the topmost layer of the salt basin. For a mild salt taste or to add at the end of cooking use table salt. Salt is a perfect souvenir of your vacation. If you go to Bretagne in France you can, for example, try to find the grey, almost moist, *sel de Guerand* and enjoy its rich taste back at home.

KALL INKOKT GÖS MED PRESSGURKA OCH HEMBAKAT KNÄCKEBRÖD
poached cold pike-perch with pressed cucumber and homemade hard bread

KALL INKOKT GÖS MED PRESSGURKA
OCH HEMBAKAT KNÄCKEBRÖD

Rör ut jästen till knäckebrödet i ljummen mjölk. Tillsätt salt, kummin eller fänkål och mjöl. Blanda till en deg. Dela degen i tjugo bitar. Rulla bitarna till bullar och låt dem jäsa i 20–30 minuter. Kavla ut varje bulle tunt, först med en slät kavel och sedan med en kruskavel. Grädda bröden i 250–300° ugn i 8 minuter. Vänd dem efter halva tiden. Ta ut dem och låt svalna på ett galler.

Skär fisken i portionsbitar. Koka upp lagen och slå den över fisken. Täck med plastfilm och låt kallna.

Skiva gurkan tunt. Salta skivorna och lägg dem under press i cirka en timme. Häll av överflödig vätska. Blanda ättika, vatten och socker. Lägg i gurkskivorna.

Förväll vårlökarna i saltat vatten. Smaksätt dem med salt och peppar.

Servera gösen med vårlökar, pressgurka och knäckebröd.

4 personer

4 göskotletter à 150 g
16 vårlökar
salt och vitpeppar

LAG
1 dl ättikssprit, 12%
2 dl strösocker
3 dl vatten
1 tsk kryddpeppar
1 lagerblad
1 morot, tunt skivad

PRESSGURKA
1/2 gurka, skalad
1 tsk salt
1 msk ättikssprit, 12%
3 msk vatten
2 msk strösocker

KNÄCKEBRÖD
50 g jäst
5 dl lättmjölk, 37°
2 tsk salt
2 tsk stött kummin eller fänkål
6 dl extra grovt rågmjöl
6 dl vetemjöl
grovt rågmjöl till utbakning

POACHED COLD PIKE-PERCH WITH
PRESSED CUCUMBER AND HOMEMADE HARD BREAD

serves 4

4 pike-perch cutlets 150g each
16 spring onions
salt and white pepper

NAGE
100 ml white vinegar
200 ml sugar
300 ml water
1tsp whole allspice
1 bay leaf
1 carrot, finely sliced

PRESSED CUCUMBER
1/2 cucumber, peeled
1 tsp salt
1 tbsp white vinegar
3 tbsp water
2 tbsp sugar

HARD BREAD
50 g fresh yeast
500 ml lukewarm skimmed
milk, 37° C
2 tsp salt
2 tsp caraway seeds or fennel
650 g extra course rye flour
630 g flour
course rye flour for kneading

Dissolve the yeast in the milk. Mix the salt, caraway seeds or fennel and flour together, then add the yeast and mix to form a soft dough. Divide into twenty pieces and roll each into a ball shape and leave to rise for 20–30 minutes. Roll each ball thinly with a rolling-pin. Place on a greased baking sheet and bake at 250–300°C oven for 4 minutes. Turn over, then bake for another 4 minutes.

Cut the fish into 4 pieces. Bring the nage up to a boil and pour over the fish. Cover with cling film and leave to cool.

Thinly slice the cucumber. Season with salt and press under a heavy weight for approximately one hour. Pour away the excess liquid, then mix the vinegar, water and sugar together. Place the cucumber slices into the mixture and sprinkle with chopped parsley.

Blanch the spring onions in boiling salted water. Season with salt and pepper.

Serve the pike-perch with the spring onions, pressed cucumber and hard bread.

NÄCKEBRÖD
ard bread

KALVCARPACCIO MED CHAMPINJONER, TRYFFEL OCH VATTENKRASSE
veal carpaccio with white mushrooms, truffle and watercress

KALVCARPACCIO MED CHAMPINJONER,
TRYFFEL OCH VATTENKRASSE

4 personer

100 g kalvytterfilé
tryffelvinägrett, se recept s.306
100 g champinjoner, skivade
50 g svart tryffel, skivad
fleur de sel (havssalt)
och vitpeppar

GARNITYR
1 kruka vattenkrasse
hyvlad parmesanost

Putsa kalvytterfilén fri från senor och hinnor. Lägg köttet i frysen i en timme.

Blanda tryffelvinägretten enligt receptet.

Marinera svamp- och tryffelskivor i tryffelvinägretten i cirka en timme.

Ta ut köttet ur frysen och skär det i tunna skivor på skärmaskin. Fördela skivorna på fyra tallrikar. Salta och peppra. Skeda över marinerad svamp och tryffel. Garnera med vattenkrasse och hyvlad parmesanost.

VEAL CARPACCIO WITH WHITE MUSHROOMS, TRUFFLE AND WATERCRESS

Remove any sinew or membranes from the veal. Place the fillet in a freezer for one hour.

Prepare the truffle vinaigrette according to the recipe.

Marinate the mushrooms and truffle slices in truffle vinaigrette for approximately one hour.

Remove the veal from the freezer and cut it into thin slices, preferably on a slicing machine. Divide the veal between four plates, season with salt and pepper, then spoon over the marinated white mushrooms and truffles. Garnish with watercress and parmesan shavings.

serves 4

100 g veal fillet
truffle vinaigrette (p.318)
100 g white mushrooms, cleaned and sliced
50 g black truffle, sliced
sea salt and white pepper

GARNISH
1 pot watercress
shavings of parmesan cheese

LÖJROM MED MANDELPOTATISPLÄTTAR

Låt löjrommen rinna av i en sil om den har varit fryst.

Koka potatisarna mjuka i saltat vatten. Häll av vattnet och pressa potatisen. Tillsätt ägg, crème fraiche, vetemjöl och citronjuice. Forma potatisblandningen till plättar och stek dem gyllenbruna i smör.

Servera löjrommen med potatisplättar, crème fraiche och rödlök. Garnera med dill.

4 personer

160 g löjrom
4 msk crème fraiche
1 rödlök, finhackad

MANDELPOTATISPLÄTTAR
5 mandelpotatisar, skalade
salt
1 ägg
2 tsk crème fraiche
1 tsk vetemjöl
några droppar citronjuice
1 msk smör

GARNITYR
dillkvistar
citronklyftor

POTATO PANCAKES WITH BLEAK ROE

serves 4

160 g bleak roe
4 tbsp crème fraiche
1 red onion, finely chopped

POTATO PANCAKES
5 almond potatoes, peeled
salt
1 egg
2 tsp crème fraiche
1 tsp flour
dash of lemon juice
1 tbsp butter

GARNISH
sprigs of dill
segments of lemon

Defrost and drain the bleak roe if frozen.

Boil the potatoes in salted water until soft. Drain the potatoes, then mash, add the egg, crème fraiche, flour and lemon juice. Shape the potato mixture into small pancakes and fry in hot butter on both sides until golden brown.

Serve the bleak roe with the potato pancakes, crème fraiche and red onion. Garnish with dill.

LÖJROM / bleak roe

Internationellt lockar kanske den storkorniga lax-
rommen mer. Men i Sverige är det en annan rom
som leder ligan – löjrommen med sina små, smakrika
korn. Den allra bästa löjrommen kommer från de
kalla vattnen utanför Kalix. Löjrom är en av få råvaror
som klarar frysförvaring utmärkt. Den kan till och
med frysas om utan att tappa smak eller konsistens.
Tina den i en liten sil, så rinner överflödig vätska av
och rommen kan formas lättare.

Though internationally the larger salmon roe are of
greater interest we feel there is another which heads
the league – the bleak roe with its small, tasty, eggs.
The best bleak roe in the world comes from the cold
waters outside Kalix in northern Sweden. Bleak roe
is one of few foods that you can freeze, thaw and
then refreeze again without losing taste or structure.
Thaw in a small strainer to get rid of excess liquid
which makes it easier to shape.

KALV- OCH KANTARELLTERRIN
MED MADEIRAVINÄGRETT

Till 1 terrin (15–20 personer)

700 g kantareller, rensade
1 msk smör
2 vitlöksklyftor, finhackade
2 msk finhackad schalottenlök
300 g finmalen kalvfärs
2 äggvitor
3 dl vispgrädde
3 msk finhackad bladpersilja
salt och vitpeppar
400 g kokt rimmad oxtunga

MADEIRAVINÄGRETT
1 1/2 dl kalvsky,
se recept s. 307
1 msk sherryvinäger
1 msk rödvinsvinäger
1/2 citron, juice
2 msk madeira
en nypa salt
4 msk förstapressad olivolja
vitpeppar

TILL SERVERING
blandad sallad

Fräs svampen i smör tillsammans med vitlök och schalottenlök. Låt blandningen svalna.

Blanda kalvfärs, äggvitor och grädde. Vänd ner svampblandningen och persiljan. Smaksätt med salt och peppar.

Skiva oxtungan tunt. Klä en enliters terrinform med plastfilm. Låt plastfilmen hänga över kanten. Fyll terrinen med färs och varva med oxtungsskivor. Stäng terrinen med den överhängande plastfilmen. Ställ in formen i 150° ugn i cirka en timme. Kontrollera att terrinen är färdig med en sticka. Vätskan som kommer från terrinen ska vara klar. Ta ut terrinen och låt den svalna över natten.

Blanda kalvsky, vinäger, citronjuice, madeira och salt till vinägretten. Vispa ner oljan droppvis och smaksätt med peppar.

Skiva kalv- och kantarellterrinen och servera den med madeiravinägrett och sallad.

KALV- OCH KANTARELLTERRIN MED MADEIRAVINÄGRETT
veal and chanterelle terrine with madeira vinaigrette

VEAL AND CHANTERELLE TERRINE
WITH MADEIRA VINAIGRETTE

1 terrine (serves 15–20)

700 g chanterelles, cleaned
1 tbsp butter
2 cloves of garlic,
finely chopped
2 tbsp finely chopped shallots
400 g boiled salt beef tongue
300 g finely minced veal
2 egg whites
300 ml single cream
3 tbsp finely chopped flat leaf
parsley
salt and white pepper

MADEIRA VINAIGRETTE
150 ml veal stock (p.319)
1 tbsp sherry vinegar
1 tbsp red wine vinegar
juice of 1/2 lemon
2 tbsp madeira
a pinch of salt
4 tbsp extra virgin olive oil
white pepper

SERVE WITH
mixed salad

Fry the chanterelles in butter together with the garlic and shallots. Leave to cool.

Mix the minced veal, egg whites and cream together. Fold in the chanterelle mixture and parsley. Season with salt and pepper.

Slice the beef tongue thinly. Line a one litre terrine with clingfilm leaving an overhang. Fill the mould with layers of the veal mixture and beef tongue. Fold over the cling film to enclose the meat. Place the mould in 150°C oven for approximately one hour. To ensure the terrine is cooked pierce gently with a cocktail stick, the juice from the terrine should be clear. Remove from the oven and leave to cool overnight.

Mix together the veal stock, vinegars, lemon juice, madeira and salt for the vinaigrette. Whisk in the oil little by little and season with salt and pepper.

Slice the terrine and serve it with the madeira vinaigrette and salad.

PLASTFOLIE / cling film

Förr fick man alltid lära sig att plast inte hörde hemma i ugnen. Numera är det en sanning med viss modifikation. Vid lägre temperaturer går det utmärkt att använda plastfolie i ugnen, se bara till att den inte kommer i direkt kontakt med ugnsväggarna. Plastfolien passar extra bra när man till exempel ska göra terriner. Smakerna stannar kvar och terrinen går lättare att lossa. Fodra formen med plastfolie och ta till så mycket att plasten hänger över kanterna rejält. Fyll formen och «stäng» sedan terrinen genom att täcka med plasten.

Originally we were told that cling film shouldn't be used in the oven. Today that is not completely correct, you may use cling film at low temperatures being careful that it doesn't touch the sides of the oven. Cling film is suitable for terrines as it helps retain the flavour and makes it easier to remove from the dish. Line a terrine mould with cling film, leaving some overhang. Fill the dish, then cover with the excess cling film to enclose the terrine.

46   KALLA

PAPRIKAMOUSSE MED ROSTAD PAPRIKA, OLIVER OCH FRITERADE LÖKRINGAR

Gnid in paprikorna med olivolja. Lägg dem på en plåt eller i en ugnssäker form. Rosta paprikorna i 225° ugn tills skalen börjar spricka, det tar cirka 10 minuter. Vänd dem efter 5 minuter. Ta ut paprikorna och lägg dem i en bunke. Täck bunken med plastfilm. Skala paprikorna när de svalnat något. Halvera dem och ta bort kärnhusen.

Skär paprikorna till moussen i mindre bitar. Lägg dem i en kastrull, slå på buljong och låt sjuda i 20 minuter. Mixa och tillsätt paprikapulver och gelatin. Passera blandningen genom en finmaskig sil. Vispa grädden och vänd ner den i paprikablandningen. Smaksätt med salt och peppar. Ställ moussen i kylen i minst en timme.

Skär en gul och en röd paprika i vackra bitar. Blanda dem med oliver, schalottenlök, oregano, förstapressad olivolja, salt och peppar.

Vänd lökringarna i tempuramix. Fritera dem i het olja.

Lägg upp paprikamoussen med en varm sked. Servera den med paprika- och olivblandningen samt friterade lökringar.

4 personer

1 gul paprika
1 röd paprika
olivolja
20 calamata-oliver
1 schalottenlök, tunt skivad
1 tsk färska oreganoblad
förstapressad olivolja
salt och vitpeppar

PAPRIKAMOUSSE
6 röda paprikor
2 dl kycklingbuljong,
se recept s. 308
1 tsk paprikapulver
3 gelatinblad, blötlagda
2 1/2 dl vispgrädde
salt och vitpeppar

FRITERADE LÖKRINGAR
1 rödlök, skivad
1 pkt tempuramix
olja till fritering

PEPPER MOUSSE WITH ROASTED PEPPER, OLIVES AND DEEP-FRIED ONION RINGS

serves 4

1 yellow pepper
1 red pepper
olive oil
20 calamata olives
1 shallot, thinly sliced
1 tsp fresh oregano leaves
extra virgin olive oil
salt and white pepper

PEPPER MOUSSE
6 red peppers
200 ml chicken stock (p.320)
1 tsp ground paprika
3 leaves of gelatine, soaked in a
little cold water
250 ml whipping cream
salt
white pepper

DEEP FRIED ONION RINGS
1 red onion, sliced
tempura mixture
frying oil

Rub the skin of all the peppers with olive oil, then place on an oven tray or in an ovenproof dish. Roast in the oven at 225°C until the skin starts to split, approximately 10 minutes, turning halfway through. Remove from the oven and place in a bowl, cover with clingfilm and leave to cool slightly. Peel the peppers, cut in half and remove all the seeds.

Cut the peppers for the mousse into small pieces. Place the pepper pieces with the chicken stock into a saucepan and simmer for 20 minutes. Mix the peppers in a food processor, add ground paprika and the gelatine from the water. Strain the mixture through a fine sieve. Whip the cream and fold into the pepper mixture. Season with salt and pepper. Place the mousse in the refrigerator for at least one hour.

Cut the yellow and red pepper into bite-size pieces and mix with the olives, shallots, oregano, extra virgin olive oil, salt and pepper.

Coat the onion rings with the tempura mixture. Deep fry in hot oil.

Spoon the pepper mousse into egg shapes using a hot spoon. Serve with the pepper and olive mixture and the deep-fried onion rings.

PAPRIKA
pepper

GETOSTMOUSSE MED RÖDBETOR OCH BASILIKA
goats' cheese mousse with beetroot and basi

GETOSTMOUSSE
MED RÖDBETOR OCH BASILIKA

Mixa getosten. Tillsätt honung och svartpeppar.
Vispa grädden och vänd ner den i ostblandningen.

Koka rödbetorna mjuka i saltat vatten. Häll av
vattnet och låt rödbetorna svalna. Skala, klyfta och
blanda dem med olivolja, balsamvinäger och
schalottenlök.

Fördela rödbetorna på tallrikarna. Lägg på getostmousse och garnera med basilika och pinjenötter.

4 personer

4 medelstora färska rödbetor
salt
2 msk förstapressad olivolja
2 msk balsamvinäger
2 schalottenlökar, skivade

GETOSTMOUSSE
200 g lagrad getost
1 tsk honung
en nypa svartpeppar
1 dl vispgrädde

GARNITYR
strimlad basilika
rostade pinjenötter
örtolja, se recept s.311

GOATS' CHEESE MOUSSE
WITH BEETROOT AND BASIL

serves 4

4 mid-sized fresh beetroot
salt
2 tbsp extra virgin olive oil
2 tbsp balsamic vinegar
2 shallots, sliced

GOATS' CHEESE MOUSSE
200 g ripe goats' cheese
1 tsp honey
a pinch of black pepper
100 ml cream

GARNISH
shredded basil
roasted pine nuts
herb oil (p. 323)

Mix the goats' cheese in a food processor. Add the honey and black pepper. Whip the cream and fold into the cheese.

Boil the beetroot in salted water until soft. Drain the water away and leave to cool. Remove the skin and cut into segments, then mix with the olive oil, balsamic vinegar and shallots.

Place the beetroot and goats' cheese mousse onto four plates. Garnish with basil and pine nuts.

GETOST/goat cheese

Märkligt nog har det franska ordet för getost, *chèvre*, kommit att stå för en speciell typ av getost, den runda «limpa» med vitt hölje och ganska sträv smak som numera finns i nästan alla delikatessdiskar. Den typen passar utmärkt till matlagning, eftersom den ger en tydlig getostsmak utan att vara för påträngande. Den går dessutom att riva, vilket de mjukare getostarna inte är lämpade för.

The French word for goats' cheese, *chèvre*, nowadays defines the round log shaped cheese found in delicatessens. This particular type of cheese is extremely suitable for cooking as the taste is clear without being strong. It can also be grated, unlike softer cheeses.

MAKRILLTERRIN MED
SENAPSSÅS OCH SPENATSALLAD

1 kg makrillfilé, skinn- och benfri
3 auberginer
1 tsk strösocker + 1 tsk salt
4 gula paprikor
4 röda paprikor
4 msk olivolja
1 msk förstapressad olivolja
3 msk fransk senap
salt och vitpeppar
20 torkade tomathalvor,
se recept s. 313
20 basilikablad
1 tsk färska timjanblad

SENAPSSÅS
3 msk crème fraiche
1 msk fransk senap
1 msk ljus buljong,
t ex grönsaks- eller musselbuljong
salt och vitpeppar

TILL SERVERING
100 g färsk späd spenat
gräslök

Skär auberginerna i ½ cm tjocka skivor på längden.
Strö socker- och saltblandningen på båda sidor och
låt dra i 30 minuter för att vattna ur.

Gnid in paprikorna i olivolja. Lägg dem på en plåt
eller i en ugnssäker form. Rosta paprikorna i 225° ugn
tills skalen börjar spricka, cirka 10 minuter. Vänd dem
efter 5 minuter. Ta ut paprikorna och lägg dem i en
bunke. Täck bunken med plastfilm. Skala paprikorna
när de svalnat något. Halvera dem, kärna ur och dela
varje halva ytterligare en gång.

Torka av auberginskivorna, peppra och stek
dem i vanlig olivolja.

Blanda förstapressad olivolja med fransk senap.
Pensla makrillfiléerna med blandningen, salta och
peppra. Stek dem i 150° ugn i cirka 5 minuter. Ta ut
filéerna och ställ dem kallt.

Klä en terrinform med plastfilm. Varva alla grönsaker, örter och makrillfiléer i formen. Stäng terrinen
med plastfilm och ställ den i press i kylen över natten.

Blanda ingredienserna till senapssåsen. Smaksätt
med salt och peppar.

Skiva terrinen och servera den med senapssås och
spenatsallad. Garnera med gräslök.

MAKRILLTERRIN MED SENAPSSÅS OCH SPENATSALLAD
mackerel terrine with mustard sauce and spinach salad

MACKEREL TERRINE WITH
MUSTARD SAUCE AND SPINACH SALAD

1 terrine (serves 10)

1 kg deboned mackerel fillets,
skins removed
3 aubergines
1 tsp sugar + 1 tsp salt
4 yellow peppers
4 red peppers
4 tbsp olive oil
1 tbsp extra virgin olive oil
3 tbsp french mustard
salt and white pepper
20 dried tomato halves (p. 325)
20 basil leaves
1 tsp fresh thyme

MUSTARD SAUCE
3 tbsp creme fraiche
1 tbsp french mustard
1 tbsp light stock, eg vegetable
or mussel
salt and white pepper

SERVE WITH
100 g fresh tender spinach
chives

Cut the aubergines in ½ cm slices lengthwise. Place on an oven tray, sprinkle with sugar and salt. Leave for 30 minutes to draw out the water and bitterness.

Rub the skin of the peppers with olive oil, then place on a oven tray. Roast in the oven at 225°C until the skin starts to split, approximately 10 minutes, turning halfway through. Place in a bowl, cover with cling film and leave to cool slightly, then peel. Cut in half, remove the seeds, then cut in half again.

Dry the aubergine with kitchen paper, season with pepper, then fry them in olive oil.

Mix the extra virgin olive oil with the french mustard and brush over the mackerel fillets. Season with salt and pepper. Roast in the oven at 150°C for approximately 5 minutes, then leave to cool.

Line a one litre terrine with cling film. Fill the terrine by layering the vegetables, herbs and mackerel. Cover with cling film and press under a heavy weight in the refrigerator overnight.

Mix the ingredients for the mustard sauce together. Season with salt and pepper.

Slice the terrine and serve with mustard sauce and spinach salad. Garnish with chives.

AUBERGINE/aubergine

Aubergine, eller äggplanta som grönsaken egentligen heter på svenska, är oerhört användbar i matlagningen. Eftersom den innehåller mycket vätska och dessutom ibland kan smaka en aning beskt gör man klokt i att ägna den lite extra omsorg. Genom att sockra lätt på snittytorna drar man ut den eventuella beskan och genom att salta drar man ut vätskan. Lägg skivorna på hushållspapper, så sugs vätskan upp på en gång. Klappa skivorna torra och börja laga.

Aubergine or eggplant though a very useful vegetable in cooking, contains a lot of liquid which can often have a bitter taste, so it is a good idea to take a little extra time in preparation. Sugar sprinkled on both sides will take away the bitterness and a little salt the excess liquid. Place on kitchen paper which will soak up the liquid before cooking.

LAXTARTAR MED PILGRIMSMUSSLA OCH CURRY
tartar of salmon with scallops and curry

LAXTARTAR MED
PILGRIMSMUSSLA OCH CURRY

Blanda salt och socker. Vänd laxfilén i blandningen
och ställ den i kylen i 24 timmar.

Blanda ingredienserna till marinaden. Skölj laxfilén och lägg den i marinaden i 12 timmar i kylen.
Ta upp laxen ur marinaden, torka av den med hushållspapper och tärna den fint. Spara 2 msk marinad
till currysåsen.

Blanda äggula, ketchup, tabasco och salt. Vispa
ner marinaden och curryoljan droppvis i äggblandningen. Vänd laxtärningarna i 2 msk av currysåsen.
Forma blandningen och lägg på tallrikar.

Stek pilgrimsmusslorna i smör hastigt på varje
sida i en het stekpanna. Salta och peppra.

Servera laxtartaren med pilgrimsmusslor, currysås, curryolja och sallad.

4 personer

500 g laxfilé, skinnfri
150 g salt
150 g strösocker
4 pilgrimsmusslor
1 msk smör
salt och vitpeppar

MARINAD
3/4 dl olivolja
1/4 dl hasselnötolja
2 lime, juice och rivet skal
4 sardellfiléer, finhackade
1 tsk finhackad persilja
1 tsk finhackad dill
1 tsk finhackad dragon
1 tsk finhackad körvel
1 tsk finhackad basilika
1 tsk grönpeppar
1 msk kapris

CURRYSÅS
1 äggula
1 tsk tomatketchup
några stänk tabasco
en nypa salt
2 msk marinad,
se recept ovan
1 msk curryolja,
se recept s. 311

TILL SERVERING
curryolja, se recept s. 311
blandad sallad

TARTAR OF SALMON
WITH SCALLOPS AND CURRY

serves 4

500 g skinless salmon fillet
150 g salt
150 g sugar
4 king scallops
1 tbsp butter
salt and white pepper

MARINADE
75 ml olive oil
25 ml hazelnut oil
juice and grated rind of 2 limes
4 anchovy fillets, finely chopped
1 tsp each of finely chopped
parsley, dill, tarragon,
chervil and basil
1 tsp green peppercorns
1 tbsp capers

CURRY SAUCE
1 egg yolk
1 tsp tomato ketchup
a dash of tabasco
a pinch of salt
2 tbsp marinade,
se recipe above
1 tbsp curry oil (p.323)

SERVE WITH
curry oil (p.323)
mixed salad

Mix the salt and sugar together. Coat the salmon fillet with the salt and sugar mixture and place in the refrigerator for 24 hours.

Mix the ingredients for the marinade together. Rinse the salmon fillet, place in the marinade for 12 hours in the refrigerator. Remove the salmon from the marinade, wipe well with kitchen paper, then cut into fine dice. Reserve 2 tbsp of the marinade for the curry sauce.

Mix together the egg yolk, ketchup, tabasco and salt. Whisk the marinade and curry oil little by little into the egg mixture. Coat the salmon dice in 2 tbsp of the curry sauce. Form the mixture and place onto the plates.

Fry the scallops quickly on both sides in butter in a hot pan. Season with salt and pepper. Serve with curry sauce, curry oil and salad.

GRAVADE STRÖMMINGAR x 3

300 g strömmingsfiléer,
skinn- och benfria
1 1/2 dl ättikssprit, 12%
6 dl vatten
1 1/2 msk salt

ÖRTSÅS
1/2 dl majonnäs
1/2 dl crème fraiche
1/2 dl gräddfil
1 msk finhackad dill
1 msk finhackad körvel
1 msk finhackad dragon
1 msk finhackad bladpersilja
1 vitlöksklyfta, finhackad
1 tsk fransk senap
salt och vitpeppar

CITRON-, KAPRIS- OCH
TIMJANSÅS
1/2 dl majonnäs
1/2 dl crème fraiche
1/2 dl gräddfil
1 citron, juice och rivet skal
2 tsk kapris
1 msk hackad timjan
salt och vitpeppar

CURRYSÅS
1/2 äpple, skalat och tärnat
1 schalottenlök, finhackad
1 msk smör
1 msk curry
1/2 dl majonnäs
1/2 dl crème fraiche
1/2 dl gräddfil
salt och vitpeppar

Blanda ättika, vatten och salt. Lägg i strömmingsfiléerna och låt dem dra i 24 timmar i kylen. Rör om då och då. Låt strömmingarna rinna av i ett durkslag.

Blanda majonnäs, crème fraiche och gräddfil till örtsåsen. Mixa örter, vitlök och senap med lite av majonnäsblandningen. Rör ihop alltsammans, smaksätt med salt och peppar och vänd ner en tredjedel av strömmingsfiléerna. Låt dra i kylen över natten.

Blanda ingredienserna till citron-, kapris- och timjansåsen. Smaksätt såsen med salt och peppar och vänd ner en tredjedel av strömmingsfiléerna. Låt dra i kylen över natten.

Fräs äpple och schalottenlök i smör. Tillsätt curry och fräs ytterligare tills äppeltärningarna är mjuka. Mixa och låt svalna. Blanda samtliga ingredienser. Smaksätt såsen med salt och peppar och vänd ner resterande strömmingsfiléer. Låt dra i kylen över natten.

Servera gärna strömmingarna med kokt färskpotatis, knäckebröd och västerbottenost.

GRAVAD BALTIC HERRING x 3

Mix together the vinegar, water and salt. Place the herring fillets in the mixture and leave for 24 hours in the refrigerator. Stir from time to time. Drain the fillets in a colander.

Mix together the mayonnaise, creme fraiche and sour cream for the herb sauce. With a little of the mayonnaise mixture, mix together the herbs, garlic and mustard in a food processor. Finally mix in the remaining mayonnaise and season with salt and pepper. Coat ⅓ of the herring with the sauce and leave in the refrigerator overnight.

Mix together the ingredients for the lemon, caper and thyme sauce. Season the sauce with salt and pepper. Coat ⅓ of the herring with the sauce and leave in the refrigerator overnight.

Sweat the apple and shallot in butter. Add the curry and sweat until the apple is soft. Blend in a food processor, then leave to cool. Stir in the remaining ingredients and season the sauce with salt and pepper. Coat ⅓ of the herring with the sauce and leave in the refrigerator overnight.

Serve the herrings with boiled potatoes, hard bread and vaesterbottencheese.

300 g herring fillets,
skin and bones removed
600 ml water
150 ml white vinegar
1 1/2 tbsp salt

HERB SAUCE
50 ml mayonnaise
50 ml creme fraiche
50 ml sour cream
1 tbsp finely chopped dill
1 tbsp finely chopped chervil
1 tbsp finely chopped tarragon
1 tbsp finely chopped
flat leaf parsley
1 clove of garlic, finely chopped
1 tsp french mustard
salt and white pepper

LEMON, CAPER
AND THYME SAUCE
50 ml mayonnaise
50 ml creme fraiche
50 ml sour cream
juice and grated rind of 1 lemon
2 tsp capers
1 tbsp chopped thyme
salt and white pepper

CURRY SAUCE
1/2 apple, peeled and diced
1 shallot, finely chopped
1 tbsp butter
1 tbsp curry
50 ml mayonnaise
50 ml creme fraiche
50 ml sour cream
salt and white pepper

GRAVADE STRÖMMINGAR X 3 OCH VÄSTERBOTTENOST
gravad baltic herring x 3 and vaesterbottencheese

STRÖMMING / baltic herring

Mitt i Kalmarsund byter *Clupea harengus* (på latin) sitt svenska namn från strömming till sill. Är man från Stockholm är det därför mest självklart att använda strömming, men även liten sill går förstås bra. Kännaren uppskattar strömming «med ögon», det vill säga hel strömming och inte maskinrensade filéer, som gärna känns urvattnade. Helst ska dessutom strömmingen anrättas med ryggbenet kvar.

In Sweden, herring (*Clupea harengus* in Latin) have two different names, depending on where it is caught. On the west coast it's called «sill», on the east coast mainly «stromming». The connoisseur prefers to have the herring cooked whole on the bone.

YCKLINGSALLAD MED MANGO OCH CHILI
hicken salad with mango and chili

KYCKLINGSALLAD MED MANGO OCH CHILI

4 personer

12 vårkycklinglår
2 msk smör
salt och svartpeppar
1 lime, juice

SALSA
1 mango
1/4 gurka
1/2 lime, juice
1 röd chilifrukt, finhackad
salt och svartpeppar

TILL SERVERING
blandad sallad

Bryn kycklinglåren i smör. Salta, peppra och stek färdigt låren i 175° ugn i 10–15 minuter. Ta ut kycklinglåren och pressa över limejuice.

Skala och tärna mangon och gurkan. Blanda tärningarna med limejuice och chili. Smaksätt med salt och peppar.

Fördela kycklinglåren och salsan på tallrikarna. Servera med blandad sallad.

CHICKEN SALAD WITH MANGO AND CHILI

Brown the chicken thighs in butter. Season with salt and pepper. Bake in the oven at 175°C for 10–15 minutes. Remove the chicken thighs and squeeze the lime juice over.

Peel and dice the mango and cucumber. Mix together with the lime juice and chili. Season with salt and pepper.

Serve the chicken thighs and salsa with a mixed salad.

serves 4

12 spring chicken thighs
2 tbsp butter
salt and black pepper
juice of 1 lime

SALSA
1 mango
1/4 cucumber
juice of 1/2 lime
1 red chili pepper,
finely chopped
salt and black pepper

SERVE WITH
mixed salad

LAXRULLE MED SYLTADE KANTARELLER
salmon roll with pickled chanterelles

LAXRULLE MED
SYLTADE KANTARELLER

Koka upp ättika, vatten, socker, schalottenlök, vitlök och lagerblad. Lägg i kantarellerna och låt dra i 12 timmar. Ta upp svampen, salta, peppra och strö över färska örter.

Dela laxfilén på längden. Salta, peppra och lägg det blötlagda gelatinbladet på en av bitarna. Lägg den andra laxbiten ovanpå. Placera den så att hela biten blir så jämn som möjligt. Lägg laxen på en bit plastfilm. Rulla ihop till en «korv» med hjälp av plastfilmen. Omslut laxrullen med aluminiumfolie. Låt den sjuda i 70° vatten eller sätt in i lika varm ugn tills den får en innertemperatur på 38°. Lägg laxen i kylen över natten.

Skiva laxrullen och servera med syltade kantareller.

4 personer

500 g laxfilé, mittbiten
salt och vitpeppar
1 gelatinblad, blötlagt

SYLTADE KANTARELLER
1/2 msk ättikssprit, 12 %
6 msk vatten
4 msk strösocker
2 schalottenlökar, skivade
1 vitlöksklyfta, finhackad
1 lagerblad
150 g kantareller, rensade
salt och vitpeppar
1 msk körvelblad
1 msk strimlad bladpersilja

SALMON ROLL WITH
PICKLED CHANTERELLES

serves 4

500 g salmon fillet,
the middle part
salt and white pepper
1 gelatin leaf,
soaked in a little cold water

PICKLED CHANTERELLES
1/2 tbsp white vinegar
6 tbsp water
4 tbsp sugar
2 shallots, sliced
1 clove of garlic, finely chopped
150 g chanterelles, cleaned
salt and white pepper
1 bay leaf
1 tbsp chervil
1 tbsp shredded flat leaf parsley

Bring vinegar, water, sugar, shallot, garlic and bay leaf up to the boil. Pour over the chanterelles and leave for 12 hours. Remove the chanterelles, season with salt and pepper and sprinkle with fresh herbs.

Cut the salmon piece lengthwise and season with salt and pepper. Remove the gelatine from the water and lay on top of one piece of salmon. Place the second salmon piece on top as evenly as possible. Lay the salmon on a piece of cling film. Roll into a sausage with the aid of the cling film. Wrap the roll with aluminium foil. Simmer in water or in an oven of the same temperature until the roll has an inside temperature of 38°C. Place the salmon roll in the refrigerator overnight.

Slice the salmon roll and serve with pickled chanterelles.

LAX/salmon

Laxen följer de skönhetsideal som förr gällde även människor: fet är vacker – och i laxens fall dessutom god. Smålax (under 4 kilo) har inte alls samma egenskaper som större lax, där fettet bidrar till den ljuva smaken. Idealvikten är 5–7 kilo. Även större lax smakar utmärkt, men skivorna blir så stora att tallriken knappt räcker till! Rå lax ska tillagas försiktigt och fortfarande ha en rejäl «kärna» kvar.

Salmon carries the ideals that once applied to human form that fat is beautiful. Not only that, in this case fat also means great taste. Small salmon weighing under 4 kilos doesn't have the same quality as the larger ones. An ideal salmon weighs around 5–7 kilos. Anything larger will still taste good but will be unwieldy to cook and plate. Raw salmon should be handled carefully and when cooked have a pink core.

VARMA
warm

STEKT ABBORRFILÉ MED
SOMMARSALLAD OCH BRYNT SMÖR

4 personer

500 g abborrfiléer
med skinn, fjällade
5 dl vatten
2 msk vitvinsvinäger
4 ägg
salt och vitpeppar
1 msk smör
1 sats brynt smörvinägrett,
se recept s. 307

SOMMARSALLAD
250 g kokt färskpotatis,
kall, skivad
50 g rädisor, skivade
50 g små blomkålsbuketter
2 tomater, skalade,
urkärnade, klyftade
50 g späd färsk spenat
100 g blandad sallad
salt och vitpeppar

GARNITYR
fint skuren gräslök

Blanda ingredienserna till salladen.

Koka upp vatten och vinäger. Knäck äggen i små koppar vid sidan om. Häll försiktigt ner äggen efter kastrullens kant när vattnet sjuder. Låt sjuda i 3–4 minuter. Lyft upp äggen och lägg dem i kallt vatten.

Salta och peppra abborrfiléerna. Stek skinnsidorna knapriga i smör i en het panna. Vänd och stek andra sidan i någon minut.

Fördela salladen på tallrikarna. Lägg fisken och äggen ovanpå. Skeda över brynt smörvinägrett och garnera med fint skuren gräslök.

STEKT ABBORRFILÉ MED SOMMARSALLAD OCH BRYNT SMÖR
Fried perch with summer salad and brown butter vinaigrette

FRIED PERCH WITH SUMMER SALAD AND BROWN BUTTER VINAIGRETTE

serves 4

500 g perch fillets
with skin on, scaled
500 ml water
2 tbsp white wine vinear
4 eggs
salt and white pepper
1 tbsp butter
brown butter vinaigrette
(p.319)

SUMMER SALAD
250 g boiled new potatoes,
cold, sliced
50 g radish, sliced
50 g small cauliflower heads
2 tomatoes, peeled, deseeded,
cut into segments
50 g tender fresh spinach
100 g mixed salad
salt and white pepper

GARNISH
finely cut chives

Mix the ingredients for the salad together.

Bring the water and vinegar up to a simmer. Break the eggs into small cups. Pour the eggs gently down the edge of the pan into the simmering water, simmer for 3–4 minutes. Remove the eggs and cool in cold water.

Season the perch fillets with the salt and pepper, then in a hot pan fry in butter skin side down until crisp. Turn the fillets over and fry for one minute more.

Divide the salad between four plates. Place the fish and eggs on top. Spoon the vinaigrette over and garnish with finely cut chives.

FJÄLLA FISK / scale fish

När vi serverar fisk med skinn är vi alltid mycket noga med att fjälla den ordentligt, så att man även kan äta det goda skinnet. Fjälla fisken hel, helst ourtagen, under kallt vatten i diskhon, då sprätter inte fjällen i väg. Använd en fiskfjällare, håll i stjärten och fjälla framåt med bestämda tag.

When serving fish with the skin on, we always descale the skin very carefully, meaning it can also be eaten. We prefer to descale while the fish is whole, under running water using a tool designed specifically for this. Hold the fish by the tail and scrape towards the head.

SPENAT- OCH RICOTTARAVIOLI MED BÖNOR OCH TOMATSÅS
spinach and ricotta ravioli with beans and tomato sauce

SPENAT- OCH RICOTTARAVIOLI
MED BÖNOR OCH TOMATSÅS

Gör en pastadeg enligt receptet.

Tina spenaten och krama ur vätskan. Fräs schalottenlök och vitlök i olivolja utan att löken får färg. Tillsätt spenaten och fräs i ytterligare någon minut. Låt svalna. Vänd ner ricottaosten, salta och peppra. Forma blandningen till bollar. Lägg dem i kylen.

Lägg de torkade bönorna i separata kastruller. Täck ordentligt med vatten. Fördela morot, purjolök, schalottenlök och kryddor i kastrullerna. Sjud bönorna mjuka i cirka en timme. Sila och plocka bort grönsakerna och kryddorna. Spola bönorna i kallt vatten.

Koka en tomatsås enligt receptet.

Kavla ut pastadegen tunt i en pastamaskin. Placera spenatbollarna i en rad med jämna mellanrum strax under degens tänkta mittlinje. Pensla degen runt om bollarna med uppvispat ägg med salt i. Vik degen över bollarna, pressa ut luften runt fyllningen och stansa sedan ut ravioln. Koka dem i någon minut i lättsaltat vatten med lite olivolja i.

Koka beurre montéen. Värm ravioln och alla bönor i den, salta och peppra. Häll av vätskan och servera ravioln och bönorna med tomatsåsen.

4 personer

pastadeg, se recept s.315
200 g fryst hel spenat
3 finhackade schalottenlökar
2 vitlöksklyftor, finhackade
2 msk olivolja
100 g ricottaost
salt och svartpeppar
tomatsås, se recept s. 312
1 ägg + 1 nypa salt till pensling
1 msk olivolja till pastavattnet
beurre montée, se recept s.312

BÖNOR
25 g torkade svarta bönor
25 g torkade vita bönor
1 morot, delad
1/2 purjolök, delad
2 hela schalottenlökar, skalade
2 timjankvistar
2 lagerblad
50 g haricots verts, förvällda
30 g förvällda och skalade bondbönor

SPINACH AND RICOTTA RAVIOLI
WITH BEANS AND TOMATO SAUCE

serves 4

pasta dough (p.327)
200 g frozen whole leaf spinach
3 shallots, finely chopped
2 cloves of garlic
2 tbsp olive oil
100 g ricotta cheese
salt and black pepper
tomato sauce (p.324)
1 egg + 1 pinch of salt
for brushing
beurre montee (p.324)

BEANS
25 g dried black beans
25 g dried white beans
1 carrot
1/2 leek
2 whole shallots, peeled
2 sprigs of thyme
2 bay leaves
50 g fine green beans, blanched
30 g blanched and peeled
broad beans

Make the pasta dough according to the recipe.

Thaw the spinach and squeeze out excess liquid. Sweat the shallots and garlic in olive oil. Add the spinach, sweat for another minute, leave to cool. Add the ricotta and season with salt and pepper. Form into teaspoon sized balls, then place in the refrigerator.

Put the dried beans into two seperate saucepans, cover with water. Divide the carrots, leeks, shallots, thyme and bay leaves between the saucepans. Simmer until soft, approximately one hour. Strain and remove the vegetables and spices. Rinse the beans under cold water.

Make a tomato sauce according to the recipe.

Roll the pasta dough thinly in a pasta machine.

Place the spinach balls evenly in a row slightly off-centre leaving an equal space between each one. Brush around the balls with egg whisked with a little salt. Fold the dough over pressing out as much air as possible. Cut into raviolis, boil in lightly salted water with a little olive oil for one minute.

Make the beurre montee. Reheat the ravioli and beans in the sauce, season with salt and pepper. Strain and serve with the tomato sauce.

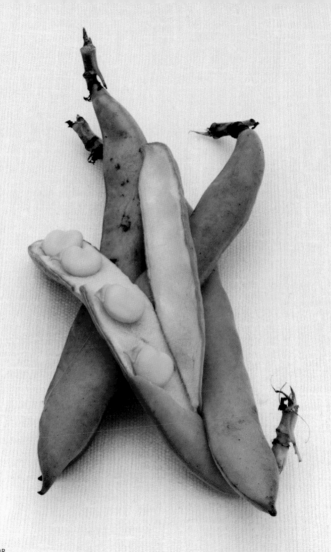

BONDBÖNOR
broad beans

BLODPUDDING MED KNAPERSTEKT FLÄSK,
ÄPPLE OCH RÅRÖRDA LINGON

1 form

5 dl svinblod
100 g fint rågmjöl
2 dl mörkt öl
2 dl ljus sirap
1 äpple, tärnat
50 g späck, tärnat
1 msk russin
1 tsk malen ingefära
1 msk torkad mejram
1 tsk malen vitpeppar
1 tsk salt
smör till stekning

TILL SERVERING
fläsk
äppelklyftor
rårörda lingon

Sila blodet. Sikta i mjöl under vispning. Tillsätt öl, sirap, äpple- och späcktärningar samt russin. Smaksätt med kryddorna. Konsistensen på smeten ska vara som filmjölk.

Klä en enliters brödform med plastfilm. Häll smeten i formen. Grädda blodpuddingen i vattenbad i 120° ugn i 1–1½ timme. Blodpuddingen är klar när den har stannat helt. Låt kallna.

Skiva blodpuddingen. Stek skivorna i lite smör. Servera dem med knaperstekt fläsk, smörstekta äppelklyftor och rårörda lingon. Blodpuddingen går också bra att frysa.

BLACK PUDDING WITH CRISPY BACON, APPLE AND PRESERVED LINGONBERRIES

1 mould

500 ml pig blood
100 g fine rye flour
200 ml dark beer
200 ml golden syrup
1 apple, diced
50 g larding bacon, diced
1 tbsp raisins
1 tsp ground ginger
1 tbsp dried marjoram
1 tsp ground white pepper
1 tsp salt
butter for frying

SERVE WITH
bacon
segments of apple
lingonberry preserve

Strain the blood. Sieve the flour into the blood whisking constantly. Add the beer, syrup, apple, bacon pieces and raisins. Add the spices. The consistency should be like sour milk.

Line a one-litre bread mould with cling film. Pour the mixture into the mould. Bake the black pudding in a water bath in a 120°C oven for 1–1½ hours. The black pudding should set completely. Leave to cool.

Slice the black pudding and fry in a little butter. Serve with crispy fried bacon, apple segments fried in butter and lingonberry preserve. Black pudding can be stored in the freezer.

BLODPUDDING/black pudding

Än en gång har skolmatsalen och industrin ställt till det. När vi talar om blodpudding är det inte de inplastade halvmånarna från snabbköpet vi menar, utan den vi gör själva. Hemgjord blodpudding är en delikatess som det tar tid att laga, men som smakar oslagbart gott.

When we refer to black pudding it is not the hard black thing wrapped in plastic found in supermarkets but a dish that, though it takes a little time to prepare, has an unbeatable taste. It is the serving of black pudding in schools and the methods of mass production that have destroyed what was once a wonderful dish.

STEKT BLÄCKFISK PROVENÇALE
fried cuttlefish provençale

STEKT BLÄCKFISK PROVENÇALE

4 personer

4 små bläckfiskar (seppia)
4 torkade tomathalvor,
se recept s. 313
2 kokta kronärtskocksbottnar
se recept s. 314
100 g haricots verts
8 färska lökar
20 niçoiseoliver
1 msk förstapressad olivolja

FYLLNING
6 schalottenlökar, finhackade
2 msk olivolja
2 vitlöksklyftor, finhackade
150 g champinjoner,
finhackade
1 citron, rivet skal av
salt och vitpeppar
4 tomater, skalade,
urkärnade, tärnade
2 msk fint strimlad bladpersilja

Skölj och rensa bläckfiskarna. Torka dem lätt med en handduk och lägg dem i kylen.

Torka tomaterna enligt receptet.

Koka kronärtskocksbottnarna enligt receptet.

Fräs schalottenlöken till fyllningen mjuk i olivolja utan att den får färg. Tillsätt vitlök och champinjoner. Koka ihop något och smaksätt sedan med citronskal, salt och peppar. Vänd ner tomattärningar och persilja på slutet. Fyll bläckfiskarna underifrån med svampfyllningen. Bryn dem i olivolja och stek färdigt dem i 175° ugn i 7–8 minuter.

Ansa och förväll haricots verts och de färska lökarna i lättsaltat vatten. Skär kronärtskocksbottnarna i mindre bitar. Blanda haricots verts, lök, kronärtskocksbottnar, torkade tomater, oliver och olivolja till en sallad.

Servera bläckfiskarna med salladen.

FRIED CUTTLEFISH PROVENÇALE

Dry the tomatoes according to the recipe.

Rinse and clean the cuttlefish, dry lightly with a tea towel. Place in the refrigerator.

Boil the artichoke hearts according to the recipe.

Sweat the shallots for the filling gently in olive oil until soft without colouring. Add the garlic and mushrooms. Cook gently for a few minutes, then sprinkle on the lemon rind and season with salt and pepper. Stir in the tomato and parsley, remove from the heat. Fill the cuttlefish from the bottom with the mushroom filling. Carefully brown the cuttlefish in olive oil, then place in a 175°C oven for 7–8 minutes.

Clean and blanch the fine green beans and onions in lightly salted, boiling water. Cut the artichoke hearts into small pieces, then mix with the green beans, onions, artichoke hearts, dried tomatoes, olives, and olive oil. Serve with the cuttlefish.

serves 4

4 small cuttlefish
4 dried tomato halves (p.325)
2 boiled artichoke hearts (p.326)
100 g fine green beans
8 small onions
20 nicoise olives
1 tbsp extra virgin olive oil

FILLING
6 shallots, finely chopped
2 tbsp olive oil
2 cloves of garlic,
finely chopped
150 g white mushrooms,
finely chopped
grated rind of 1 lemon
salt and white pepper
4 tomatoes, peeled,
deseeded, diced
2 tbsp finely shredded
flat leaf parsley

BLÄCKFISK/cuttle fish

Om fler vågade prova så skulle de upptäcka hur lätt det är att laga bläckfisk och hur god smaken är. Fråga bara fiskhandlaren hur just den sorts bläckfisk du köper ska behandlas. Vissa sorter ska bankas möra, andra kan ätas nästan naturella, en del behöver lång koktid, andra ska anrättas snabbt. Generellt gäller att bläckfisk har bra hållbarhet, jämfört med andra «blötdjur».

Ask your fishmonger what to do with the specific type of octopus you buy. Some need to be tenderised, others you can enjoy almost raw, some need to be cooked for hours, others are ready after a few minutes. In general octopus keeps well in the refrigerator, at least compared to other «molluscs».

GÖDKALVMEDALJONG MED KRONÄRTSKOCKSBARIGOU
prime veal medallion with artichoke barigou

GÖDKALVMEDALJONG
MED KRONÄRTSKOCKSBARIGOULE

Skär skockbottnarna rena från blad och skägg.
Klyfta dem. Fräs sidfläsk, schalottenlök och korianderfrön i lite olivolja. Tillsätt skockbottnarna och
fräs ytterligare någon minut. Slå på vin och buljong
och koka upp. Lägg i morötterna och smaksätt med
vitlök, salt, peppar och resterande olivolja. Låt sjuda
i cirka 15 minuter eller tills skockorna är mjuka.

Skär köttet i portionsbitar. Gnid in dem med salt
och peppar. Bryn bitarna i smör tillsammans med
salviablad. Stek färdigt i 150° ugn i 4–5 minuter. Ta
ut och låt köttet vila i 5–10 minuter i aluminiumfolie innan det serveras med kronärtskocksbarigoule.

4 personer

600 g gödkalvfilé
salt och vitpeppar
1 msk smör
5 salviablad

KRONÄRTSKOCKSBARIGOULE
6 små kronärtskockor
50 g rökt sidfläsk, skuret i stavar
2 schalottenlökar, skivade
1 tsk korianderfrön, krossade
1/2 dl förstapressad olivolja
2 dl vitt vin
4 dl kycklingbuljong,
se recept s. 308
4 små morötter
1 vitlöksklyfta, hackad
salt och vitpeppar

PRIME VEAL MEDALLION
WITH ARTICHOKE BARIGOULE

serves 4

600 g prime topside veal fillet
salt and white pepper
1 tbsp butter
5 sage leaves

ARTICHOKE BARIGOULE
6 small artichokes
50 g smoked bacon,
cut into strips
2 shallots, sliced
1 tsp coriander seeds, crushed
50 ml extra virgin olive oil
200 ml white wine
400 ml chicken stock (p.320)
4 small carrots
1 clove of garlic, chopped
salt and white pepper

Remove the hearts from the artichokes and cut into segments. Fry bacon, shallots and coriander seeds in a little olive oil. Add the artichokes hearts and fry for another minute. Add wine, stock and bring to the boil. Add the carrots, garlic and season with salt and pepper, then add the rest of the olive oil, simmer for approximately 15 minutes or until the artichoke hearts are soft.

Cut the meat into portion sized pieces, season with salt and pepper. Brown the pieces in hot butter together with the sage leaves. Place in a 150°C oven for 4–5 minutes or until ready. Remove the meat from the oven and let it rest for 5–10 minutes under foil, then serve with the artichoke barigoule.

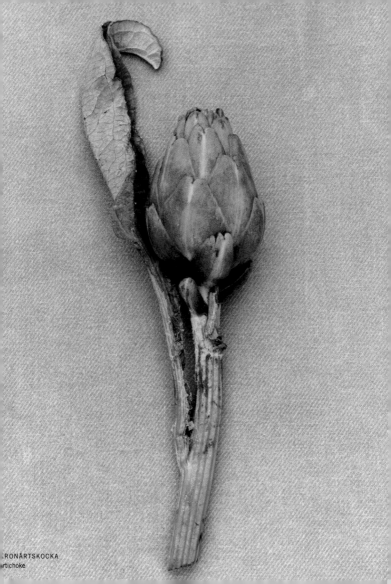

KRONÄRTSKOCKA
artichoke

CANNELLONI MED MANGOLD, JORDÄRTSKOCKSCRÈME OCH TOPPMURKLOR

Gör en pastadeg enligt receptet.

Förväll toppmurklorna i lättsaltat vatten. Dela dem på längden och skölj dem fyra gånger i kallt vatten. Låt dem rinna av.

Skär mangoldbladen rena från grova stammar. Grovstrimla bladen och fräs dem i smör med schalottenlök och vitlök. Salta och peppra.

Kavla ut pastadegen tunt. Skär degen i rektangulära plattor, cirka 8 x 12 cm. Koka degplattorna, några i taget, i 10 sekunder i saltat vatten. Kyl dem i isvatten.

Skala och skiva jordärtskockorna. Fräs skivorna i smör med schalottenlök i en kastrull. Slå på buljong och grädde. Koka jordärtskockorna mjuka. Mixa och passera dem genom en finmaskig sil. Smaksätt crèmen med salt och peppar.

Fördela mangoldblandningen på degplattorna. Rulla dem till cannelloni, lägg dem på ett ugnssäkert fat och värm dem i 150° ugn i 6 – 8 minuter.

Fräs toppmurklorna i smör med schalottenlök och vitlök. Salta och peppra.

Servera cannelloni med jordärtskockscrème och toppmurklor. Garnera med lite persilja.

4 personer

pastadeg, se recept s. 315
1 mangoldstånd
1 msk smör
5 schalottenlökar, hackade
2 vitlöksklyftor, hackade
salt och vitpeppar

TOPPMURKLOR
50 g toppmurklor
1 msk smör
1 schalottenlök, finhackad
1 vitlöksklyfta, finhackad
salt och vitpeppar

JORDÄRTSKOCKSCRÈME
300 g jordärtskockor
1 msk smör
3 schalottenlökar, skivade
5 dl kycklingbuljong,
se recept s. 308
2 dl grädde
salt och vitpeppar

GARNITYR
hackad bladpersilja

CANNELLONI WITH SWISS CHARD, JERUSALEM ARTICHOKE CREAM AND MORELS

serves 4

pasta dough (p. 327)
1 bunch swiss chard
1 tbsp butter
5 shallots, chopped
2 cloves of garlic, chopped
salt and white pepper

MORELS
50 g morels
1 tbsp butter
1 shallot, finely chopped
1 clove of garlic,
finely chopped
salt and white pepper

JERUSALEM ARTICHOKE
CREAM
300 g jerusalem artichokes
1 tbsp butter
3 shallots, sliced
500 ml chicken stock, (p. 320)
200 ml cream
salt and white pepper

GARNISH
chopped flat leaf parsley

Make the pasta dough according to the recipe. Blanch the morels in lightly salted water. Cut lengthwise, rinse four times in cold water, drain. Discard the white stalk of the chard and coarsely chop the leaves into strips. Fry in hot butter with shallots and garlic. Season with salt and pepper.

Thinly roll the pasta dough and cut into pieces, 8 x 12 cm. Cook a few at a time in boiling salted water for 10 seconds, cool quickly in iced water. Peel and slice the jerusalem artichokes. Heat the butter in a large saucepan and sweat the artichoke and shallots until softened. Add the stock and cream. Boil until the artichokes are completely soft. Blend with a hand mixer or food processor and strain through a fine sieve. Season with salt and pepper.

Divide the swiss chard mixture between each piece of dough and roll into cannellonis. Place in an ovenproof dish and bake at 150°C for 6–8 minutes. Sweat the morels in butter with shallots and garlic. Season with salt and pepper. Serve the cannelloni with the jerusalem artichoke cream and morels. Garnish with the parsley.

MURKLOR/morels

Numera använder vi enbart toppmurklor. Stenmurklan
må vara en delikatess, men efter fem förvällningar à
10 minuter finns fortfarande 9–11 procent av det
ursprungliga giftet (gyromitrin) kvar. Och vid det laget
har murklan totalt förlorat sitt gastronomiska värde.

Nowadays we only use the edible «top» morels.
The other kind,«stone» morel, may be delicious,
but after you have parboiled it five times for 10
minutes 9–11 percent of the poison gyromitrin is
still there. By that time the morel has lost all of its
culinary appeal.

BRÄSERAT LAMMLÄGG
MED BÖNOR OCH PATA NEGRA-SKINKA

4 personer

4 lammlägg
5 msk smör
1 morot, tärnad
1 gul lök, hackad
2 vitlöksklyftor, hackade
1 liter kalvsky, se recept s. 307
1 purjolök,
den vita delen, tärnad
1 liten timjankvist
8 vitpepparkorn
1 lagerblad
salt och vitpeppar
gremolata, se recept s. 314
20 smålökar, skalade
1/2 msk strösocker
1 dl spritärter
4 skivor pata negra-skinka,
strimlade

BÖNOR
50 g torkade
vita och svarta bönor
1 morot
en bit purjolök
2 hela schalottenlökar
2 timjankvistar
2 lagerblad
2 skivor bacon
salt

Bryn lammläggen i 4 msk smör tillsammans med morot, lök och vitlök. Slå på kalvsky. Tillsätt purjolök, timjan, vitpeppar och lagerblad. Låt sjuda under lock tills läggen är möra, det vill säga i cirka 2 timmar. Köttet ska släppa från benen. Ta upp läggen och koka ihop skyn till hälften. Sila och smaksätt med salt och peppar.

Lägg de vita och svarta bönorna i separata kastruller. Täck ordentligt med vatten. Fördela morot, purjolök, schalottenlök, timjan, lagerblad och bacon i kastrullerna. Sjud bönorna mjuka i cirka en timme. Sila och plocka bort grönsakerna, kryddorna och baconskivorna. Smaksätt bönorna med salt.

Gör gremolatan enligt receptet.

Bryn smålökarna i resterande smör. Strö över socker och låt karamellisera. Stek dem därefter mjuka i 175° ugn i cirka 5 minuter.

Vänd ner lökarna, bönorna och spritärter i skyn.

Servera lammläggen med sky, strimlad pata negra-skinka och gremolata.

BRÄSERAT LAMMLÄGG MED BÖNOR OCH PATA NEGRA-SKINKA
braised lamb shanks with beans and pata negra

BRAISED LAMB SHANKS
WITH BEANS AND PATA NEGRA

serves 4

4 lamb shanks
5 tbsp butter
1 carrot, diced
1 onion, chopped
2 cloves of garlic, chopped
1 litre veal stock, (p. 319)
white of 1 leek, diced
1 small sprig of thyme
8 white peppercorns
1 bay leaf
salt and white pepper
gremolata, (p. 326)
20 baby onions, peeled
1/2 tbsp caster sugar
100 ml shelled fresh peas
4 slices pata negra, shredded

BEANS
25 g dried white beans
25 g dried black beans
1 carrot
a piece of leek
2 whole shallots
2 sprigs of thyme
2 bay leaves
2 slices of bacon
salt

Brown the lamb shanks in 4 tbsp butter with the carrot, onion and garlic. Pour the veal stock over and add the leek, thyme, white pepper and bay leaf. Cover and simmer until the shanks are tender, approximately 2 hours or until the meat falls easily from the bone. Remove the lamb and reduce the broth by half. Strain and season with salt and pepper.

Put the white and the black beans in separate saucepans, cover with cold water and divide the carrot, leek, shallots, thyme, bay leaves and bacon between the two. Simmer until the beans are soft, about one hour. Strain and remove the vegetables, spices and the bacon. Season the beans with salt.

Make the gremolata according to the recipe.

Brown the onions in the rest of the butter, sprinkle with sugar. Bake in the oven at 175°C, until soft and caramelised, approximately 5 minutes. Add the onions, beans and peas to the broth.

Serve the lamb shanks with the broth, shredded pata negra and gremolata.

SMÖR / butter

Stänker det när du steker i smör? Försök att skira/klara smöret först. Genom att smälta smöret och skumma bort allt som flyter upp till ytan får du ett renare smör, perfekt att steka i. När vi ska servera smält smör, till exempel till fisk, så bryner vi det alltid. Då kommer den underbart nötiga smörsmaken verkligen fram.

When frying with butter, do you find it splashes all over the kitchen? Then first clarify the butter by melting it and skimming away everything that floats to the surface. Now you have a clean butter to cook with and perfect for frying. When we serve melted butter, for example with fish, we always brown it, creating a rich nutty taste.

UGNSBAKAD VÄSTERHAVSTORSK I CLAMCHOWDER MARYLAND
oven-baked cod in mussel chowder

UGNSBAKAD VÄSTERHAVSTORSK
I CLAMCHOWDER MARYLAND

4 personer

600 g västerhavstorsk
6 dl musselbuljong,
se recept s. 309
2 bakpotatisar
4 sticklökar, ansade
2 schalottenlökar, finhackade
2 vitlöksklyftor, finhackade
musslor från buljongkoket
2 msk osaltat smör
1 msk vispgrädde
salt och vitpeppar

GARNITYR
2 tomater
4 baconskivor

Koka musselbuljong enligt receptet. Plocka bort musslorna från skalen. Spara musslorna.

Skålla och skala tomaterna till garnityret. Kärna ur dem och tärna tomatköttet. Tärna och knapersteck baconet.

Skala och skär potatisen i centimeterstora tärningar. Koka dem och sticklökarna mjuka i lite av musselbuljongen. Låt schalottenlök och vitlök koka med. Lyft upp potatistärningarna och sticklökarna och lägg dem i djupa tallrikar.

Fördela musslorna i tallrikarna.

Skär torsken i portionsbitar. Sjud dem i lättsaltat vatten i 8–10 minuter. Lägg fisken på musslorna.

Värm och mixa resterande musselbuljong med smör och grädde. Smaksätt med salt och peppar. Häll buljongen över fisken.

Garnera torskbitarna med tomat och bacon.

OVEN-BAKED COD
IN MUSSEL CHOWDER

Prepare the mussel stock according to the recipe. Remove the mussels from the shells and place to one side. Discard the shells.

Blanch and peel the tomatoes for the garnish, remove the seeds and dice the flesh. Dice the bacon and fry until crisp.

Peel and cut the potatoes into 1 cm cubes. Boil the potatoes with the spring onions, shallot and garlic in a little mussel stock until soft. Remove the potatoes and spring onions and divide with the mussels between 4 soup plates.

Cut the fish into 4 pieces. Simmer in lightly salted water for 8–10 minutes. Place the fish on the mussels and vegetables.

Warm up the remaining mussel stock, then mix in a food processor with butter and cream. Season with salt and pepper. Pour over the fish. Garnish with tomatoes and bacon.

serves 4

600 g cod
600 ml mussel stock (p. 321)
2 baking potatoes
4 spring onions
2 shallots, finely chopped
2 cloves of garlic, finely chopped
mussels from the stock
2 tbsp unsalted butter
1 tbsp cream
salt and white pepper

GARNISH
2 tomatoes
4 slices of bacon

KANINSADEL MED SPARRIS OCH KRONÄRTSKOCKO
saddle of rabbit with asparagus and artichok

KANINSADEL MED SPARRIS
OCH KRONÄRTSKOCKOR

Skär loss ryggfilén och kappan i ett stycke från benet
på kaninsadlarna.

Fräs svamp, schalottenlök, vitlök, persilja och
dragon i 1 msk smör. Smaksätt med rivet citronskal,
salt och peppar. Fördela svampblandningen på
kappan intill ryggfilén. Vik ihop kappan och filén till
ett paket och rulla till en korv med hjälp av aluminiumfolie.

Koka rödvinssås enligt receptet.

Lägg de inrullade kaninrullarna i en ugnssäker
form. Ställ den i 200° ugn i 10–12 minuter. Ta ut
formen ur ugnen och låt rullarna vila i 5 minuter. Ta
bort folien och bryn rullarna gyllenbruna i resterande smör i en het stekpanna innan de ska serveras.

Skär skockbottnarna rena från blad och skägg.
Koka bottnarna mjuka i saltat vatten och citronjuice.
Skär bottnarna i tårtbitar och fräs dem i olivolja
innan de ska serveras.

Skala sparrisen och koka den mjuk i saltat vatten.

Servera kaninrullarna med rödvinssås, kronärtskockor och sparris.

4 personer

2 kaninsadlar
200 g champinjoner,
finhackade
3 schalottenlökar, finhackade
2 vitlöksklyftor, finhackade
1 msk finhackad bladpersilja
1/2 msk finhackad dragon
2 msk smör
1 citron, juice och rivet skal
salt och vitpeppar
rödvinssås, se recept s. 312
4 små kronärtskockor
olivolja
16 gröna sparrisar

SADDLE OF RABBIT
WITH ASPARAGUS AND ARTICHOKE

serves 4

2 saddles of rabbit
200 g white mushrooms,
finely chopped
3 shallots, finely chopped
2 cloves of garlic, finely chopped
1 tbsp finely chopped
flat leaf parsley
1/2 tbsp finely
chopped tarragon
2 tbsp butter
juice and grated rind of 1 lemon
salt and white pepper
red wine sauce, (p. 324)
4 small artichokes
olive oil
16 green asparagus spears

Remove the rabbit fillet with the skin flaps, in one piece from the bone.

Sweat the mushrooms, shallots, garlic, parsley and tarragon in half of the butter. Flavour with the grated lemon rind, salt and pepper. Spread the mushroom mixture over the fillet. Roll the fillet with the skin into a sausage shape and wrap tightly with aluminium foil.

Prepare the red wine sauce according to the recipe.

Put the rabbit rolls into an ovenproof dish. Bake at 200°C for 10–12 minutes. Remove from the oven and rest for 5 minutes. Heat the remaining butter, remove the foil and brown in hot butter before serving.

Remove the hearts from the artichokes and boil until soft in salted water with lemon juice added. Cut each heart into quarters and fry gently in olive oil.

Peel the asparagus and boil until soft in salted water.

Serve the rabbit rolls with red wine sauce, artichokes and asparagus.

SPARRIS/asparagus

Skala vit sparris extra noga, tills den tvärstrimmiga strukturen syns. På så sätt slipper man trista trådar och kan njuta av hela sparrisen. Den gröna sparrisen är inte lika trådig, den kan man ansa snabbare. För att akta topparna och hålla sparrisen rak binder vi den i portionsstora knippen innan den kokas, sju normalstora sparrisar per knippe brukar vara lagom.

White asparagus needs to be peeled really well, until you can see the streaky coloured structure of the stem. Doing this will ensure that you can eat and enjoy the whole asparagus without the tough fibrous skin. Green asparagus is less difficult to deal with. To prevent the tips from getting damaged in cooking we tie about seven spears together with kitchen string before boiling them.

STEKT KALVBRÄSS MED HAVSKRÄFTOR OCH KRÄFTBRÄSERAD PERSILJEROT

4 personer

150 g kalvbräss
2 dl havskräftsfond,
se recept hummerfond s. 310
2 medelstora persiljerötter
3 msk smör
1/2 msk hackad dragon
1/2 dl mjölk
12 havskräftstjärtar, skalade
salt och vitpeppar
olivolja

LAG
1/2 gul lök, finhackad
1 selleristjälk, fint tärnad
1 liten morot, fint tärnad
1 msk olivolja
1 lagerblad
5 vitpepparkorn
2 dl torrt vitt vin

Koka en havskräftsfond enligt receptet för hummer-fond. Byt ut hummerskalen mot kräftskal.

Spola kalvbrässen i kallt vatten i 5 minuter. Förväll den i kokande vatten och kyl av den i kallt vatten. Plocka brässen fri från de yttersta hinnorna.

Fräs grönsakerna till lagen i olivolja. Lägg i brässen och kryddorna och slå på vin. Koka i 5 minuter. Ta kastrullen från spisen och låt dra i 10 minuter under lock. Lyft upp brässen och skär den i portionsbitar.

Skala och ansa persiljerötterna. Skär rötterna i fina bitar och bryn dem i 1 msk smör. Slå på havskräftsfond och sjud rötterna mjuka. Lyft upp och lägg dem på ett fat. Strö över hackad dragon. Mixa havskräftsfonden med mjölk och 1 msk smör innan den ska serveras.

Bryn kalvbrässen i resterande smör i en het panna. Salta och peppra.

Halstra havskräftstjärtarna i lite olivolja. Salta och peppra.

Fördela kalvbräss, havskräftstjärtar och persilje-rötter på tallrikarna. Slå på havskräftsfond.

EKT KALVBRÄSS MED HAVSKRÄFTOR OCH KRÄFTBRÄSERAD PERSILJEROT
ed sweetbread with langoustines and langoustine braised parsnip

FRIED SWEETBREAD WITH LANGOUSTINES
AND LANGOUSTINE BRAISED PARSNIPS

serves 4

150 g sweetbreads
200 ml langoustine stock, (p. 322)
2 medium sized parsnips
3 tbsp butter
1/2 tbsp chopped tarragon
50 ml milk
12 langoustine tails, peeled
salt and white pepper
olive oil

NAGE
1/2 onion, finely chopped
1 celery stalk, finely diced
1 small carrot, finely diced
1 tbsp olive oil
1 bay leaf
5 white peppercorns
200 ml dry white wine

Prepare the langoustine stock according to the recipe for lobster stock using langoustine shells instead of lobster shells.

Rinse the sweetbread in cold water for 5 minutes. Blanch in boiling water and cool quickly in cold water, remove the outer membrane.

Sweat the vegetables for the nage in olive oil. Add the sweetbread, spices and wine. Boil for 5 minutes, remove from the heat, cover with a lid and leave for 10 minutes. Remove the sweetbread and cut into portion-sized pieces.

Peel the parsnips and cut into chunks. Brown in half of the butter, then pour the langoustine stock over and simmer until soft. Remove the parsnips from the stock, place in a dish and sprinkle with chopped tarragon. In a food processor mix the langoustine stock with milk and 1 tbsp of butter before serving. In a hot pan, brown the sweetbread in the remaining butter, season with salt and pepper. Fry the langoustine tails in olive oil and season with salt and pepper. Divide the sweetbread, langoustine tails and parsnips between four plates and pour the langoustine stock over.

VÄGA RÄTT/weighty reasons

Många tror att kockar alltid lagar mat på en höft och aldrig mäter eller väger speciellt noga. Ibland är det kanske så, men vill du vara säker på att få samma resultat varje gång du lagar en rätt är det viktigt att följa angivna mått. Speciellt om du bakar kan bara några gram för mycket eller för lite förändra hela slutresultatet. Så, investera i en liten elektronisk våg. Det tjänar både du och maten på.

A lot of people tend to think that chefs always cook haphazardly, never using scales. It's like that sometimes but if you want to get the same result every time you cook it is important to follow the recipe, especially when baking, a few tablespoons can change the result. So let your next investment be in a small electronic scale, a gain for you and for the food.

HALSTRADE PILGRIMSMUSSLOR MED VITLÖKSCRÊM
fried king scallops with garlic cream

HALSTRADE PILGRIMSMUSSLOR
MED VITLÖKSCRÈME

Skär potatisen till chipsen tunt på en skärmaskin eller mandolin. Fritera skivorna gyllenbruna i olja. Salta och peppra.

Koka potatisen till vitlökscrèmen mjuk i vatten. Häll av vattnet. Koka upp mjölk med en vitlöksklyfta i. Lägg potatisen i mjölken och mixa. Tillsätt olivolja, salt och peppar.

Koka russinen i vatten i några minuter och häll av vattnet. Blanda russinen med kapris, vinäger och olivolja.

Halstra pilgrimsmusslorna i smör och olivolja, någon minut på varje sida. Salta och peppra.

Servera pilgrimsmusslorna med vitlökscrème och russin. Garnera med ett potatischips.

4 personer som tilltugg

4 pilgrimsmusslor
smör + olivolja
salt och vitpeppar
1 msk vita russin
1 tsk kapris
1 tsk sherryvinäger
1 tsk förstapressad olivolja

CHIPS
1 mandelpotatis
olja till fritering
salt och svartpeppar

VITLÖKSCRÈME
1 mandelpotatis, skalad
1 1/2 dl mjölk
1 vitlöksklyfta
1/2 dl förstapressad olivolja
salt och vitpeppar

FRIED KING SCALLOPS
WITH GARLIC CREAM

serves 4

4 scallops
butter + olive oil
salt and white pepper
1 tbsp raisins
1 tsp capers
1 tsp sherry vinegar
1 tsp extra virgin olive oil

CHIPS
1 almond potato
oil for frying
salt and black pepper

GARLIC CREAM
1 almond potato, peeled
150 ml milk
1 clove of garlic
50 ml extra virgin olive oil
salt and white pepper

Cut the potato into chips using a cutter or mandolin. Deep-fry in hot oil until golden brown. Remove from the oil and season with salt and pepper.

Boil the potato for the garlic cream in water until soft. Drain the water. Bring the milk to the boil with the clove of garlic. Put the boiled potato in the milk and blend together with a hand blender. Add olive oil, salt and pepper.

Boil the raisins in water for a couple of minutes, drain, then add the capers, vinegar and olive oil.

Fry the scallops in hot butter and olive oil, a minute on each side. Season with salt and pepper.

Serve the scallops with the garlic cream and raisins. Garnish with chipped potatoes.

POTATIS /potatoes

Eftersom mandelpotatis lätt kokar sönder passar den extra bra till puré. Men läs en gång till på påsen innan du köper mandelpotatis. Den riktigt gula färgen får bara mandelpotatis från Norrland, där den växer långsamt och får rik smak. Mandelpotatis från Skåne, däremot, kan vara både blek och betydligt mer smaklös.

We prefer a specific type of potatoes, grown in the northern parts of Sweden where it grows very slowly. It is called mandelpotatis (almond potatoes) and is extremely easy to overcook, therefore we mostly serve it mashed! Yellow in colour and rich in taste, *Estnia* and *Belle de Fontenay* are similar.

GÖDKALVLEVER MED
RÖDBETSVINÄGRETT OCH SALVIA

4 personer

4 skivor gödkalvlever
50 g haricots verts
12 sticklökar
12 salviablad, strimlade
salt och vitpeppar

RÖDBETSVINÄGRETT
150 g färska rödbetor, skalade
1 dl balsamvinäger
salt och vitpeppar
2 msk förstapressad olivolja

Tärna rödbetorna och koka dem mjuka i balsamvinäger. Ta bort kastrullen från värmen. Salta,
peppra och tillsätt olivoljan droppvis.

Ansa haricots verts och sticklökar och koka dem
mjuka i lättsaltat vatten. Blanda dem sedan med salvia.

Grilla kalvlevern i en het panna, cirka 2 minuter
på varje sida. Salta och peppra.

Servera kalvlevern med grönsaker och rödbetsvinägrett.

GÖDKALVLEVER MED RÖDBETSVINÄGRETT OCH SALVIA
Prime calves' liver with beetroot vinaigrette and sage

PRIME CALVES' LIVER WITH
BEETROOT VINAIGRETTE AND SAGE

serves 4

4 slices of prime calves liver
50 g green beans
12 spring onions
12 sage leaves, shredded
salt and white pepper

BEETROOT VINAIGRETTE
150 g fresh beetroots, peeled
100 ml balsamic vinegar
salt and white pepper
2 tbsp extra virgin olive oil

Dice and boil the beetroot in the balsamic vinegar until soft. Remove the saucepan from the heat and little by little add salt, pepper and olive oil.

Prepare the green beans and spring onions and boil in lightly salted water until soft, drain, then mix with the sage.

Grill the calves' liver in a hot pan, for approximately 2 minutes on each side. Season with salt and pepper.

Serve the liver with the vegetables and beetroot vinaigrette.

ÖRTER/ herbs

Färska kryddörter är ett trivsamt tillskott till det moderna köket. Förutom våra gamla vänner dill, persilja och gräslök kan vi numera året runt botanisera bland basilika, koriander, salvia, citronmeliss, rosmarin, timjan, oregano, mynta, fransk dragon ... Odla själv på sommaren, köp växthusodlade krukor på vintern.

One of the most welcome newcomers in the kitchen is the use of fresh herbs. There are our old friends dill, parsley and chives, however now we can enjoy fresh basil, sage, lemon balm, rosemary, thyme and tarragon. All of these can be grown in pots during the summer and are available year-round in the supermarket.

TONFISK MED APELSINBRÄSERAD ENDIVE OCH CH
tuna with orange braised belgian endive and cl

TONFISK MED APELSINBRÄSERAD ENDIVE OCH CHILI

Gör basilikaoljan enligt receptet för örtolja.

Skär endiverna i mindre bitar. Lägg dem i en kastrull. Strö över socker, apelsinskal och slå på apelsin- och citronjuice. Koka upp under lock. Ta bort kastrullen från värmen och låt dra utan omrörning i 10 minuter. Tillsätt chili.

Skär tonfisken i portionsbitar. Pensla dem med olivolja och grilla hastigt båda sidorna i en het panna. Salta och peppra.

Grilla havskräftstjärtarna. Salta och peppra.

Servera tonfisken med havskräftstjärtar, endiver och apelsinlag. Garnera med basilikaolja.

4 personer

600 g tonfiskfilé
12 havskräftstjärtar
3 endiver
1 msk strösocker
1 apelsin, juice och rivet skal
1/2 citron, juice
1 knivsudd färsk hackad chili
1 msk olivolja
salt och svartpeppar

GARNITYR
basilikaolja,
se recept örtolja s. 311

TUNA WITH ORANGE BRAISED
BELGIAN ENDIVE AND CHILLI

serves 4

600 g tuna fillet
12 langoustine tails
3 Belgian endives
1 tbsp caster sugar
juice and grated rind of 1 orange
juice of 1/2 lemon
tiny pinch of chopped chilli
1 tbsp olive oil
salt and black pepper

GARNISH
basil oil,
make as herb oil (p. 323)

Make the basil oil according to the recipe for herb oil.

Cut the endives into small pieces. Place in a saucepan, sprinkle with the sugar and orange rind, pour over the orange and lemon juice. Cover and bring to the boil. Remove the saucepan from the heat and leave to stand without stirring for 10 minutes. Add the chilli.

Cut the tuna fillet into portions, brush with olive oil and grill quickly on both sides in a hot grill pan. Season with salt and pepper.

Grill the langoustine tails and season with salt and pepper.

Serve the tuna with the langoustines, endive and orange nage. Garnish with basil oil.

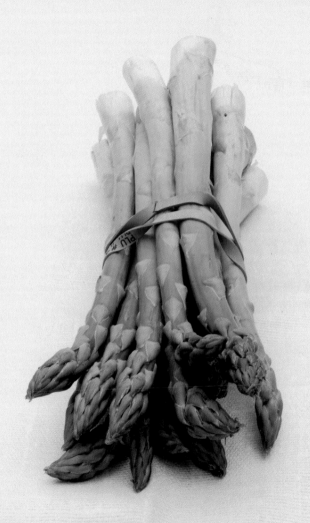

GRÖN SPARRIS
green asparagus

SPARRISRISOTTO
MED BONDBÖNOR OCH SVAMP

4 personer

risotto, se recept s. 313
8 gröna sparrisar,
skalade och skurna i mindre bitar
8 vita sparrisar,
skalade och skurna i mindre bitar
50 g skalade bondbönor
50 g blandad svamp
1 msk smör
salt och vitpeppar

Förväll sparrisen i saltat vatten. Kyl bitarna i isvatten.

Följ grundreceptet för risotto. Vänd ner sparris och bondbönor mot slutet och låt dem bli varma. Spara även några sparrisbitar och bondbönor till garnering.

Fräs svampen i smör. Salta och peppra.

Servera sparrisrisotton med svampen.

SPARRISRISOTTO MED BONDBÖNOR OCH SVAMP
asparagus risotto with broad beans and mushrooms

ASPARAGUS RISOTTO
WITH BROAD BEANS AND MUSHROOMS

serves 4

risotto, (p. 325)
8 green asparagus spears,
peeled and cut into small pieces
8 white asparagus spears,
peeled and cut into small pieces
50 g peeled broad beans
50 g mixed mushrooms
1 tbsp butter
salt and white pepper

Blanch the asparagus in salted water. Cool in iced water.

Follow the recipe for risotto. Reserve a few asparagus pieces and broad beans for garnish. Add the remaining asparagus and broad beans to the risotto towards the end of cooking to warm them through.

Fry the mushrooms in butter. Season with salt and pepper.

Serve the asparagus risotto with the mushrooms and garnish.

SVAMP/ mushrooms

När det är svampsäsong har vi ofta rätter med
svamp på matsedeln. För den som plockar mycket
svamp kan en liten elektrisk torkapparat vara en bra
investering. De flesta ätbara svampar passar att
torka. Trattkantareller torkar dessutom bra även
utan torkapparat, bred bara ut dem luftigt och vänta
några dagar. Förvara svampen mörkt i lufttäta bur-
kar. När svampen ska användas smular du antingen
ner den direkt i grytan eller såsen som redning eller
så blötlägger du svampen en stund i vatten och
använder den sedan som färsk svamp.

When in season we often have dishes with mushrooms
on the menu. For those who pick a lot of mushrooms
a small electric dryer may be a good investment. Most
edible mushrooms are suitable for drying. The dark
autumn chanterelle is perfect for this even without a
dryer. Simply spread the mushrooms on a piece of
paper in a dry airy place and leave for a few days.
Store dried mushrooms in dark, air-tight pots. When
you use the mushrooms either crumble them directly
into the pot or sauce or let them soak in water for a
short time and then use as fresh mushrooms.

BRÄCKT RIMMAD OXBRINGA MED MANDELPOTATIS- OCH SVAMPKOMPOTT SAMT PERSILJEBULJONG
fried salted brisket with almond potato and mushroom compote and parsley bouillon

BRÄCKT RIMMAD OXBRINGA MED MANDELPOTATIS-
OCH SVAMPKOMPOTT SAMT PERSILJEBULJONG

Lägg oxbringan i en kastrull och täck den ordentligt med kallt vatten. Koka upp och skumma väl. Tillsätt bouquet garni, persilja och kryddor. Låt sjuda i cirka 1½ timme. Lyft upp köttet, täck det med plastfilm och lägg det under press i kylen över natten. Sila buljongen och ställ även den kallt.

Koka potatisen mjuk i lättsaltat vatten. Stek svampen i smör i en het panna. Tillsätt schalottenlök mot slutet. Smaksätt svampen med persilja, salt och peppar. Mosa potatisen med en gaffel. Blanda potatis och svamp. Smaksätt med ost, salt och peppar.

Värm buljongen från köttkoket. Mixa mjölk och persilja. Vispa ner mjölkblandningen och smöret i buljongen.

Skiva oxbringan. Stek skivornas båda sidor hastigt utan fett i en het panna.

Servera oxbringan med mandelpotatis- och svampkompott samt persiljebuljong.

4 personer

800 g rimmad oxbringa
1 bouquet garni,
se recept s. 314
1 lagerblad
5 persiljestjälkar
1 msk vitpepparkorn

KOMPOTT
500 g mandelpotatisar, skalade
100 g blandad svamp
1 msk smör
1 msk finhackad schalottenlök
1 msk hackad bladpersilja
salt och vitpeppar
20 g västerbottenost, riven

PERSILJEBULJONG
4 dl buljong från köttkoket
1/2 dl mjölk
1 dl grovhackad bladpersilja
1 msk smör

TILL SERVERING
kokta morötter
kokta gröna bönor

FRIED SALTED BRISKET WITH ALMOND POTATO AND MUSHROOM COMPOTE AND PARSLEY BOUILLON

serves 4

800 g salted brisket
1 bouquet garni (p. 326)
1 bay leaf
5 sprigs of flat leaf parsley
1 tbsp white peppercorns

COMPOTE
500 g almond potatoes, peeled
100 g mixed mushrooms
1 tbsp butter
1 tbsp finely chopped shallots
1 tbsp chopped flat leaf parsley
salt and white pepper
20 g vaesterbotten cheese, grated

PARSLEY BOUILLON
400 ml liquid
from the boiled meat
50 ml milk
100 ml coarsely chopped
flat leaf parsley
1 tbsp butter

SERVE WITH
boiled carrots
boiled green beans

Put the brisket in a large saucepan and cover with cold water. Bring to a boil and skim frequently. Add bouquet garni and spices and simmer for 1 ½ hours. Remove the meat, strain and reserve the broth somewhere cool. Cover the meat with cling film and place under a weight overnight in the refrigerator.

Boil the potatoes until soft in lightly salted water. Fry the mushrooms in butter in a hot pan, add the shallots towards the end of cooking, sprinkle on the parsley and season with salt and pepper. Mash the potatoes with a fork. Mix the potatoes and mushrooms together. Add the cheese and season with salt and pepper.

Bring the meat broth to a boil. Blend the milk and parsley in a food processor. Whisk the milk mixture and butter into the boiling broth.

Slice the brisket. Fry quickly on each side in a hot dry pan.

Serve the beef with the potato and mushroom compote and parsley bouillon.

OXBRINGA/brisket of beef

Även om den tar lite tid att koka är oxbringa verklig snabbmat när den serveras. Bara att skiva upp och bräcka hastigt eller värma i lite buljong. Tänk på att rimmad oxbringa ger salt buljong, spara bara lite av den. Färsk bringa, däremot, kokas med grönsaker och ger en utmärkt buljong. Oxbringa behöver koka längre än man tror. Om du kan lyfta hela bringan med en köttgaffel är köttet inte färdigkokt. Om du däremot behöver ta stöd av en hålslev är bringan korrekt kokt. Låt kallna under press.

Even if it takes a little time to prepare, brisket of beef is really fast food to serve. Just slice it, fry it quickly or heat it in a little stock. Just remember that salted brisket of beef gives a very salt broth, so use carefully. On the contrary, fresh brisket of beef is cooked with lots of vegetables and the broth has a superb taste. Brisket of beef needs to boil longer than you think! If you can lift it up in one piece with a big fork it's not ready. However if you need a slotted spoon to lift it – then it's perfectly cooked! Leave to cool under a heavy weight.

GRÖNSAKSBRIOCHE MED TOMATVINÄGRETT

4 personer

5 torkade tomathalvor,
se recept s. 313
2 kokta kronärtskocksbottnar,
se recept s. 314
tomatvinägrett, se recept s. 306
6 vita sparrisar
salt
15 svarta oliver
6 vitlöksklyftor
1/2 dl olivolja
1 kvist rosmarin
1/2 sats briochedeg,
se recept s. 317
5 basilikablad
1 ägg
fleur de sel (havssalt)

Torka tomaterna enligt receptet.

Koka kronärtskockorna enligt receptet.

Blanda tomatvinägretten enligt receptet.

Koka sparrisen mjuk i saltat vatten. Kärna ur oliverna.

Förväll vitlöksklyftorna med skal i vatten. Lyft upp dem och koka dem sedan mjuka i olivolja med rosmarin.

Följ receptet för briochebröd tills degen har jäst i 3 timmar. Kavla ut degen och lägg på sparris, oliver och basilikablad. Rulla ihop och pensla på ägg. Strö över havssalt. Skär några snitt i degen och stick ner de kokta vitlöksklyftorna. Grädda briochen i 175° ugn i 20–25 minuter. Låt den svalna.

Skiva grönsaksbriochen och servera den med tomatvinägrett.

GRÖNSAKSBRIOCHE MED TOMATVINÄGRETT
Vegetable brioche with tomato vinaigrette

GRÖNSAKSBRIOCH
vegetable brioch

VEGETABLE BRIOCHE
WITH TOMATO VINAIGRETTE

Dry the tomatoes according to the recipe.

Boil the artichoke hearts according to the recipe.

Prepare the tomato vinaigrette according to the recipe.

Boil the asparagus until soft in salted water. Pit the olives.

Blanch the cloves of garlic in boiling water. Remove from the water, then gently fry in olive oil with the rosemary.

Make the brioche according to the recipe and leave to rise for three hours. Roll out the dough. Place the asparagus, olives and basil leaves on the dough and roll up. Brush with egg and sprinkle with sea salt. Slash the top of the dough a few times and drop the garlic into the cuts. Bake the brioche in a 175°C oven for 20–25 minutes. Leave to cool.

Slice the brioche and serve with tomato vinaigrette.

serves 4

5 dried tomato halves (p. 325)
2 boiled artichoke hearts (p.326)
tomato vinaigrette (p. 318)
6 white asparagus
salt
15 black olives
6 cloves of garlic with skin on
50 ml olive oil
1 sprig of rosemary
1/2 batch of
brioche dough (p.330)
5 basil leaves
1 egg
fleur de sel (sea salt)

STEKT MARULK MED PARMASKINKA, SALVIA OCH TOMATRISOTTO

4 personer

4 marulkskotletter à 200 g
risotto, se recept s. 313
6 tomater
4 torkade tomathalvor,
se recept s. 313
salt och vitpeppar
12 salviablad
4 tunna skivor parmaskinka
1 msk olivolja + 1 msk smör

Följ grundreceptet för risotto, men använd bara halva mängden kycklingbuljong som mixas med 6 tomater och sedan silas genom en finmaskig sil innan du kokar risotton.

Torka tomaterna enligt receptet.

Salta och peppra marulkskotletterna. Placera tre salviablad ovanpå och linda en parmaskinksskiva runt varje kotlett. Bryn dem runt om i olivolja och smör i en het panna. Stek dem färdigt i 150° ugn i 8–10 minuter.

Servera marulkskotletterna med tomatrisotto. Garnera med de torkade tomathalvorna.

STEKT MARULK MED PARMASKINKA, SALVIA OCH TOMATRISOTTO
Fried monkfish cutlet with parma ham, sage and tomato risotto

FRIED MONKFISH CUTLET
WITH PARMA HAM, SAGE AND TOMATO RISOTTO

serves 4

4 monkfish cutlets 200 g each
risotto (p. 325)
6 tomatoes
4 dried tomato halves (p. 325)
salt and white pepper
12 leaves of sage
4 thin slices of parma ham
1 tbsp olive oil + 1 tbsp butter

Follow the base recipe for risotto using only half the chicken stock blended in a food processor with 6 tomatoes and strained trough a fine sieve.

Dry the tomatoes according to the recipe.

Season the monkfish cutlets with salt and pepper. Place three sage leaves on each and wrap with a slice of parma ham. In a hot pan brown the cutlets in olive oil and butter. Bake in a 150°C oven for 8–10 minutes.

Serve the monkfish cutlets with tomato risotto. Garnish with the dried tomato halves.

MARULK / monkfish

Letar du efter fiskdiskens fulaste fisk är chansen stor att du väljer marulken med sitt enorma huvud och sin gapande mun. Men skenet bedrar, smaken på det fasta köttet är så god att den förr kallades «fattig-manshummer». I dag är den knappast ett budget-alternativ, men vill man lyxa är den lätt att tillaga eftersom den saknar tvärgående ben och är tålmodig även om den får koka lite för länge. Till skillnad från lax, som gärna får ha lite «kärna» kvar, bör marulk vara ordentligt tillagad för att bli riktigt mör.

Look for the most ugly fish at the fishmonger and there is a good chance that you have chosen monk-fish with its enormous head and big mouth. Don´t let this put you off, the meat tastes so delicious that in the old days monkfish used to be called «poor mans lobster» .Today monkfish is hardly a bargain, more a luxury. You will find it is easy to cook owing to the absence of lateral bones. It's also a very patient fish, even if you cook it a little too long. In fact contrary to salmon which can be served a little pink, for tender monkfish it needs to be cooked right through.

KÅLDOLMAR MED ANKCONFIT, SVAMP OCH PERSILJER
stuffed cabbage rolls with duck confit, mushrooms and parsn

KÅLDOLMAR MED ANKCONFIT,
SVAMP OCH PERSILJEROT

Koka rödvinssåsen enligt receptet.

Förväll vitkålsbladen i lättsaltat vatten. Ta upp,
kyl dem i isvatten och skär bort den hårda biten på
stammen. Plocka köttet från anklåret och skär det i
mindre bitar. Stek kantarellerna i smör i en het
panna. Tillsätt schalottenlök och vitlök mot slutet.
Salta, peppra och strö över persilja. Låt svalna.
Tärna ankleverterrinen och blanda den med kantarellerna och anklåret. Fördela blandningen på vitkålsbladen och forma till dolmar. Värm dem i 150°
ugn i 10 minuter.

Tärna och förväll persiljerötterna i lättsaltat vatten.

Stek trumpetsvampen i smör i en het panna.
Tillsätt persiljerotstärningarna och schalottenlöken
mot slutet. Salta och peppra.

Servera kåldolmarna med trumpetsvamp och
persiljerötter.

4 personer

2 persiljerötter
salt och vitpeppar
150 g svart trumpetsvamp
1 msk smör
2 schalottenlökar, skivade

KÅLDOLMAR
4 vitkålsblad
salt och vitpeppar
confit på 2 anklår
200 g kantareller
1 msk smör
2 schalottenlökar, finhackade
1/2 vitlöksklyfta, finhackad
1 msk fint strimlad bladpersilja
200 g ankleverterrin,
se recept s. 23

TILL SERVERING
rödvinssås, se recept s. 312
potatispuré

STUFFED CABBAGE ROLLS
WITH DUCK CONFIT, MUSHROOMS AND PARSNIPS

serves 4

2 parsnips
salt and white pepper
150 g trompette mushroom
1 tbsp butter
2 shallots, sliced

STUFFED CABBAGE ROLLS
4 leaves of white cabbage
salt and white pepper
confit from 2 duck thighs
200 g chanterelles
1 tbsp butter
2 shallots, finely chopped
1/2 clove of garlic, finely chopped
1 tbsp finely shredded
flat leaf parsley
200 g foie gras terrine (p. 24)

SERVE WITH
red wine sauce (p. 324)
potato purée

Make the red wine sauce according to the recipe.

Blanch the cabbage leaves in lightly salted water. Remove and cool in iced water and remove the hard stalk. Remove the meat from the duck thigh and cut into small pieces. Fry the chanterelles in butter in a hot pan, add shallots and garlic towards the end of cooking. Season with salt and pepper and sprinkle with parsley. Leave to cool. Dice the duck liver terrine and mix with the chanterelles and duck confit. Divide the mixture between the cabbage leaves and form into rolls. Heat through in a 150°C oven for 10 minutes.

Dice, then blanch the parsnips in lightly salted water.

Fry the mushrooms in butter in a hot pan. Add the parsnips and shallots towards the end of cooking. Season with salt and pepper.

Serve the cabbage rolls with the trompette mushrooms and parsnips.

CONFIT/confit

Ett gammalt sätt att bevara kött är att koka det långsamt och sedan täcka det med fett. Mest klassisk är confit på anka, eftersom köttet blir oerhört mört och avger riktligt med gott fett. En nygjord confit måste mogna i ett par veckor innan den avnjuts. Sedan håller den i flera månader, om man bara ser till att ytan hela tiden är täckt av fett. Delikatessaffärer har färdig confit, för den som vill gå en genväg men ändå njuta av den mjälla smaken.

This is an old way of preserving meat. First it is cooked very slowly, then covered with fat. The most classical is confit made with duck, because the meat is very tender and renders a lot of delicious fat. A freshly made confit must rest for a couple of weeks before eating, but it can then last for months if kept covered with fat. To enjoy the wonderful taste one short cut is to buy it ready made from a delicatessen.

VARMA VÅRPRIMÖRER
MED BLOMKÅLSCRÈME OCH CURRY

4 personer

8 färska gula lökar
8 vårlökar
12 späda morötter
4 vita sparrisar
8 gröna sparrisar
salt
2 medelstora eller 4 små kokta
kronärtskocksbottnar,
se recept s. 314
200 g färskpotatis
beurre montée, se recept s. 312
fleur de sel (havssalt)

BLOMKÅLSCRÈME
1 msk finhackad schalottenlök
1 tsk curry
1 msk smör
50 g blomkål, i mindre bitar
1 dl grönsaksbuljong
se recept s. 308
2 dl vispgrädde
salt och vitpeppar

Ansa lökarna, morötterna och sparrisarna. Koka dem mjuka var för sig i saltat vatten. Kyl i isvatten.

Koka kronärtskockorna enligt receptet.

Koka potatisen mjuk i saltat vatten.

Fräs schalottenlök och curry i smör utan att löken får färg. Tillsätt blomkålen och fräs i ytterligare någon minut. Slå på buljong och grädde och sjud blomkålen mjuk. Mixa och passera genom en finmaskig sil. Smaksätt crèmen med salt och peppar.

Gör beurre montée enligt receptet och värm de kylda grönsakerna i den. Fördela grönsakerna på tallrikar, strö över havssalt och skeda över blomkålscrème.

VARMA VÅRPRIMÖRER MED BLOMKÅLSCRÈME OCH CURRY
Warm spring vegetables with cauliflower cream and curry

WARM SPRING VEGETABLES
WITH CAULIFLOWER CREAM AND CURRY

serves 4

8 small onions
8 spring onions
12 tender carrots
4 white asparagus spears
8 green asparagus spears
salt
2 mid-sized or
4 small artichoke hearts (p. 326)
200 g new potatoes
beurre montee (p. 324)
fleur de sel (sea salt)

CAULIFLOWER CREAM
1 tbsp finely chopped shallots
1 tsp curry
1 tbsp butter
50 g cauliflower, in small pieces
100 ml vegetables stock (p. 321)
200 ml cream
salt and white pepper

Clean, then boil separately in salted water, the onions, carrots and asparagus. Cool in iced water.

Cook the artichokes according to the recipe.

Cook the potatoes until soft in salted water.

Sweat the shallots and curry in butter. Add the cauliflower and sweat for another minute. Add the stock and cream and simmer until the cauliflower is soft. Mix in a food processor and strain through a fine sieve. Season the cream with salt and pepper.

Make a beurre montée according to the recipe and reheat the vegetables in the sauce. Divide the vegetables between the plates, sprinkle with sea salt and spoon the cauliflower cream over.

ÅRSTIDER / seasons

Förr styrdes våra matvanor mycket mer av årstiderna. Skafferiet var en tydlig avspegling av vad som växte på åkrarna för tillfället eller vad man hade tagit vara på och konserverat. Även om det mesta numera finns att tillgå året runt vill vi gärna följa säsongerna. Frossa i primörer på våren, njuta av bär och örter på sommaren och skörda rotfrukter på hösten, att använda hela vintern.

In the old days our way of eating varied much more depending on the seasons. The cupboard was like a mirror of the harvest of what you had taken care of and preserved. We like to follow the seasons even though nowadays you can find most fresh products all year round. Feast on early vegetables in the spring, enjoy fruits and fresh herbs in the summer, harvest various root vegetables in the autumn for use all winter.

HALSTRAD GRAVAD LAX MED
SENAPSSTUVAD POTATIS OCH SPENAT

4 personer

600 g lax, mittbit
1 msk strösocker
1 msk salt
1 tsk krossad vitpeppar
1 knippe dill
2 msk matolja
200 g späd färsk spenat
1/2 msk smör
salt och vitpeppar

STUVAD POTATIS
500 g färskpotatis
några dillkvistar
2 dl vispgrädde
1 msk senap
1 tsk strösocker
3 msk rödvinsvinäger
3 dl matolja
salt och vitpeppar

Gnid in laxbiten med socker, salt, peppar och dill-stjälkar (hacka och spara dillvipporna till senare). Låt stå i rumstemperatur i ett par timmar så att sockret smälter något. Lägg fisken i en plastpåse, knyt ihop och lägg den i kylen i minst 24 timmar. Vänd den efter halva tiden.

Koka potatisen mjuk i saltat vatten med några dillkvistar i. Koka ihop grädden till hälften. Vispa ihop senap, socker och vinäger. Tillsätt oljan droppvis. Rör ner senapssåsen i grädden och smaksätt med salt och peppar. Vänd ner potatisen i såsen och håll den varm utan att den kokar.

Skär laxen i portionsbitar. Stek varje sida i 2 minuter i olja.

Fräs spenaten i smör. Salta och peppra.

Servera laxen med spenat och senapsstuvad potatis. Garnera med dill.

GRILLED GRAVAD LAX WITH
MUSTARD STEWED POTATOES AND SPINACH

serves 4

600 g salmon
cut from the middle
1 tbsp salt
1 tsp crushed white pepper
1 bunch of dill
2 tbsp cooking oil
200 g tender fresh spinach
1/2 tbsp butter
salt and white pepper

STEWED POTATOES
500 g new potatoes
a couple of dill sprigs
200 ml cream
1 tbsp mustard
1 tsp sugar
3 tbsp red wine vinegar
300 ml cooking oil
salt and white pepper

Remove the dill leaves from the stalks. Chop the leaves and reserve for later. Rub the flesh of the salmon with sugar, salt, pepper and dill sprigs. Leave at room temperature for a couple of hours until the sugar melts a little. Put the fish in a plastic bag, tie and place in the refrigerator for at least 24 hours turning once.

Boil the potatoes until soft in salted water with a few sprigs of dill. Reduce the cream by half. Whisk the mustard, sugar and vinegar together, add the oil a little at a time whisking constantly. Fold the mustard sauce into the cream and season with salt and pepper. Gently fold the potatoes into the sauce and keep warm without boiling.

Cut the salmon into portions. Fry for 2 minutes on each side in oil.

Cook the spinach in butter until wilted. Season with salt and pepper.

Serve the salmon with spinach and potatoes. Garnish with dill.

BLANCHERA/blancher

Ordet betyder «göra vit» på franska. Lägg råvarorna i kokande, lättsaltat vatten och koka i en halv minut, inte längre. Spola dem därefter i kallt vatten, så att kokprocessen avstannar. Passar bland annat när man vill ha knapriga, men ändå tillagade, grönsaker.

From the French verb meaning «make white». Add foods to boiling, salted water and boil for 30 seconds, no longer. Cool the foods quickly under running cold water to stop the cooking process. This method is ideal when you want crisp, yet cooked, vegetables.

HALSTRAD ANKLEVER MED VINÄGERKOKTA KÖRSBÄ

fried foie gras with infused cherri

HALSTRAD ANKLEVER
MED VINÄGERKOKTA KÖRSBÄR

Koka upp vatten, vinäger, socker och kanel i en
kastrull. Lägg i körsbären, ta bort kastrullen från
värmen och låt dra över natten.

Plocka anklevern fri från blodådror. Skär anklevern i skivor, salta och peppra. Stek dem hastigt i
en het panna.

Servera anklevern med körsbär.

4 personer

320 g anklever
salt och vitpeppar

VINÄGERKOKTA KÖRSBÄR
300 g färska körsbär
1 1/4 dl vatten
2 1/2 dl rödvinsvinäger
1 1/4 dl strösocker
1 kanelstång

FRIED FOIE GRAS WITH INFUSED CHERRIES

serves 4

320 g fresh duck foie gras
salt and white pepper

INFUSED CHERRIES
300 g fresh cherries
125 ml water
250 ml red wine vinegar
125 ml sugar
1 cinnamon stick

In a saucepan bring the water, vinegar, sugar and cinnamon to a boil. Add the cherries, remove from the heat and leave to soak overnight.

De-vein the liver. Slice and season with salt and pepper. Fry quickly in a hot pan.

Serve the duck liver with cherries.

ANKLEVER / foie gras

Trots den omdiskuterade tvångsmatningen är *foie gras*, «fet lever», alltjämt en populär delikatess. Förr dominerade gåslevern i det klassiska köket, numera har intresset mer vänts mot anklevern. Den är visserligen mindre men har tydligare smak. Pröva att steka en skiva färsk gås- eller anklever hastigt i het panna. Det är våldsamt gott, som att äta sufflé! Spara fettet som bildats i pannan till annan matlagning, till exempel till röd- eller surkål.

Despite the controversial feeding of birds for foie gras, «fat-liver» is still a popular delicacy. At one time the majority of the livers were from the goose, now it tends to be mainly from duck. Although the duck liver is smaller than goose the flavour is more intense. Try frying a slice of goose or duck liver quickly in a hot pan. It is extremely tasty, like eating a souffle. Save the fat from the pan to use in other dishes such as sauerkraut.

GLASERAD VIT SPARRIS MED VÄSTERBOTTENOST
glazed white asparagus with vaesterbotten cheese

GLASERAD VIT SPARRIS
MED VÄSTERBOTTENOST

4 personer

400 g vit sparris, skalad
5 dl kalvsky, se recept s. 307
1 msk finhackad schalottenlök
salt och vitpeppar
1 msk förstapressad olivolja
40 g västerbottenost

Dela upp sparrisen i fyra knippen och bind ihop dem knippe för knippe. Koka sparrisen mjuk i rikligt med saltat vatten. Kyl i isvatten och klipp upp snörena.

Koka ihop kalvskyn tillsammans med schalottenlök tills 1 ½ dl återstår. Smaksätt med salt och peppar. Sila såsen.

Värm sparrisen i såsen. Tillsätt olivolja. Fördela sparrisen på varma tallrikar. Hyvla över västerbottenost och servera.

GLAZED WHITE ASPARAGUS
WITH VAESTERBOTTEN CHEESE

Divide the asparagus into 4 bundles and tie together with string. Boil the asparagus until soft in plenty of salted water. Cool quickly in iced water, then untie the bundles.

Reduce the veal stock together with shallots until 150 ml remains. Season with salt and pepper, strain.

Heat the asparagus in the sauce. Add the olive oil. Divide the asparagus between four hot plates, place slices of cheese on top and serve.

serves 4

400 g white asparagus, peeled
500 ml veal stock (p. 319)
1 tbsp finely chopped shallots
salt and white pepper
1 tbsp extra virgin olive oil
40 g vaesterbotten cheese

STEKT PIGGVARSRYGG MED
OXMÄRG OCH SURKÅL

4 personer

800 g piggvarsrygg, skinnfri
40 g oxmärg
2 dl kycklingbuljong,
se recept s. 308
salt och vitpeppar
2 msk klarat smör
1 msk fint skuren gräslök
1 nypa grovsalt
1 msk finhackad schalottenlök

SURKÅL

800 g vitkål, strimlad
4 dl vitt vin
1 msk salt
1 msk strösocker
1 dl ättikssprit, 12%
1/2 gul lök, finhackad
1 msk gåsfett
1 lagerblad
3 enbär
5 dl kycklingbuljong,
se recept s. 308
(salt och vitpeppar)

Lägg vitkålstrimlorna i en bunke. Tillsätt vin, salt, socker och ättika. Täck med plastfilm och låt kålen ligga under press i rumstemperatur i 5 dagar. Rör om kålen och ställ den sedan i kylen i en vecka.

Skölj kålen i kallt vatten. Låt rinna av. Fräs lök i gåsfett i en kastrull utan att löken får färg. Tillsätt kålen, lagerblad och enbär. Slå på buljong och låt sjuda i cirka en timme. Kålen ska inte bli alldeles mjuk. Smaksätt eventuellt med salt och peppar.

Skär åtta tunna skivor av oxmärgen till garnityr. Spara resten till såsen.

Koka ihop kycklingbuljongen till hälften. Vispa ner resterande oxmärg innan såsen ska serveras. Smaka av med salt och peppar.

Skär fisken i portionsbitar. Salta, peppra och bryn dem i klarat smör. Stek färdigt i 175° ugn i cirka 10–12 minuter.

Servera piggvaren med surkål och sås. Garnera med oxmärgsskivorna.

STEKT PIGGVARSRYGG MED OXMÄRG OCH SURKÅL
fried turbot back with beef marrow and sour cabbage

FRIED TURBOT BACK
WITH BEEF MARROW AND SOUR CABBAGE

serves 4

800 g turbot back, without skin
40 g beef marrow
200 ml chicken stock (p. 320)
salt and white pepper
2 tbsp clarified butter
1 tbsp finely cut chives
1 pinch coarse salt
1 tbsp finely chopped shallots

SOUR CABBAGE
800 g white cabbage, shredded
400 ml white wine
1 tbsp salt
1 tbsp sugar
100 ml white vinegar
1/2 onion, finely chopped
1 tbsp goose fat
1 bay leaf
3 juniper berries
500 ml chicken stock (p. 320)
salt and white pepper (optional)

Put the cabbage into a bowl, add wine, salt, sugar and white vinegar. Weight the cabbage down, cover with cling film and leave for five days at room temperature. Stir the cabbage and place in the refrigerator for one week.

Rinse the cabbage in cold water, drain. In a saucepan sweat the onion in goose fat. Add the cabbage, bay leaf and juniper berries. Pour the stock over and simmer for approximately one hour. The cabbage should not become too soft. Season with salt and pepper if using.

Cut eight thin slices of the marrow for garnish, save the rest for the sauce.

Reduce the chicken stock by half. Whisk in the rest of the marrow before serving. Season with salt and pepper.

Cut the fish into portions. Season with salt and pepper and brown in clarified butter, then cook until ready in a 175°C oven for 10–12 minutes.

Serve the turbot with the sour cabbage and sauce. Garnish with the slices of marrow.

FOND / stock

Fond eller buljong, två ord för samma sak: en god bas för såser, soppor och smaksättning som kan kokas av såväl kött, fågel och fisk som grönsaker och skaldjur. Om du ändå tar dig tid att koka egen fond – koka en rejäl sats och frys in den i små byttor eller istärningspåsar. Den håller minst ett år i frysen. Koka gärna ihop den ordentligt, så tar den mindre plats. Mest användbara är fonder kokade av kyckling eller skaldjur.

Good stocks can be made from meat, poultry, fish, vegetables or seafood. If you are taking the time to make a good stock, why not make a huge potful. This can then be stored in smaller containers in the freezer, keeping for up to a year. Heavily reduce the stock and it will take up less space. Stocks from poultry and seafood tend to be the most useful.

LAMMKARRÉ OCH LAMMBRÄSS MED PETIT POIS À LA FRANÇAIS
rack of lamb and sweetbreads with petit pois à la françaisi

LAMMKARRÉ OCH LAMMBRÄSS
MED PETIT POIS À LA FRANÇAISE

Spola lammbrässen under kallt vatten i 5 minuter.
Förväll den i kokande vatten och kyl den sedan i
kallt. Plocka brässen fri från de yttersta hinnorna.

Fräs grönsakerna till lagen i olivolja. Lägg i
brässen, slå på vin och kryddor. Koka i 5 minuter. Ta
bort kastrullen från värmen och låt dra i 10 minuter
under lock. Lyft upp brässen och skär den i portionsbitar. Sila buljongen och koka ihop den till 2 dl.
Vispa i smör innan den ska serveras.

Salta och peppra lammkarrén. Bryn den hel i
olivolja tillsammans med en vitlöksklyfta. Stek färdigt köttet i 150° ugn i 10–12 minuter. Låt köttet vila
i 10 minuter.

Bryn lammbrässbitarna i hälften av smöret. Salta
och peppra.

Fräs bacon, schalottenlök och spritärter i resterande smör. Vänd ner romansallad och smaksätt
med salt och peppar.

Skär lammkarrén i portionsbitar. Servera dem
med lammbräss, ärter och sås.

4 personer

200 g lammbräss
600 g lammkarré med ben
salt och vitpeppar
1 msk olivolja
1 vitlöksklyfta
1 msk osaltat smör
40 g bacon, strimlat
1/2 dl finhackad schalottenlök
200 g spritärter, förvällda
5 blad romansallad,
fint strimlade

LAG
1/2 gul lök, finhackad
1 selleristjälk, fint tärnad
1 liten morot, fint tärnad
1/2 msk olivolja
2 dl torrt vitt vin
1 lagerblad
5 vitpepparkorn
2 msk smör

RACK OF LAMB AND SWEETBREADS
WITH PETIT POIS À LA FRANÇAISE

serves 4

200 g lamb sweetbreads
600 g rack of lamb
salt and white pepper
1 tbsp olive oil
1 clove of garlic
1 tbsp unsalted butter
40 g bacon, shredded
50 ml finely chopped shallots
200 g green peas, blanched
5 romaine salad leaves,
finely shredded

NAGE
1/2 onion, finely chopped
1 stalk of celery, finely diced
1 small carrot, finely diced
1/2 tbsp olive oil
200 ml dry white wine
1 bay leaf
5 white peppercorns
2 tbsp butter

Rinse the lamb sweetbreads in cold water for 5 minutes. Blanch in boiling water and cool rapidly in cold water. Remove the outer membrane.

Fry the vegetables for the nage in olive oil. Add the sweetbread, wine and spices. Boil for 5 minutes. Remove the saucepan from the heat and leave covered with a lid for 10 minutes. Remove the sweetbread and cut into portions. Strain and reduce the stock until 200 ml remains. Whisk in the butter before serving.

Season the lamb with salt and pepper. Brown the whole piece in olive oil together with a clove of garlic. Roast in a 150°C oven for 10–12 minutes, remove from the oven and leave to rest for 10 minutes.

Brown the lamb sweetbread pieces in half of the butter. Season with salt and pepper.

Fry bacon, shallots and green peas in the remaining butter. Stir in the the romaine salad and season with salt and pepper.

Cut the lamb into portions and serve with the sweetbreads, green peas and sauce.

LAMM / lamb

En av våra absolut bästa råvaror. Lammet äter det naturen bjuder och köttet smakar ljuvligt och mjällt. Numera finns det färskt lamm att tillgå under större delen av året, eftersom uppfödarna har förlängt lamningsperioden.

Lamb is one of our best products. The lamb eats what nature has to offer creating tender, tasty meat. Nowadays you can find fresh lamb almost all yearround as producers have prolonged the breeding season.

FOCACCIA MED GRILLADE GRÖNSAKER

4 personer

1 liten zucchini
1 fänkålsstånd
1/2 aubergine
4 torkade tomater,
se recept s. 313
4 msk olivolja
salt och vitpeppar
1 citron, juice och rivet skal
1/2 vitlöksklyfta, finhackad
1 tsk hackad dragon
rucolasallad

FOCACCIA
15 g jäst
1 3/4 dl vatten, 37°
1 tsk strösocker
1 tsk salt
1 tsk finhackad rosmarin
450 g vetemjöl
smör till form
6 msk förstapressad olivolja
+ 1 msk vatten
grovsalt

Rör ut jästen i ljummet vatten. Tillsätt socker, salt, rosmarin och mjöl. Arbeta till en smidig deg. Låt degen jäsa till dubbel storlek, vilket tar cirka 30 minuter. Kavla ut degen och placera den i en smord pajform. Låt den jäsa i ytterligare 30 minuter. Gör gropar med fingertopparna i degen. Häll på olivolje- och vattenblandningen och strö över grovsalt. Grädda brödet i 200° ugn i 25–30 minuter.

Skiva zucchinin, fänkålen och auberginen i ½ cm tunna skivor. Pensla alla grönsaker, även de torkade tomaterna, med hälften av olivoljan och grilla dem. Salta och peppra. Blanda 2 msk olivolja med citronjuice, citronskal, vitlök och dragon. Vänd de grillade grönsakerna i blandningen och servera dem och rucolasallad med focaccian.

FOCACCIA MED GRILLADE GRÖNSAKER
Focaccia with grilled vegetables

FOCACCIA WITH GRILLED VEGETABLES

serves 4

1 small courgette
1 fennel bulb
1/2 aubergine
4 dried tomatoes (p. 325)
4 tbsp olive oil
salt and white pepper
juice and grated rind
of 1 lemon
1/2 clove of garlic, finely chopped
1 tsp chopped tarragon
rucola salad

FOCACCIA
15 g fresh yeast
175 ml water
1 tsp sugar
1 tsp salt
1 tsp finely chopped
rosemary
450 g flour
butter for the mould
6 tbsp extra virgin olive oil
1 tbsp water
coarse salt

Dissolve the yeast in lukewarm water. Add sugar, salt, rosemary and flour. Work to form a smooth dough. Leave to rise until double in size, approximately 30 minutes. Roll out the dough and place on the bottom of a greased pie dish. Leave to rise for another 30 minutes.

Using your fingertips make indentations in the dough. Mix together the oil and water and pour over the dough and sprinkle with coarse salt. Bake in a 200°C oven for 25–30 minutes.

Cut the courgette, fennel bulb and aubergine into ½ cm thick slices. Brush all the vegetables, including the dried tomatoes, with olive oil, then grill them. Season with salt and pepper. Mix 2 tbsp olive oil with lemon juice, lemon rind, garlic and tarragon. Turn the grilled vegetables in the mixture and serve with the focaccia and rucola salad.

FOCACCIA/focaccia

Nästan varje del av världen har ett platt bröd med mycket smak: från Mellanöstern kommer *pitabrödet*, i Indien bakas *chapati* och *naan*. I Mexiko gräddar man *tortillas*, i Östafrika fungerar *injera* både som bröd och tallrik och i Sverige kavlar vi *tunnbröd*. I Italien bakar man *focaccia* i långpanna, ett bröd som girigt suger åt sig olivolja och olika smaksättningar tack vare de täta gropar man gör med fingrarna i brödkakan innan den gräddas.

Almost every part of the world has its own version of flat bread. In the Middle East, *pita*, in India *chapati*. The Mexicans have *tortillas* and in Africa *injera* which also serves as a plate. In Sweden we make *hard bread*. The Italians however have *focaccia*, baked in oven trays and with various flavourings, it is drenched in olive oil through the indentations in the surface of the bread which is one of its distinctive features.

GRILLAD ENTRECÔTE MED STEKTA KRONÄRTSKOCKOR, AUBERGINE, GREMOLATA OCH OLIVSK
grilled entrecôte with fried artichokes, aubergine and olive gra

GRILLAD ENTRECÔTE MED STEKTA KRONÄRTSKOCKOR, AUBERGINE, GREMOLATA OCH OLIVSKY

Skiva auberginen tunt, gärna i skärmaskin. Strö socker- och saltblandningen på båda sidor av skivorna och låt dra i 30 minuter för att vattna ur.

Gör gremolata enligt receptet.

Koka ihop kalvsky och vin till hälften tillsammans med schalottenlök. Sila och tillsätt oliver. Vispa i olivolja innan skyn ska serveras. Smaksätt med salt och peppar.

Torka aubergineskivorna med hushållspapper och fritera dem i olja.

Koka vitlöksklyftorna mjuka med skal i smör, cirka 5 minuter.

Stek de kokta kronärtskocksbottnarna i olivolja. Salta och peppra.

Salta, peppra och grilla entrecôten. Servera köttet med kronärtskockor, aubergine och vitlök. Skeda gremolata och olivsky runt om.

4 personer

4 skivor entrecôte à 200 g
1/2 aubergine
1 tsk strösocker + 1 tsk salt
gremolata, se recept s. 314
matolja till fritering
4 vitlöksklyftor
50 g smör
4 kokta små kronärtskockor,
se recept s. 314
1 msk olivolja
salt och vitpeppar

OLIVSKY
1 1/2 dl kalvsky,
se recept s. 307
1 1/2 dl torrt vitt vin
1 msk finhackad schalottenlök
100 g urkärnade niçoiseoliver,
hackade
1 msk förstapressad olivolja
salt och vitpeppar

GRILLED ENTRECÔTE WITH FRIED ARTICHOKES, AUBERGINE, GREMOLATA AND OLIVE GRAVY

serves 4

4 slices of entrecôte 200 g each
1/2 aubergine
1tsp sugar +1 tsp salt
gremolata (p.326)
oil for deep frying
4 cloves of garlic
50 g butter
4 small boiled artichokes (p.326)
1 tbsp olive oil
salt and white pepper

OLIVE GRAVY
150 ml veal stock (p. 321)
150 ml dry white wine
1 tbsp finely chopped shallots
100 g pitted niçoise olives, chopped
1 tbsp extra virgin olive oil
salt and white pepper

Slice the aubergine thinly with the aid of a mandolin. Sprinkle with the sugar and salt mixture on both sides and leave for 30 minutes to draw out the water and bitterness.

Make the gremolata according to the recipe.

Reduce the veal stock and wine together by half with the shallots. Strain and add the olives. Whisk in the olive oil before serving the gravy. Season with salt and pepper.

Wipe the aubergine slices with kitchen paper and deep-fry them in hot cooking oil.

Sweat the garlic until soft approximately 5 minutes in hot butter.

Fry the boiled artichokes in olive oil. Season with salt and pepper.

Season the entrecôte with salt and pepper and grill to desired cooking. Serve the entrecôte with artichokes, aubergine and garlic. Drizzle gremolata and olive gravy around.

ENTRECÔTE / entrecôte

Glöm inte uttalet: «angträkått»! Ordet betyder «mellan sidorna», det vill säga en fin entrecôte ska alltså innehålla både fett och senor. Det vackert röda köttet finns mellan tre olika muskelpaket. Entrecôte är det enda möra framdelsköttet, men det räcker, en god entrecôte är oslagbar.

It is important to note the meaning of the word, Entrecôte – «between the sides» – meaning that the meat should contain both fat and sinew. The beautiful red meat is found between three different muscles. Entrecôte is the only tender meat from the front part of the animal and when it's good, it's impossible to beat.

SVAMPFRITTATA
mushroom frittata

SVAMPFRITTATA

4 personer

8 ägg
4 msk vatten
salt och vitpeppar
200 g svamp, t ex kantareller
1 msk smör
2 msk finhackad schalottenlök
1 vitlöksklyfta, finhackad
1 dl finstrimlad bladpersilja

Vispa ihop ägg, vatten, salt och peppar. Ställ blandningen åt sidan.

Stek svampen i smör i en het panna. Tillsätt schalottenlök och vitlök mot slutet. Salta, peppra och blanda i lite av persiljan.

Smält smöret i en het panna. Stek fyra omeletter på ena sidan. Ställ därefter in pannan i ugn under grillelementet i någon minut istället för att vända omeletterna. Lägg omeletterna på tallrikarna. Fördela svampen på omeletterna och strö över resterande persilja.

MUSHROOM FRITTATA

Whisk the eggs, water, salt and pepper, place to one side.

Fry the mushrooms in butter in a hot pan. Add the shallots and garlic towards the end of cooking. Season with salt and pepper and sprinkle with some of the parsley.

Fry four thin omelettes in butter in a hot pan. Place under a hot grill for one minute. Divide the mushrooms between the omelettes, sprinkle with the remaining parsley and serve.

serves 4

8 eggs
4 tbsp water
salt and white pepper
200 g wild mushrooms,
eg. chanterelles
1 tbsp butter
2 tbsp finely chopped shallots
1 clove of garlic,
finely chopped
100 ml finely shredded
flat leaf parsley

STEKT LAXFILÉ MED APELSINKARAMELLISERAD FÄNKÅL, HUMMER OCH JUNGFRUSÅS

4 personer

600 g laxfilé med skinn, fjällad
2 kokta humrar
1 fänkålsstånd
3 apelsiner
rivet skal av 1 apelsin
1 stjärnanis
jungfrusås, se recept s.306
2 tsk strösocker
salt och vitpeppar
2 msk klarat smör

Skala hummerstjärtarna och klorna. Halvera stjärtarna.

Halvera fänkålsståndet och skär bort roten. Skiva fänkålen. Pressa apelsinerna och förväll skivorna i hälften av apelsinjuicen tillsammans med stjärnanis.

Gör en jungfrusås enligt receptet.

Smält sockret i en tjockbottnad kastrull till en karamell. Tillsätt resterande apelsinjuice samt rivet skal från en apelsin. Värm fänkålen och hummerdelarna i karamellen.

Skär fisken i portionsbitar. Salta, peppra och stek skinnsidan knaprig i klarat smör. Vänd och stek andra sidan i någon minut.

Servera laxen med fänkål och hummer. Skeda jungfrusåsen runt om.

TEKT LAXFILÉ MED APELSINKARAMELLISERAD FÄNKÅL, HUMMER OCH JUNGFRUSÅS
ed salmon fillet with orange caramelised fennel, lobster and sauce vièrge

FRIED SALMON FILLET WITH ORANGE
CARAMELISED FENNEL, LOBSTER AND SAUCE VIÈRGE

serves 4

600 g salmon fillet skin-on,
scaled
2 boiled lobsters
1 fennel bulb
juice of 3 oranges
grated rind of 1 orange
1 star anise
sauce vièrge (p. 318)
2 tsp sugar
salt and white pepper
2 tbsp clarified butter

Peel the lobster tails and claws. Cut the tails in half.

Cut the fennel in half and remove the root. Slice and blanch in half of the orange juice with the star anise.

Make a sauce vièrge according to the recipe.

In a thick bottomed saucepan make a caramel from sugar. Add the remaining orange juice and orange rind. Reheat the fennel and lobster in the caramel sauce.

Cut the fish into portions. Season with salt and pepper, in a hot pan fry the salmon skin side down in clarified butter until crisp. Turn the salmon over and fry for one minute more.

Serve the salmon with fennel and lobster surrounded by the sauce vièrge.

SJUDA / simmer

Det är inte bara färskpotatis som smakar bäst av att få plumsa ner i kokande vatten. Genom att lägga råvarorna (fisk, kött eller grönsaker) i kokande vätska, i stället för i kall, stänger man porerna snabbare och smakämnena bevaras bättre. Koka upp, sänk därefter temperaturen och sjud sakta tills allt är klart.

It's not only new potatoes where it is preferable to cook in boiling water. By placing ingredients (fish, meat and vegetables) into boiling liquid rather than cold, the food is sealed much quicker and more flavour is retained. So, for the best results, boil the liquid, add the food, reduce the temperature and simmer until ready.

HONUNG- OCH KRYDDSTEKT ANKBRÖST MED ANKSKOJS OCH RÖDBETSCRUD
honey and spice fried duck breast with duck scouse and beetroot crud

HONUNG-OCH KRYDDSTEKT ANKBRÖST
MED ANKSKOJS OCH RÖDBETSCRUDITÉ

Skär de råa rödbetorna i tunna skivor. Blanda dem med resterande ingredienser till en crudité. Låt dra i minst en timme i rumstemperatur.

Stöt saltet och kryddorna till glasyren i en mortel. Blanda dem med honungen.

Koka rödvinssåsen enligt receptet.

Snitta fettet på ankbrösten i diagonala rutor. Bryn båda sidor i en stekpanna utan fett. Stek färdigt ankbrösten i 175° ugn i cirka 5 minuter. Ta ut dem ur ugnen och häll över glasyren. Öka värmen i ugnen till 250°. Ställ in ankbrösten i ugnen i någon minut och låt dem bli krispiga. Ta ut dem och låt dem vila i 5 minuter.

Koka mandelpotatisen mjuk i lättsaltat vatten. Häll av vattnet från kastrullen och passera potatisen. Koka upp mjölken. Blanda den, smöret och varmrökt ankbröst med potatisen. Smaksätt med persilja, salt och peppar.

Skiva ankbrösten och servera med ankskojs och rödbetscrudité.

4 personer

2 ankbröst
rödvinssås, se recept s. 312

RÖDBETSCRUDITÉ
100 g färska rödbetor, skalade
2 msk balsamvinäger
1 msk förstapressad olivolja
1 tsk rivet citronskal
salt och vitpeppar

GLASYR
1 krm fleur de sel (havssalt)
1 krm guineapeppar
eller svartpeppar
1 krm korianderfrön
1 krm fänkålsfrön
1 stjärnanis
2 msk apelsinblomshonung

ANKSKOJS
200 g mandelpotatis, skalad
salt och vitpeppar
2 dl mjölk
2 msk smör
50 g varmrökt ankbröst, tärnat
1 msk fint strimlad bladpersilja

HONEY AND SPICE FRIED DUCK BREAST
WITH DUCK SCOUSE AND BEETROOT CRUDITÉ

serves 4

2 duck breasts
red wine sauce (p. 324)

BEETROOT CRUDITÈ
100 g fresh beetroots, peeled
2 tbsp balsamic vinegar
1 tbsp extra virgin olive oil
1 tsp grated lemon rind
salt and white pepper

GLAZE
1 pinch fleur de sel (sea salt)
1 pinch guinea pepper
or black pepper
1 pinch coriander seeds
1 pinch fennel seeds
1 star anise
2 tbsp orange flower honey

DUCK SCOUSE
200 g almond potatoes, peeled
salt and white pepper
200 ml milk
2 tbsp butter
50 g warm-smoked duck breast, diced
1 tbsp finely shredded flat leaf parsley

Thinly slice the beetroots and mix with the rest of the ingredients for the crudité. Leave to soak for at least one hour at room temperature.

Pound the salt and spices for the glaze in a mortar and mix with the honey.

Make a red wine sauce according to the recipe.

Score the fat on the duck breasts to create diagonal squares. Brown both sides in a hot dry frying pan. Roast in 175° C oven for approximately 5 minutes. Remove from oven and rest for 5 minutes.

Boil the potatoes until soft in lightly salted water. Drain the potatoes in a colander. Bring the milk up to a boil. Mix the milk, butter and diced smoked duck breast with the potatoes. Season with parsley, salt and pepper.

Slice the duck breast and serve with duck scouse and beetroot crudité.

ANKA / duck

Det finns både många olika raser och olika storlekar
av anka. Men gemensamt för dem är att det smakrika köttet är fett och därför passar söta och syrliga
tillbehör extra bra.

There are many types of duck and varying sizes. What
they all have in common is rich, tasty meat which
goes so well with sweet and sour accompaniments.

UGNSBAKAD HÄLLEFLUNDRA MED OSTRON OCH GRÖNSAKSVINÄGRETT

4 personer

600 g hälleflundrafilé
salt och vitpeppar
12 –16 ostron
vetemjöl och ströbröd
till panering
1 ägg
2 msk klarat smör

GRÖNSAKSVINÄGRETT
1/2 grön paprika, fint tärnad
1/2 röd paprika, fint tärnad
1 vitlöksklyfta, finhackad
2 msk finhackad schalottenlök
1 tsk fint tärnad ingefära
salt
1/2 citron, juice
några droppar tabasco
1 dl förstapressad olivolja
1 tsk finhackad dragon
1 tsk fint strimlad bladpersilja

Förväll paprikan, vitlöken, schalottenlöken och ingefäran i separata kastruller. Kyl och låt rinna av. Blanda dem och smaksätt med salt, citron och tabasco. Tillsätt olivolja, dragon och persilja.

Skär fisken i portionsbitar. Salta, peppra och lägg bitarna i en smord ugnssäker form och ställ in den i 150° ugn i cirka 10 minuter.

Öppna ostronen och ta ut dem ur skalen. Vänd dem i mjöl, ägg och sist i ströbröd. Stek ostronen hastigt i klarat smör i en het panna.

Värm grönsaksvinägretten i en kastrull.

Servera hälleflundran med ostron och ljummen grönsaksvinägrett.

UGNSBAKAD HÄLLEFLUNDRA MED OSTRON OCH GRÖNSAKSVINÄGRETT
oven baked halibut with oysters and vegetable vinaigrette

OVEN BAKED HALIBUT WITH OYSTERS
AND VEGETABLE VINAIGRETTE

serves 4

600 g halibut fillet
salt and white pepper
12–16 fresh oysters
flour and bread
crumbs for coating
1 egg
2 tbsp clarified butter

VEGETABLE VINAIGRETTE
1/2 green pepper, finely diced
1/2 red pepper, finely diced
1 clove of garlic, finely chopped
2 tbsp finely chopped shallots
1 tsp finely diced ginger
salt
juice of 1/2 lemon
a dash of tabasco
100 ml extra virgin olive oil
1 tsp finely chopped tarragon
1 tsp finely chopped
flat leaf parsley

Blanch the pepper, garlic, shallot and ginger in separate saucepans. Cool and strain. Mix the vegetables together, then season with salt, lemon juice and tabasco, add the olive oil, tarragon and parsley.

Cut the fish into portions, season with salt and pepper, place in a buttered ovenproof dish and bake in a 150°C oven for approximately 10 minutes.

Remove the oysters from the shell and roll them in flour, dip in the egg, then coat in breadcrumbs. In a hot pan fry quickly in clarified butter.

Heat the vinaigrette in a saucepan.

Serve the halibut with oysters and lukewarm vegetable vinaigrette.

KOKT LAMMBRINGA I DILLSÅS MED PRIMÖRE
boiled breast of lamb in dill sauce with spring vegetabl

KOKT LAMMBRINGA
I DILLSÅS MED PRIMÖRER

Rulla och bind upp lammbringan. Lägg rullen i en kastrull och täck den ordentligt med kallt vatten. Salta, koka upp och skumma väl. Tillsätt bouquet garni och kryddor. Låt köttet sjuda mört under lock i cirka en timme. Lyft upp köttet och täck det med plastfilm. Koka ihop buljongen tills en tredjedel återstår.

Koka upp ättika, socker och dillstjälkar (hacka och spara dillvipporna till senare). Ta kastrullen av spisen och låt dra i 20 minuter. Sila.

Blanda smör och mjöl till en kula. Vispa ner kulan i lammbuljongen som redning och låt koka i 10 minuter. Smaksätt med ättiks- och dillreduktionen, lite i taget tills balansen mellan sötma och syra är behaglig.

Ansa morötter och lök. Koka dem mjuka i lättsaltat vatten.

Skiva lammbringan. Vänd ner grädde och hackad dill i såsen och häll den över köttet. Servera med primörer, nykokt potatis och örtolja.

4 personer

800 g tunn, benfri lammbringa
1 msk salt
1 bouquet garni,
se recept s. 314
1 lagerblad
1 msk vitpepparkorn
1 dl ättikssprit, 12 %
1 msk strösocker
2 knippen dill
1 msk smör + 1 msk vetemjöl
till redning
1 dl vispgrädde, lätt vispad

TILL SERVERING
12 små morötter
12 små färska lökar
500 g färskpotatis, kokt
örtolja, se recept s. 311

BOILED BREAST OF LAMB IN DILL SAUCE WITH SPRING VEGETABLES

serves 4

800 g boneless breast of lamb
1 tbsp salt
1 bouquet garni (p. 326)
1 bay leaf
1 tbsp white peppercorns
100 ml white vinegar
1 tbsp sugar
2 bunches of dill
1 tbsp butter + 1 tbsp flour
for thickening
100 ml cream, lightly whisked

SERVE WITH
12 small carrots
12 small onions
500 g new potatoes, boiled
herb oil, (p. 323)

Roll and tie the breast of lamb securely. Place into a large saucepan and cover with cold water. Add the salt and bring to a boil, skim well. Add the bouquet garni, bay leaf and peppercorns. Cover with a lid and simmer for one hour until tender, approximately one hour. Remove the meat from the broth and cover with cling film. Reduce the broth until only ⅓ remains.

Remove the dill leaves from the stalks. Chop the leaves and reserve for later. Bring the vinegar, sugar and dill sprigs to a boil, remove from the heat and leave to infuse for 20 minutes, then strain. Bring the lamb broth to a boil.

Mix the butter and flour together and whisk into the broth. Boil hard for 10 minutes. Gradually add the vinegar and dill reduction to create a good balance between sweet and sour.

Clean the carrots and onion, then boil until soft in lightly salted water.

Slice the breast of lamb. Gently fold the sauce into the cream and add the chopped dill. Serve with spring vegetables, boiled new potatoes and herb oil.

BOUQUET GARNI/bouquet garni

Att samla alla kryddörter i en liten bukett kom den franske kocken Pierre de Lune på redan för 300 år sedan. Då var det ett sätt att undvika den på den tiden så vanliga överkryddningen. Vi har förfinat hans ursprungliga idé en aning, och vår bouquet garni är till och med så god att vi brukar äta den ljummen med sallad när vi har lyft upp det mjukkokta lilla paketet ur kastrullen.

300 years ago the French chef Pierre de Lune devised this way of gathering seasonings together into a small bouquet intended to avoid the over seasoning of food which was common then. We have improved his original bouquet a little and our version is so tasty that we eat it with a salad after it has been cooked.

SVAMPTOAST

4 personer

600 g blandad svamp
2 msk smör
2 msk finhackad schalottenlök
2 vitlöksklyftor, finhackade
salt och vitpeppar
4 skivor brioche,
se recept s. 317
1 msk strimlad bladpersilja

Stek svampen i smör i en het panna. Tillsätt schalottenlök och vitlök mot slutet. Salta och peppra.

Stek eller rosta briocheskivorna. Fördela svampen
på skivorna, garnera med persilja och servera.

WAMPTOAST
Ishroom toast

MUSHROOM TOAST

serves 4

600 g mixed wild mushrooms
2 tbsp butter
2 tbsp finely chopped shallots
2 cloves of garlic,
finely chopped
salt and white pepper
4 slices brioche (p. 330)
1 tbsp shredded flat leaf parsley

Fry the mushrooms in butter in a hot pan, add the shallots and garlic towards the end of the cooking. Season with salt and pepper.

Fry or toast the brioche slices. Place the mushrooms on the brioche and garnish with parsley and serve.

LOCK / lid

Lock eller inte? Regeln är egentligen enkel: vill man att vätska ska koka bort har man inte lock. Vill man däremot ångkoka eller bräsera (det vill säga först bryna, sedan sjuda i lite vätska) lägger man på ett lock. En gyllene medelväg är att göra ett lock av smörpapper med ett litet hål i mitten. Då sprids värmen i kastrullen samtidigt som överflödig vätska dunstar.

Lid or not? The rule is simple, if you want to get rid of liquid you cook without a lid and if you want to steam or braise (frying quickly, then boiling in a little liquid or broth) you use a lid. A useful way between the two is to make a lid from a piece of greaseproof paper with a small hole in the middle. The steam can circulate in the pot but the hole allows the excess to evaporate.

SÖTA
sweet

PÄRONSUFFLÉ MED STJÄRNANIS OCH VANILJGLASS

4 personer

strösocker + smör till formar
80 g päronpuré
0,8 dl vatten
2 cl Williamine, päronlikör
16 g potatismjöl
1/2 mald stjärnanis
100 g äggvitor
30 g strösocker

TILL SERVERING
vaniljglass,
se recept crème anglaise s. 316

Gör en vaniljglassgrund enligt receptet. Frys i en glassmaskin.

Smörj och sockra 4 suffléformar.

Koka upp päronpuré, vatten och Williamine. Vispa i potatismjöl och koka upp igen. Ta bort kastrullen från värmen. Tillsätt stjärnanis och häll över blandningen i en bunke.

Vispa äggvitor och socker. Vänd försiktigt ner de vispade äggvitorna i päronpurén. Fyll suffléformarna med päronblandningen. Grädda suffléerna i 200° ugn i 8 minuter.

Servera päronsuffléerna med vaniljglass.

PÄRONSUFFLÉ MED STJÄRNANIS
pear soufflé with star anise

PEAR SOUFFLÉ WITH STAR ANISE AND VANILLA ICE CREAM

serves 4

butter + caster sugar
for the soufflé mould
80 g pear purée
80 ml water
20 ml Poire Williamine liqueur,
16 g potato flour
1/2 ground star anise
100 g egg whites
30 g caster sugar

FOR SERVING
vanilla ice cream, (p. 328)

Make a vanilla ice cream base according to the recipe and freeze in an ice cream machine.

Butter 4 soufflé moulds and coat in caster sugar.

Bring the pear purée, water and liqueur up to a boil. Whisk in the potato flour and bring to the boil again. Remove the saucepan from the heat. Add the star anise and pour the mixture into a large bowl.

Whisk the egg whites with the sugar. Carefully fold the whipped egg whites into the pear purée. Fill the soufflé moulds with the pear mixture. Cook in the oven at 200°C for 8 minutes.

Serve the pear soufflés immediately with vanilla ice cream.

SOCKER / sugar

Strösocker, bitsocker, florsocker, farinsocker, råsocker… Det är skillnad i smak och egenskaper på
olika sorters socker, allra tydligast märks det på
råsockret (oraffinerat rörsocker). För att till exempel
crème brûlée ska få rätt yta blandar man råsocker
eller farinsocker med strösocker. Den som vill stila
lite extra köper Moscovado-socker från Västindien
som har en mycket särpräglad smak.

There are huge differences in taste depending on
what type of sugar you use – caster sugar, sugar
cubes, icing sugar, farine, brown sugar… Take
crème brûlée for example. For a perfect result blend
caster sugar with brown sugar. For an even more
exciting result use Moscovado sugar from the West
Indies to give a very distinct taste to the brûlée.

ANANAS- OCH ÄPPELSAVARIN MED KANEL OCH VANIL
pineapple and apple savarin with cinnamon and vanil

ANANAS- OCH ÄPPELSAVARIN MED KANEL OCH VANILJ

Gör en vaniljglassgrund. Frys i en glassmaskin.

Skär äpplet till chipsen i tunna skivor. Koka upp vatten och socker. Låt skivorna ligga i sockerlagen i 10 minuter. Lägg dem på en silpatduk och låt torka i 100° ugn i ett par timmar.

Skala, kärna ur och halvera tre äpplen. Skär dem i tunna skivor på skärmaskin eller mandolin. Lägg skivorna på en smord plåt. Pensla dem med klarat smör och strö över socker. Sätt in äppelskivorna i 225° ugn tills de får lite färg. Klä 4 savarinformar med plastfilm. Fodra formarna med äppelskivorna, lite omlott. Låt skivorna hänga över formarnas kanter.

Skala och tärna ananas och äpple fint till fyllningen. Stek i smör, vanilj och honung tills de får färg. Tillsätt äppelcidervinäger och kanel. Ta bort pannan från värmen och låt svalna. Fördela fyllningen i savarinformarna och stäng dem med hjälp av de överhängande äppelskivorna.

Mixa smör och vanilj. Koka ihop socker och vinäger till en färglös karamell. Tillsätt ananasjuice och koka ihop till hälften. Vispa ner vaniljsmöret.

Servera savarinen med ljummen vaniljvinägersås och vaniljglass. Garnera med äppelchips.

4 personer

3 stora Granny Smith-äpplen
1 dl klarat smör
40 g strösocker

FYLLNING
1/2 ananas
1 stort Granny Smith-äpple
30 g smör
1 vaniljstång, urskrapad
1 1/2 msk honung
1 msk äppelcidervinäger
1 nypa malen kanel

ÄPPELCHIPS
1 Granny Smith-äpple
1,2 dl vatten
100 g strösocker

VANILJVINÄGERSÅS
50 g smör
1/2 vaniljstång, urskrapad
50 g strösocker
3/4 dl äppelcidervinäger
2 1/2 dl färskpressad ananasjuice

TILL SERVERING
vaniljglass,
se recept crème anglaise s. 316

PINEAPPLE AND APPLE SAVARIN
WITH CINNAMON AND VANILLA

serves 4

3 large Granny Smith apples
100 ml clarified butter
40 g caster sugar

FILLING
1/2 pineapple, peeled
1 large Granny Smith apple
30 g butter
seeds of 1 vanilla pod
1 1/2 tsp honey
1 tbsp apple cider vinegar
1 pinch of ground cinnamon

APPLE CHIPS
1 Granny Smith apple
120 ml water
100 g caster sugar

PINEAPPLE SAUCE
50 g butter
seeds from 1/2 vanilla pod
50 g caster sugar
75 ml apple cider vinegar
250 ml fresh pineapple juice

FOR SERVING
vanilla ice cream,
make as crème anglaise (p. 328)

Make a vanilla ice cream base according to the recipe and freeze in an ice cream machine.

Cut the apple for the chips into thin slices. Bring the water and sugar to a boil, add the apple slices and leave to soak for 10 minutes. Place the apple slices on a non-stick baking mat and dry in the oven at 100°C for a few hours. Peel three apples, cut in half and remove the seeds. Cut into thin slices. Place the slices on a buttered oven tray. Brush with clear butter and sprinkle with sugar. Bake at 225°C until lightly coloured. Line four savarin moulds with cling film, then the apple slices, overlapping each one slightly leaving an overhang at the top. Peel and cut the pineapple and apple for the filling into small dice. Fry in butter, vanilla and honey until lightly coloured. Add the vinegar and cinnamon. Remove from the heat and leave to cool.

Divide the filling between the moulds and fold over the overhanging apple slices to cover. Mix the butter with the vanilla. Reduce the vinegar and sugar to a colourless caramel. Add pineapple juice and reduce by half. Whisk in the vanilla butter. Serve the savarin with lukewarm pineapple sauce.

VANILJ / vanilla

Utan socker spelar det ingen roll hur mycket vanilj du skrapar ner i desserten. Det är nämligen sockret som «löser» vaniljsmaken. Dela stången på längden med en vass kniv och skrapa ner innehållet i kastrullen. Låt sedan även själva stången koka med för att få ut maximal smak.

Without sugar it doesn't matter how much vanilla you add to a dessert. It's the sugar that «loosens» the taste of vanilla. Cut the pod lengthwise with a sharp knife and scrape the contents into the pan together with the pod to get maximum taste.

KASTANJECRÈME MED TUNNA CHOKLADFLARN OCH KASTANJER I KARAMELL
chestnut cream with thin chocolate biscuits and chestnuts in caramel

KASTANJECRÈME MED TUNNA CHOKLADFLARN
OCH KASTANJER I KARAMELL

4 personer

chokladflarn, se recept s. 316

KASTANJECRÈME
1/2 sats crème pâtissière,
se recept s. 317
150 g kastanjepuré
1 dl vispgrädde

KARAMELL
1 dl vatten
ett stänk citronjuice
100 g strösocker
12 kastanjer, kokta

Gör chokladflarn enligt receptet.

Koka ½ dl vatten, citronjuice och socker till en karamell. Tillsätt resterande vatten och vänd ner kastanjerna. Låt svalna.

Följ receptet för crème pâtissière. Smaksätt den med kastanjepuré och passera blandningen genom en finmaskig sil. Vispa grädden och vänd ner den i kastanjecrèmen.

Varva chokladflarn och kastanjecrème. Garnera med kastanjer i karamell.

CHESTNUT CREAM WITH THIN CHOCOLATE BISCUITS AND CHESTNUTS IN CARAMEL

Make the chocolate biscuits according to the recipe.

Boil 50 ml water with lemon juice and sugar to create a caramel. Add the rest of the water and fold in the chestnuts. Leave to cool.

Follow the recipe for crème pâtissière. Flavour with the chestnut puree and strain the mixture through a fine sieve. Whip the cream and fold into the chestnut cream.

Layer the chocolate biscuits and chestnut cream. Garnish with the caramel chestnuts.

serves 4

chocolate biscuits (p. 328)

CHESTNUT CREAM
1/2 batch crème pâtissière (p.329)
150 g chestnut puree
100 ml cream

CARAMEL
100 ml water
a dash of lemon juice
100 g sugar
12 chestnuts, boiled

JORDGUBBAR
MED CITRONCRÈME I SMÖRDEG

4 personer

400 g jordgubbar, halverade
100 g smördeg
1 tsk vispgrädde + 1 äggula
till pensling
florsocker
1 msk hackade pistaschnötter
1 tsk pärlsocker

CITRONCRÈME
1,2 dl färskpressad citronjuice
3 citroner, rivet skal
165 g strösocker
3 ägg
225 g rumstempererat smör,
tärnat

JORDGUBBSCOULIS
100 g jordgubbar
2 msk strösocker
1 tsk färskpressad citronjuice

Blanda citronjuice, -skal, socker och ägg till citron-crèmen i en kastrull. Koka upp försiktigt under vispning tills det tjocknar. Ta kastrullen från värmen, vispa i smör och låt svalna.

Koka upp jordgubbar, socker och citronjuice till coulin. Mixa och passera blandningen genom en finmaskig sil. Vänd ner de halverade jordgubbarna.

Skär ut fyra smördegsplattor i önskad storlek. Pensla dem med grädd- och ägguleblandningen. Grädda smördegsplattorna i 225° ugn i 5–6 minuter. Sänk värmen till 175° och grädda klart i ytterligare cirka 5 minuter. Ta ut plattorna ur ugnen och pudra över florsocker. Ställ tillbaka dem i ugnen tills flor-sockret har smält.

Klyv varje smördegsplatta i en över- och underdel. Fördela jordgubbarna på underdelarna. Lägg en klick citroncrème på jordgubbarna och placera ett smördegslock överst. Strö över hackade pistasch-nötter och pärlsocker.

JORDGUBBAR MED CITRONCRÈME I SMÖRDEG
Strawberries with lemon cream in puff pastry

STRAWBERRIES WITH
LEMON CREAM IN PUFF PASTRY

serves 4

400 g strawberries, halved
100 g puff pastry
1 tsp cream + 1 egg yolk
icing sugar
1 tbsp chopped pistachio nuts
1 tsp sugar pearls

LEMON CREAM
120 ml freshly squeezed
lemon juice
grated rind of 3 lemons
165 g sugar
3 eggs
225 g butter
at room temperature, diced

STRAWBERRY COULIS
100 g strawberries
2 tbsp sugar
1 tsp freshly squeezed
lemon juice

Stir together the lemon juice, rind, sugar and egg for the lemon cream in a saucepan. Bring gently to a boil whisking constantly until thickened. Remove the saucepan from the heat. Mix the butter and lemon cream together, then leave to cool.

Bring strawberries, sugar and lemon juice for the coulis up to a boil. In a food processor blend together, then strain through a fine sieve. Coat the halved strawberries in the coulis.

Cut four pieces of puff pastry in any desired shape. Brush with the cream and egg yolk mixture. Bake in a 225°C oven for 5–6 minutes. Lower the temperature to 175°C and bake until ready, approximately 5 minutes. Remove from the oven and coat with icing sugar. Return to the oven until the icing sugar has melted.

Cut each puff pastry piece into two lengthwise. Place strawberries on one piece, cover with lemon cream, then cover with the remaining pastry. Sprinkle with chopped pistachio nuts and sugar pearls.

SMÖRDEG / puff pastry

Att göra egen smördeg är ett äventyr som kräver mycket erfarenhet. Därför har vi valt recept till den här boken till vilka även färdigköpt smördeg passar. Ofta innehåller butikernas smördeg margarin, vilket gör den lättare att handskas med, samtidigt som det kan vara knepigare att få den perfekt gräddad. Så passa den noga när den är i ugnen, ytan ska vara riktigt mörkbrun och alla lager ska vara ljusbruna.

To make your own puff pastry is an adventure for which you need a lot of experience! Therefore for the recipes in this book we have chosen to use ready made puff pastry. Ready made puff pastry often contains margarine making it easier to handle but it can be a little tricky to cook correctly. So watch it carefully, puff pastry is cooked when the top is evenly dark brown and all the layers are light brown.

JORDGUBBAR I RÖDV
strawberries in red w

JORDGUBBAR I RÖDVIN

Koka upp vin och socker. Ta bort kastrullen från värmen och tillsätt apelsinskalet och myntabuketten.
Låt dra i 30 minuter under lock. Sila.

Rensa och halvera jordgubbarna. Lägg dem i
rödvinslagen och låt dra i en timme. Tillsätt fint
strimlad mynta innan jordgubbarna ska serveras.

4 personer

400 g jordgubbar
7 1/2 dl rött vin
200 g strösocker
2 apelsiner, rivet skal
10 myntablad,
bundna till en bukett

GARNITYR
5 myntablad, fint strimlade

STRAWBERRIES IN RED WINE

serves 4

400 g strawberries
750 ml red wine
200 g sugar
grated zest of 2 oranges
10 mint leaves, tied together

GARNISH
5 mint leaves, finely shredded

Bring wine and sugar to a boil. Remove the saucepan from the heat and add the orange zest and mint. Leave to infuse for 30 minutes covered with a lid. Strain.

Clean and half the strawberries. Add to the red wine and orange mixture and leave to infuse for one hour. Add finely shredded mint leaves just before serving.

JORDGUBBAR / strawberries

Äntligen har producenterna upptäckt att jordgubbar kan smaka också, att de inte bara ska vara röda, ge rik skörd och tåla långa transporter. Var frågvis och hitta din egen favoritsort! Jordgubbar passar ihop med många andra smaker. Mest klassisk är kombinationen jordgubbar och apelsinskal, men pröva även att blanda sockrade jordgubbar med lime, alkohol (rött vin eller olika likörer) eller vanilj.

Finally strawberry growers have realised that strawberries must not only look good with a deep rich red colour and have a long shelf life, they must also taste good! Strawberries with orange zest is a classical combination but also try sweetened strawberries together with lime, red wine, different liqueurs, or vanilla.

CHOKLADNAPOLEON

4 personer

24 färska hallon

CHOKLADPLATTOR
300 g mörk choklad, finhackad

DRAGONANGLAIS
1/2 sats crème anglaise,
se recept s. 316
1 msk finhackad dragon

CHOKLADMOUSSE
200 g mörk choklad, hackad
1/2 dl varmt vatten
1 ägg
2 äggulor
85 g strösocker
3 dl vispgrädde
2 äggvitor

Temperera chokladen till plattorna genom att först värma halva mängden choklad till 48–50°. Rör sedan ner resterande choklad. Rör tills temperaturen är 27–28°. Värm därefter upp chokladen till 31–32°. Häll ut den på en marmorskiva och skär ut 16 tunna rektanglar, 6½ x 6 cm.

Gör crème anglaise enligt receptet. Tillsätt dragon medan krämen är varm. Kyl den sedan.

Smält chokladen till moussen tillsammans med vatten i mikrovågsugn eller vattenbad. Blanda ägg, äggulor och 60 g socker. Vispa till hårt skum i vattenbad. Vänd ner äggblandningen i chokladen. Låt svalna. Vispa grädden och vänd ner den i chokladblandningen. Vispa äggvitorna och tillsätt resterande socker lite i taget. Vänd ner äggvitorna i chokladblandningen och låt stå i kylen i 2 timmar.

Varva chokladplattor, chokladmousse och hallon. Servera med dragonanglaise runt om.

CHOKLADNAPOLEON
chocolate napoleon

CHOCOLATE NAPOLEON

serves 4

24 fresh raspberrries

CHOCOLATE TILES
300 g dark chocolate,
finely chopped

TARRAGON ANGLAISE
1/2 batch crème anglaise (p.328)
1 tbsp finely chopped
tarragon

CHOCOLATE MOUSSE
200 g dark chocolate, chopped
50 ml hot water
1 egg
2 egg yolks
85 g sugar
300 ml whipped cream
2 egg whites

Temper the dark chocolate to create chocolate tiles by heating half the quantity of chocolate to 48–50°. Stir in the rest of the chocolate. Stir until the temperature is 27–28°. Heat again to 31–32°. Pour the chocolate onto a marble board and cut 16 thin rectangles, 6½ x 6 cm.

Make the crème anglaise according to the recipe. Add tarragon while the cream is still warm. Leave to cool.

Melt the chocolate for the mousse with water in a microwave or in a water bath. Mix eggs, egg yolks and 60 g of sugar. Whisk to a hard foam in a water bath. Fold the egg mixture into the chocolate. Leave to cool. Whisk the cream and fold into the chocolate mixture. Whisk the egg whites and add the remaining sugar a little at a time. Fold the egg whites into the chocolate mixture and leave in the refrigerator for 2 hours.

Layer the chocolate squares, chocolate mousse and raspberries. Serve the Napoleon surrounded by the tarragon anglaise.

CHOKLAD /chocolate

När Cortéz kom till Mexiko år 1519 blev han serverad den kungliga drycken *xocoatl* (choklad) vid Montezumas hov. Spanjorerna «tackade för senast» genom att döda Montezuma och erövra hans stad ...
I dag är choklad en hel vetenskap och vårt intresse för högkvalitativ choklad bara ökar. Ska man smälta choklad i vattenbad gäller det att vara försiktig. Vattnet ska knappt sjuda, annars kan chokladen bli grynig. Lättast är att smälta chokladen i mikrougn.

When Cortez first arrived in Mexico in 1519 he was served the royal drink *xocoatl* at Montezumas court. The Spaniards way to say «thank you» was to kill him and conquer his city...! Today chocolate is pure science and our interest for chocolate of good quality only increases. To melt chocolate over hot water (bain marie) you have to be careful. The water should hardly simmer, otherwise the chocolate can become granular. The easiest way is to melt it in the microwave.

CRÈME BRÛLÉE

Vispa äggulor, socker och vanilj lätt. Tillsätt grädde och mjölk. Sila och fyll portionsformar med blandningen. Placera formarna på ett galler och ställ dem i 90° ugn tills äggblandningen har stannat. Ta ut dem och låt kallna.

Sikta farinsocker över brûléerna och karamellisera sockret under grillelementet i ugnen eller med en gasolbrännare. Servera genast.

4 personer

180 g äggulor
150 g strösocker
3 vaniljstänger, urskrapade
7 1/2 dl grädde
2 1/2 dl mjölk
farinsocker

CRÈME BRÛLÉE

serves 4

180 g egg yolks
150 g caster sugar
seeds from 3 vanilla pods
750 ml cream
250 ml milk
brown sugar

Lightly whisk the egg yolks, sugar and vanilla. Add cream and milk. Strain and fill individual dishes with the egg mixture. Bake at 90°C until the eggs are just set. Remove from the oven and cool.

Sift the brown sugar over the brûlée and caramelise under a hot grill, hot oven or with a blow torch. Serve immediately.

CRÈME BRÛLÉE/crème brûlée

På senare år har fransk, kall crème caramel fått hård konkurrens av len crème brûlée med varmt, knaprigt sockertäcke, speciellt på restauranger utanför Frankrike. Denna variant har egentligen sitt ursprung i den spanska desserten *crema catalana*. En perfekt crème brûlée är en verklig njutning, så har man också speciella crème brûlée-sällskap världen över som listar var den bästa puddingen finns: perfekt gräddad utan bubblor och med ett täcke så exakt karamelliserat att den kittlande smaken nästan är på gränsen att slå över i bränt.

The French crème caramel is served cold in small individual pots. Whereas outside France what is becoming more and more popular is the delicate crème brûlée with its covering of warm, crisp melted sugar which has origins in the Spanish *crema catalana*. A perfect crème brûlée is a true pleasure with societies worldwide listing the most perfect creme brûlée – perfectly cooked without any bubbles and with a cover of caramel, the taste of which has to be so exact having a slight tickling tone and just on the edge of being burnt.

BABA MED KÖRSBÄR OCH KIRSCHGLA
baba with cherries and kirsch ice cre

BABA MED KÖRSBÄR OCH KIRSCHGLASS

Gör en vaniljglassgrund enligt recept. Smaksätt den med Kirschwasser innan den fryses i en glassmaskin.

Värm mjölken till babadegen fingervarm. Lös jästen i mjölken och tillsätt lite av mjölet. Ställ åt sidan några minuter på en varm plats. Tillsätt resterande mjöl, socker, ägg, salt och soltorkade körsbär när jäsningen har kommit igång. Blanda ihop till en deg. Gör ett hål i degen. Häll det brynta smöret i hålet och låt degen jäsa till dubbel volym. Knåda sedan degen tills smöret har absorberats helt. Fyll en spritspåse med degen. Spritsa den i portionsstora smorda och mjölade savarinformar. Fyll dem till hälften. Låt dem jäsa till dubbel volym. Grädda i 175° ugn i cirka 15 minuter. Lossa dem från formarna och låt svalna på galler.

Koka körsbären, socker, vatten och citronjuice till coulin i 20 minuter. Passera dem genom en finmaskig sil. Red av med maizenamjöl.

Koka upp alla ingredienser till kryddlagen utom ananasjuicen, som tillsätts när lagen har svalnat. Värm kryddlagen före servering och lägg i bakverken. Låt dem ligga i lagen och svälla i cirka 3–4 minuter.

Servera med kirschglass. Skeda körsbärscoulis runt om. Garnera med körsbär.

4 personer

BABA
2 dl mjölk, 37°
20 g jäst
450 g vetemjöl
40 g strösocker
5 ägg
15 g salt
100 g brynt smör
300 g soltorkade körsbär, hackade
smör + vetemjöl till formar

KÖRSBÄRSCOULIS
500 g körsbär, urkärnade
200 g strösocker
1 dl vatten
1 citron, juice
1 msk maizenamjöl

KRYDDLAG
175 g strösocker
5 dl vatten
1/2 vaniljstång
1/2 kanelstång
1 stjärnanis
1 citrongräs
1/2 apelsin, rivet skal
1/2 citron, rivet skal
1 1/2 dl ananasjuice, färskpressad

TILL SERVERING
vaniljglass, se recept s. 316
1/2 dl Kirschwasser
färska urkärnade körsbär

BABA WITH CHERRIES AND KIRSCH ICE CREAM

serves 4

BABA
200 g milk
20 g fresh yeast
450 g flour
40 g sugar
5 eggs
15 g salt
100 g brown butter
300 g sun dried cherries, chopped
butter + flour for moulds

CHERRY COULIS
500 g fresh cherries, pitted
200 g sugar
100 ml water
juice of 1 lemon
1 tbsp cornflour

SPICE SYRUP
175 g sugar
500 ml water
1/2 vanilla pod
1/2 cinnamon stick
1 star anise
1 lemon grass
grated rind of 1/2 orange
grated rind of 1/2 lemon
150 ml freshly squeezed pineapple juice

SERVE WITH
vanilla ice cream (p. 328)
50 ml Kirsch liqueur
fresh pitted cherries

Make a vanilla ice cream base according to the recipe, flavour with Kirsch before freezing in an ice cream machine.

Heat the milk for the baba dough until lukewarm. Dissolve the yeast in the milk and add a little flour. Put aside for a few minutes in a warm place. Add the rest of the flour, sugar, eggs, salt and sundried cherries once fermentation has started. Form into a dough. Make a hole in the dough and pour in the brown butter. Leave to rise until doubled in volume. Knead the dough until the butter is completely incorporated.

Fill a piping bag with the dough and pipe halfway up buttered, floured, individual savarin moulds. Leave to double in volume. Bake in a 175C° oven for approximately 15 minutes. Remove from the moulds and leave to cool on a rack. Boil the cherries, sugar, water and lemon juice together for 20 minutes. Strain through a fine sieve. Thicken with the cornflour. Bring all ingredients for the spice syrup, except the pineapple juice, up to a boil. Leave to cool, then add the pineapple juice. Reheat the syrup before serving, add the babas and leave to soak for 3–4 minutes to soak up the nage. Serve with the kirsch ice cream surrounded by cherry coulis.

BABA/baba

Det finns åtminstone två teorier om hur de ryska små, runda savarinliknande kakorna har fått sitt namn: Antingen syftar det på att ryska barn kallar mormor eller farmor för *babusjka* eller *baba* och att de gärna pysslar om barnbarnen med just den här typen av mjuka bakverk. Eller så kommer namnet av att kakorna liknar just runda, krumma gummor.

There are at least two theories how the small, round savarin-like Russian cakes derived their name. Either that Russian children call their grandmothers *babusjka* or *baba* and they like to spoil their grandchildren with these sponge cakes or they got their name because the cakes look like bent old women.

CAPPUCCINOGLASS MED MANDELSKUM
OCH MADELEINEKAKOR

4 personer

CAPPUCCINOGLASS
5 dl mjölk
1 dl espressokaffe
2 msk nescafépulver
7 äggulor
120 g strösocker

MANDELSKUM
200 g mandel, skållad, hackad
100 g strösocker
5 dl mjölk
2 gelatinblad, blötlagda
1 msk amaretto (mandellikör)

TILL SERVERING
kakao
madeleinekakor,
se recept s. 316

Koka upp mjölken till glassen och tillsätt allt kaffe. Vispa äggulor och socker till dubbel volym. Slå den varma mjölken över ägg- och sockerblandningen under vispning. Häll tillbaka alltsammans i kastrullen. Värm försiktigt under omrörning tills blandningen tjocknar. Gör ett rosenprov, se s. 247. Blandningen får inte koka. Ta bort kastrullen från värmen, sila och kyl snabbt. Frys i en glassmaskin.

Rosta mandeln i en stekpanna. Tillsätt socker och låt det smälta till en karamell. Slå på mjölk, rör om och låt sjuda i 10 minuter. Sila och tillsätt gelatin och amaretto. Låt svalna och fyll en sifon med blandningen.

Varva glass och kakao i kaffekoppar. Tillsätt skum och servera genast med madeleinekakor.

CAPPUCCINOGLASS MED MANDELSKUM OCH MADELEINEKAKOR
cappuccino ice cream with almond foam and madeleine cookies

CAPPUCCINO ICE CREAM WITH ALMOND FOAM
AND MADELEINE COOKIES

serves 4

CAPPUCCINO ICE CREAM
500 ml milk
100 ml espresso coffee
2 tbsp instant coffee
7 egg yolks
120 g sugar

ALMOND FOAM
200 g almonds,
peeled, chopped
100 g sugar
500 ml milk
2 leaves of gelatine, soaked
1 tbsp amaretto (almond liqueur)

SERVE WITH
cocoa powder
madeleine cookies (p. 328)

Bring the milk for the cappuccino ice cream to the boil and add all the coffee. Whisk the egg yolks and sugar together until doubled in volume. Pour the hot milk onto the egg and sugar mixture whisking constantly. Place back in the saucepan, stir constantly until the mixture thickens, see p. 247. Do not allow to boil. Strain, then cool quickly. Freeze in an ice cream machine.

Roast the almonds in a frying pan. Add sugar and melt to form a caramel. Pour the milk over the caramel, stir, then simmer for 10 minutes. Strain and add the gelatine and amaretto. Leave to cool, fill a siphon with the mixture.

Put the ice cream and cocoa powder in layers in coffee cups. Spray the siphoned foam on top and serve it immediately with madeleine cookies.

MADELEINEKAKOR / madeleines

Den franske författaren Marcel Proust (1871–1922) är kanske den som mest förknippas med de fina mördegskakorna. Från 1905 arbetade han med den väldiga romansviten «På spaning efter den tid som flytt» (*A la recherche du temps perdu*). Proust var egentligen ganska ointresserad av mat, men ett gäng madeleinekakor brukade muntra upp honom när arbetet med de 16 böckerna i sviten kändes tungt.

The French author Marcel Proust (1871–1922) is maybe the person most closely related to these delicate buttery cakes. From 1905 he worked on his enormous series of novels – *Remembrance of Things Past*. He was rather disinterested in food, but a couple of madeleines would cheer him up when the work involved in 16 novels became too heavy.

CLAFOUTI
clafout

CLAFOUTIS

Blanda siktat florsocker och mandelmjöl med smör och salt till mördegen. Tillsätt äggulor och slutligen mjöl. Arbeta snabbt till en deg. Täck degen med plastfilm och låt vila 30 minuter i kylen. Kavla ut mördegen tunt och klä två smorda pajformar med den. Täck degen med aluminiumfolie och lägg på ett lager torra ärter eller bönor. Förgrädda i 175° ugn i 20 minuter. Ta ut pajerna, lyft bort aluminiumfolien och ärterna/bönorna och låt pajskalen svalna.

Vispa ihop äggulor, socker, maizenamjöl och vispgrädde. Sila blandningen genom en finmaskig sil.

Lägg aprikoshalvorna på pajskalen. Slå på äggblandningen. Grädda i 175° ugn tills äggblandningen har stannat, det tar cirka 20 minuter. Ta ut pajerna, pudra över lite florsocker och ställ in dem under ugnens grillelement tills florsockret har smält.

Servera pajerna varma.

2 pajer

5 äggulor
200 g strösocker
15 g maizenamjöl
3 1/4 dl vispgrädde
600 g halverade och urkärnade färska aprikoser
florsocker

MÖRDEG
40 g florsocker
40 g mandelmjöl
160 g mjukt smör
1 nypa salt
2 äggulor
200 g vetemjöl

Makes 2 tarts

5 egg yolks
200 g sugar
15 g cornflour
325 ml cream
600 g halved and pitted apricots
icing sugar

RICH SHORTCRUST PASTRY
40 g icing sugar
40 g ground almonds
160 g soft butter
1 pinch of salt
2 egg yolks
200 g flour

In a food processor mix the sifted icing sugar and ground almonds with the butter and salt for the pastry. Add the egg yolks and finally the flour quickly to form a dough. Cover with cling film and leave to rest for 30 minutes in the refrigerator. Roll the dough thinly and line two greased tart tins with the pastry. Cover the dough with aluminium foil and then a layer of dried peas or beans. Par-bake in a 175°C oven for 20 minutes. Take the pie shells from the oven, remove the foil and the peas/beans and leave to cool.

Whisk egg yolks, sugar, cornflour and cream together. Strain through a fine sieve.

Place the apricot halves on the pie shells, cut-side down. Pour the egg mixture over. Bake in 175°C oven until the eggs are set, for approximately 20 minutes. Remove the tarts from the oven, powder with icing sugar and place under a hot grill until the sugar has melted.

Serve the tarts warm.

ROSENPROVET/coating the spoon

Hur tjock ska dessertsåsen eller smeten vara innan man slutar vispa? Ett enkelt test är att röra med en träslev, lyfta upp sleven med botten upp och dra med ett finger längs baksidan. När såsen inte går ihop igen, utan lämnar en liten «gata» är den lagom tjock. Sluta vispa och kyl snabbt, annars klumpar sig såsen. Från början blåste kockarna på baksidan av en sked; när en ros bildades var såsen klar. Vårt sätt är inte lika romantiskt, men betydligt enklare.

How do you tell when a sauce is thick enough to stop whisking? One easy way is to take a wooden spoon, pass it through the sauce, then on the back of the spoon make a line with your finger. When the finger mark leaves an indentation it's time to stop whisking and cool the sauce. Originally chefs blew on the back of a spoon and when the hole looked like a rose, the sauce was ready. Our way doesn't sound as romantic but it is easier.

GOTLÄNDSK SAFFRANSPANNKAKA
MED SALMBÄR

8–10 personer

1 1/4 dl rundkornigt ris
2 1/2 dl vatten
3 1/2 dl grädde
3 1/2 dl mjölk
2 krm salt
2 msk honung
1 pkt saffran (1/2 g)
1 dl hackad mandel
3 bittermandlar, hackade
1 dl russin
3 ägg
smör till formen

TILL SERVERING
100 g salmbär
50 g strösocker
vispgrädde

Koka ris och vatten under lock i cirka 10 minuter tills vattnet har kokat in. Tillsätt grädde, mjölk och salt. Låt koka i 30 minuter under lock till en lös gröt. Blanda i honung, saffran, mandel, bittermandel och russin. Låt svalna.

Rör ner äggen i gröten, ett i taget. Häll blandningen i smorda portionsformar. Grädda i 200° ugn i cirka 20 minuter tills smeten har stannat. Låt svalna.

Värm salmbär och socker.

Servera saffranspannkakan med salmbär och vispad grädde.

GOTLÄNDSK SAFFRANSPANNKAKA MED SALMBÄR
saffron pancake from gotland with blackberries

SAFFRON PANCAKE FROM GOTLAND
WITH BLACKBERRIES

serves 8–10

100 g pudding rice
250 ml water
350 ml cream
350 ml milk
2 pinches salt
2 tbsp honey
1/2 g saffron
75 g chopped almonds
3 bitter almonds, chopped
50 g raisins
3 eggs
butter for the mould

SERVE WITH
100 g blackberries
50 g sugar
whipped cream

Boil the rice and water covered with a lid, until all the water has evaporated, approximately 10 minutes. Add the cream, milk and salt. Boil for 30 minutes covered with a lid, to create a porridge-like consistency. Stir in the honey, saffron, almonds and raisins. Leave to cool.

Stir the eggs into the rice, one at a time. Pour the mixture into buttered portion sized moulds. Bake in a 200°C oven for approximately 20 minutes until set. Leave to cool.

Heat up the blackberries and sugar.

Serve the saffron pancake with blackberries and whipped cream.

SILPATDUK / silpat mat

Silpatduk är en ugnstålig silikonduk som inget fastnar på, ett slags evighetsbakplåtspapper som ofta används i proffskök. För hemmamatlagare finns teflonark att köpa i större livsmedelsbutiker. Investera i ett sådant och du slipper smörja plåtar i fortsättningen.

These revolutionary non-stick, oven-proof baking sheets completely replace greaseproof paper. However they are usually only found in professional kitchens. At home it is possible to buy Teflon coated sheets in larger stores and supermarkets which will completely render useless the need for grease baking sheets and pans again.

RÖDA BÄR I CHAMPAGNEGE
red berries in champagne je

RÖDA BÄR I CHAMPAGNEGELÉ

4 personer

4 dl champagne
140 g strösocker
1/2 citron, juice
1 vaniljstång, urskrapad
1 1/2 gelatinblad, blötlagt
20 körsbär,
halverade och urkärnade
20 hallon
40 smultron
8 jordgubbar, halverade

GARNITYR
4 myntablad, strimlade

Koka upp champagne, socker, citronjuice och vanilj. Rör ner gelatinet och sila blandningen genom en finmaskig sil. Låt svalna.

Fördela bären i portionsskålar. Häll champagnegelén över bären precis när den håller på att stelna. Garnera med mynta och servera.

RED BERRIES IN CHAMPAGNE JELLY

Bring the champagne, sugar, lemon juice and vanilla to a boil. Stir in the gelatine and strain the mixture through a fine sieve. Leave to cool.

Divide the berries into portion sized dishes. Pour the champagne jelly over the berries just before it starts to set. Garnish with mint leaves and serve.

serves 4

400 ml champagne
140 g sugar
juice of 1 /2 lemon
seeds from 1 vanilla pod
1 1/2 leaves of gelatine, soaked in cold water
20 cherries, halved and pitted
20 raspberries
40 wild strawberries
8 strawberries, halved

GARNISH
4 leaves of mint, shredded

CHOKLADTRYFFEL

1 sats

5 dl vispgrädde
325 g ljus choklad, hackad
325 g mörk choklad, hackad
(Grand Marnier)
kakao

Koka upp grädden. Vänd ner chokladen och smaksätt eventuellt med Grand Marnier. Låt blandningen stå i kylen över natten. Forma chokladsmeten och rulla tryfflarna i kakao. Servera dem rumstempererade.

CHOKLADTRYFFEL
chocolate truffles

CHOCOLATE TRUFFLES

1 batch

500 ml cream
325 g light chocolate, chopped
325 g dark chocolate, chopped
Grand Marnier liqueur (optional)
cocoa powder

Bring the cream to a boil. Fold in the chocolate and flavour with Grand Marnier (if using). Leave in the refrigerator overnight. Shape the chocolate mixture and roll the truffles in cocoa powder. Serve at room temperature.

FATTIGA RIDDARE MED KRYDDKOKTA PÄRON OCH KRYDDGLAS
poor knights with spicy boiled pears and spicy ice crea

FATTIGA RIDDARE MED
KRYDDKOKTA PÄRON OCH KRYDDGLASS

Koka upp mjölken till kryddglassen. Tillsätt kryddorna och låt dra under lock i 20 minuter, sila. Vispa äggulor och socker till dubbel volym. Slå den varma mjölken över ägg- och sockerblandningen under vispning. Häll tillbaka alltsammans i kastrullen. Värm försiktigt under omrörning tills blandningen tjocknar. Gör ett rosenprov, se s. 251. Blandningen får inte koka. Ta bort kastrullen från värmen, sila och kyl snabbt. Frys i en glassmaskin.

Skala, halvera och kärna ur päronen. Koka upp vatten och socker. Tillsätt allt utom farinsocker och lägg i päronhalvorna. Låt päronen sjuda mjuka under ett smörpapperslock, i 15–20 minuter. Skär päronen i klyftor.

Blanda mjölk, öl, ägg och farinsocker till en smet. Vänd briocheskivorna i smeten och stek dem gyllenbruna i klarat smör.

Värm päronklyftorna i en stekpanna. Strö över farinsocker.

Fördela päronen på briocheskivorna. Servera med kryddglass.

4 personer

2 skivor brioche,
se recept s. 317
2 1/2 dl mjölk
1 1/4 dl öl
1 ägg
40 g farinsocker
2 msk klarat smör

KRYDDGLASS
5 dl mjölk
1 tsk malen kanel
1 tsk krossade korianderfrön
1 stjärnanis
1 tsk fänkålsfrön
1 tsk malen ingefära
6 äggulor
110 g strösocker

KRYDDKOKTA PÄRON
4 fasta päron
1 liter vatten
300 g strösocker
2 kanelstänger
1 tsk fänkålsfrön
1 tsk korianderfrön
1 stjärnanis
1 tsk farinsocker

POOR KNIGHTS WITH
SPICY BOILED PEARS AND SPICY ICE CREAM

serves 4

2 slices brioche (p. 330)
250 ml milk
125 ml beer
1 egg
40 g brown sugar
2 tbsp clarified butter

SPICY ICE CREAM
500 ml milk
1 tsp ground cinnamon
1 tsp crushed coriander seeds
1 star anise
1 tsp fennel seeds
1 tsp ground ginger
6 egg yolks
110 g sugar

SPICY BOILED PEARS
4 firm pears
1 litre water
300 g sugar
2 cinnamon sticks
1 tsp fennel seeds
1 tsp coriander seeds
1 star anise
1 tsp brown sugar

Bring the milk for the spicy ice cream to the boil. Add the spices and leave covered for 20 minutes, strain. Whisk the egg yolks and sugar together until doubled in volume. Pour the hot milk onto the egg and sugar mixture whisking constantly. Place back in the saucepan, stir constantly until the mixture thickens see p. 251. Do not allow to boil. Remove the saucepan from the heat, strain and cool quickly. Freeze in an ice cream machine.

Peel, half and remove the pips from the pears. Bring water and sugar to the boil, add all the spices except the brown sugar then add the pears. Leave the pears to simmer until soft covered with a grease-proof paper lid for 15–20 minutes. Cut the pears into segments.

Mix the milk, beer, egg and brown sugar to a smooth batter. Coat the brioche slices with the batter and fry until golden brown in clarified butter.

Heat the pear segments in a frying pan. Sprinkle with brown sugar.

Place the pear segments on the brioche slices. Serve with the spicy ice cream.

FATTIGA RIDDARE/poor knights

Fattiga riddare är en direktöversättning från tyskans *arme Ritter*, men även i England finns efterrätten *poor knights*. Rätten dyker upp i kokböckerna runt mitten av 1800-talet. Namnet syftar troligen på att det under ett stiligt yttre (rustningen respektive sockertäcket) kan dölja sig något ganska enkelt (en vanlig bondgrabb respektive en skiva bröd, som ibland nog hade hunnit bli gott och väl dagsgammal...). Även Shakespeare skrev om fattiga riddare. I andra delen av Henrik IV serveras «withered knights».

Poor knights is a direct translation from the german name *arme Ritter* and the dessert first appears in cookbooks around 1850. The name probably refers to the fact that behind something which looks marvelous (the armour or the sugar coating) can hide something rather ordinary (a simple farmer boy or a two-day old slice of bread, ...). Even Shakespeare wrote about poor knights, in the second part of Henry IV they serve «withered knights».

MILLEFEUILLES MED KARAMELLKOKT PÄRON
OCH KARDEMUMMACRÈME

4 personer

4 fasta päron
flytande karamell,
se recept s. 315
3 dl vatten
250 g smördeg
florsocker

KARDEMUMMACRÈME
1/2 sats crème pâtissière,
se recept s. 317
2 dl vispgrädde
nymalen kardemumma

Skala, halvera och kärna ur päronen. Gör en fly-tande karamell enligt receptet. Slå på vatten och låt päronhalvorna sjuda mjuka under ett smörpappers-lock, 15–20 minuter. Klyfta päronen.

Gör crème pâtissière enligt receptet. Vispa grädden och vänd ner den i crèmen. Smaksätt med nymalen kardemumma.

Kavla ut smördegen 2 mm tjock. Lägg degen på en plåt och placera en plåt ovanpå så att degen ligger i press. Grädda smördegen i 200° ugn i 30 minuter. Degen ska bli brun. Ta ut plåtarna och skär degen i 16 rektanglar. Pudra över florsocker och ställ in dem i ugnen tills sockret har smält.

Varva smördegsplattor, kardemummacrème och päronklyftor.

MILLEFEUILLES MED KARAMELLKOKT PÄRON OCH KARDEMUMMACRÈME
millefeuilles with caramel pears and cardamon cream

MILLEFEUILLES WITH CARAMEL PEARS
AND CARDAMOM CREAM

serves 4

4 firm pears
liquid caramel (p. 327)
300 ml water
250 g puff pastry
icing sugar

CARDAMOM CREAM
1/2 batch of crème pâtissière
(p. 329)
200 ml whipping cream
freshly ground cardamom

Peel, half and remove the pips from the pears and make a liquid caramel according to the recipe. Pour the water onto the caramel and let the pears simmer in the caramel under a greaseproof paper lid until soft, 15–20 minutes. Cut the pears into segments.

Make a crème patissière according to the recipe. Whisk the cream and fold into the crème pâtissière. Season with freshly ground cardamom.

Roll the puff pastry until 2 mm thick. Place the pastry on an oven tray and place another tray on top. Bake the pastry in a 200°C oven for 30 minutes. The pastry should be brown. Remove from the oven and cut the pastry into 16 rectangles. Powder with icing sugar and return to the oven until the icing sugar melts.

Layer the puff pastry with the cardamom cream and pear segments.

FLYTANDE KARAMELL/caramel

Hur lyckas kockarna smälta sockret utan att det blir grynigt och kristalliserat? Knepet är enkelt: tillsätt ett stänk vinäger eller citron, så smälter sockret till en slät karamell. Undvik dessutom att röra i sockret innan det har smält. Skulle det stänka mycket runt kanterna kan du i stället pensla försiktigt med en brödpensel doppad i vatten eller citronsaft.

How do chefs manage to melt sugar without it crystallising? It's easy, add a dash of vinegar or lemon juice to the sugar and it will melt to a smooth caramel. Also avoid stirring the sugar while it is melting. If you find you have sugar around the edges of the pan, use a pastry brush, dipped in water or lemon juice and brush carefully.

VARM CHOKLADMOUSS
warm chocolate mous

VARM CHOKLADMOUSSE

Smält choklad och smör i ett vattenbad. Tillsätt äggulor och kakao. Låt svalna.

Vispa äggvitor och socker till hårt skum. Vänd ner äggvitorna i chokladblandningen. Fördela smeten i ugnssäkra portionsformar och grädda i 180° ugn i 3–5 minuter. Ta ut dem, pudra över florsocker och servera genast.

4 personer

100 g mörk choklad
50 g smör
3 äggulor
15 g kakao
3 äggvitor
50 g strösocker

GARNITYR
florsocker

WARM CHOCOLATE MOUSSE

serves 4

100 g dark chocolate
50 g butter
3 egg yolks
15 g cocoa powder
3 egg whites
50 g sugar

GARNISH
icing sugar

Melt the chocolate and butter in a water-bath. Add egg yolks and cocoa powder. Leave to cool.

Whisk the egg whites and sugar until stiff. Fold the egg whites into the chocolate. Divide the mixture into ovenproof portion sized dishes and bake in a 180C° oven for 3–5 minutes. Remove from the oven, powder with icing sugar and serve immediately.

STARKA

strong

BELLINI (apéritif)

1/2 vit persika
5 cl persikojuice från burk
4 cl färskpressad citronjuice
2 cl Peachtree, persikolikör
3 dl krossad is
champagne

Blanda fruktkött, fruktjuicer, Peachtree och krossad is i en blender till en sorbetliknande konsistens. Fyll ett champagneglas till hälften med blandningen. Fyll upp glaset med champagne som rörs ner med en rörsked. Servera genast.

BELLINI (apéritif)

BELLINI (apéritif)

1/2 white peach
50 ml juice from tinned peaches
40 ml freshly squeezed lemon juice
20 ml Peachtree, peach liqueur
300 ml crushed ice
champagne

Mix the peach, fruit juices, peach liqueur and crushed ice in a blender to a sorbet like consistency. Half fill a champagne glass with the mixture and top up with champagne and stir. Serve immediately.

CHARMER (apéritif)

CHARMER (apéritif)

2 1/2 cl Scotch whisky
2 cl Blå curacao
1 1/2 cl Martini dry
4 droppar Angostura bitter
is

Fyll ett rörglas med is. Slå på whisky, Blå curacao och Martini dry. Rör om och sila ner i ett martiniglas.

CHARMER (apéritif)

Fill a mixing glass with ice. Pour the whisky over the ice followed by Blue curacao and Martini dry. Stir and strain into a martini glass.

25 ml Scotch whisky
20 ml Blue curacao
25 ml Martini dry
4 drops Angostura bitter
ice

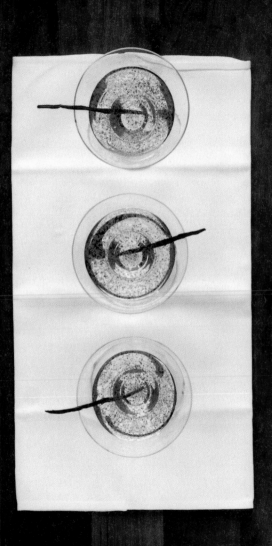

VANILLA CHOCOLATE (after dinne

VANILLA CHOCOLATE (after dinner)

Fyll ett rörglas med is. Slå på vodka och Creme de cacao. Rör om och sila ner i ett martiniglas. Pudra över kakao och garnera med en vaniljstång.

3 cl Smirnoff black vodka
3 cl Creme de cacao, vit
is
kakao
vaniljstång

VANILLA CHOCOLATE (after dinner)

3o ml Smirnoff black vodka
30 ml white Creme de cacao
ice
cocoa powder
vanilla pod

Fill a mixing glass with ice. Pour the vodka over the ice followed by the Crème de cacao. Stir and strain into a martini glass. Sprinkle with cocoa and garnish with a vanilla pod.

NORTH FACE (apéritif)

NORTH FACE (apéritif)

3 cl Smirnoff black vodka
2 cl Lakka, hjortronlikör
1 cl Smirnoff cream
is
1 färskt hjortron

Fyll ett rörglas med is. Slå på vodka, Lakka och Smirnoff cream. Rör om och sila ner i ett martini-glas. Garnera med ett färskt hjortron.

NORTH FACE (apéritif)

Fill a mixing glass with ice. Pour the vodka over the ice followed by Lakka and Smirnoff cream. Stir and strain into a martini glass. Garnish with a fresh cloud berry.

30 ml Smirnoff black vodka
20 ml Lakka, cloud berry liqueur
10 ml Smirnoff cream
ice
1 fresh cloud berry

MOJITO (long drink)

8–9 myntablad
3 cl sockerlag på rörsocker
1/2–3/4 lime, klyftad
krossad is
6 cl rom, ljus eller mörk
sodavatten

Stöt myntablad i sockerlag direkt i glaset. Använd gärna en trämortel. Lägg i limeklyftor och stöt lite till.

Fyll glaset med krossad is och rom. Täck glaset och skaka. Toppa med sodavatten och garnera med myntablad.

MOJITO (long drink)

MOJITO (long drink)

8–9 mint leaves
30 ml cane syrup
1/2–3/4 of a lime cut in segments
crushed ice
60 ml dark or light rum
soda water

Directly in a glass pound the mint leaves s into the syrup using a wooden mortar. Add the lime segments and pound a little more. Fill the glass with crushed ice and rum. Cover the glass and shake. Top with soda water and garnish with mint leaves.

ROB ROY (apéritif)

Fyll ett rörglas med is. Slå på whisky, Martini rosso och Angostura bitter. Rör om och sila ner i ett martiniglas. Garnera med ett rött cocktailbär.

4 cl Scotch whisky
2 cl Martini rosso
4 droppar Angostura bitter
is
1 rött cocktailbär

BRANDY ALEXANDER (after dinner)

Fyll en shaker med is. Slå på konjak, Creme de cacao, mjölk och vispgrädde. Skaka, sila och häll blandningen i ett martiniglas. Pudra över kakao.

3 cl konjak
3 cl Creme de cacao, vit
1 1/2 cl mjölk
1 1/2 cl vispgrädde
is
kakao

ROB ROY (apérit

BRANDY ALEXANDER (after dinner)

ROB ROY (apéritif)

40 ml Scotch whisky
20 ml Martini rosso
4 drops Angostura bitter
ice
1 red cocktail cherry

Fill a mixing glass with ice. Pour the whisky over the ice followed by Martini rosso and Angostura bitter. Stir and strain into a martini glass. Garnish with a red cocktail cherry.

BRANDY ALEXANDER (after dinner)

3o ml brandy
30 ml Creme de cacao, white
15 ml milk
15 ml cream
ice
cocoa powder

Fill a cocktail shaker with ice. Pour the brandy over the ice followed by Creme de cacao, milk and cream. Shake, strain and pour the mixture into a martini glass. Sprinkle with cocoa.

CHE GUEVARA (long drink)

CHE GUEVARA (long drink)

6 cl Bacardi limone
8 myntablad
1/2 lime, klyftad
2 cl rörsocker
4 droppar Angostura bitter
ginger ale

Stöt myntablad, limeklyftor, rörsocker, Bacardi limone och Angostura bitter i en shaker. Använd gärna en trämortel. Tillsätt is. Skaka och häll upp i highballglas. Fyll upp glaset med ginger ale. Rör om med en drinkpinne.

CHE GUEVARA (long drink)

In a cocktail shaker pound the mint leaves, lime segments, cane sugar, Bacardi limone and Angostura bitter using a wooden mortar. Add the ice. Shake and pour into a highball glass. Top up the glass with ginger ale. Stir with a cocktail stirrer.

60 ml Bacardi limone
8 mint leaves
1/2 a lime cut into segments
20 ml cane sugar
4 drops Angostura bitter
ginger ale

CHAMPAGNE COCKTAIL (apéritif)

CHAMPAGNE COCKTAIL (apéritif)

Stänk några droppar Angostura bitter på sockerbi-
ten. Lägg den i ett champagneglas. Fyll upp glaset
med champagne.

några droppar Angostura bitter
1 sockerbit
champagne

CHAMPAGNE COCKTAIL (apéritif)

a few drops Angostura bitter
1 sugar cube
champagne

Sprinkle a few drops of Angostura bitter onto the sugar cube. Place into a champagne glass and fill with champagne.

CHAMPAGNE COCKTAIL (apérit

PRESIDENT COCKTAIL (apéritif)

Fyll en shaker med krossad is. Slå på rom, Triple sec, Martini dry och några droppar Grenadine. Skaka och häll upp i martiniglas. Garnera med ett rött cocktailbär.

3 1/2 cl ljus rom
1 1/2 cl Triple sec, citruslikör
1/2 cl Martini dry
några droppar Grenadine
krossad is
1 rött cocktailbär

PRESIDENT COCKTAIL (apéritif)

35 ml light rum
15 ml Triple sec, citrus liqueur
5 ml Martini dry
a few drops Grenadine
crushed ice
1 red cocktail cherry

Fill a cocktail shaker with crushed ice. Pour the rum over the ice followed by Triple sec, Martini dry and a few drops of Grenadine. Shake and pour into a martini glass. Garnish with a red cocktail cherry.

BASER
base

VINÄGRETT

1 msk balsamvinäger
3 msk olivolja
en nypa salt
vitpeppar

Blanda vinäger och salt. Vispa ner olja droppvis. Smaksätt med peppar.

TOMATVINÄGRETT

2 mogna tomater
1 tsk tomatpuré
1 tsk sherryvinäger
1/2 schalottenlök, hackad
1 liten vitlöksklyfta, hackad
1 dl olivolja
salt och svartpeppar

Halvera tomaterna och gröp ur och släng kärnhusen. Mixa tomatköttet med tomatpuré, vinäger, schalottenlök och vitlök. Vispa ner olja droppvis. Sila och smaksätt med salt och peppar.

JUNGFRUSÅS

1 citron, skinnfria klyftor
2 apelsiner, skinnfria klyftor
10 basilikablad
1 tsk korianderfrön
2 dl förstapressad olivolja

Mixa citron- och apelsinklyftorna med basilika, korianderfrön och olivolja.

TRYFFELVINÄGRETT

1 liten svart tryffel
1/2 dl tryffeljuice
1 citron, juice
1 msk sherryvinäger
salt och vitpeppar
2 1/2 dl rapsolja
1/2 dl vatten

Mixa tryffel och tryffeljuice. Tillsätt citronjuice, vinäger, salt och peppar. Vispa ner olja och kokhett vatten droppvis.

BRYNT SMÖRVINÄGRETT

Koka ihop vinägern till hälften.

Bryn smöret nötbrunt. Vispa ner smöret, citronjuicen och olivoljan i vinägern och smaksätt med salt och peppar.

1 dl balsamvinäger
1 msk osaltat smör
1 tsk färskpressad citronjuice
1 msk förstapressad olivolja
salt och vitpeppar

KALVSKY

Bryn kalvbenen hårt i en långpanna i 225° ugn i cirka 30 minuter. Bred tomatpuré på benen mot slutet. Slå bort allt överflödigt fett ur långpannan och lägg över benen i en rymlig kastrull. Koka ur långpannan med lite vatten och häll det i kastrullen. Täck benen med kallt vatten. Koka upp och skumma väl.

Klyv en hel vitlök på mitten, tvärs över klyftorna. Skär morot, lök och rotselleri i mindre bitar. Bryn en av vitlökshalvorna med grönsakerna i olja i en het panna. Lägg de brynta grönsakerna, purjolök och kryddor i kastrullen. Låt sjuda i 6–8 timmar utan lock. Skumma då och då. Fyll på vatten så att benen alltid är täckta. Sila skyn och koka ihop den till hälften.

Till 1 liter färdig sky

1 kg kalvben
3 msk tomatpuré
1/2 vitlök
1 morot
2 gula lökar
200 g rotselleri
1 msk matolja
1 purjolök, i bitar
1 tsk torkad timjan
2 lagerblad
10–12 vitpepparkorn

LJUS KALVBULJONG

Till 1 liter färdig buljong

1 kg kalvben
1 tsk salt
1 bouquet garni (se s. 314)
2 lagerblad
10–12 vitpepparkorn
ett par persiljekvistar

Lägg kalvbenen i en rymlig kastrull och täck dem med kallt vatten. Koka upp, salta och skumma väl.

Tillsätt bouquet garni och kryddorna i kastrullen. Låt sjuda i 4–5 timmar utan lock. Skumma då och då. Fyll på vatten så att benen alltid är täckta. Sila buljongen och koka ihop den till hälften.

KYCKLINGBULJONG

Till 1 liter färdig buljong

2 kycklingskrov
1 tsk salt
1 bouquet garni (se s. 314)
2 lagerblad
10–12 vitpepparkorn
ett par persiljekvistar
1 rosmarinkvist

Skölj skroven ordentligt. Lägg dem i en rymlig kastrull och täck dem med kallt vatten. Koka upp, salta och skumma väl.

Tillsätt bouquet garni och kryddor. Låt sjuda i 4–5 timmar utan lock. Skumma då och då. Fyll på vatten så att skroven alltid är täckta. Sila buljongen och koka ihop den till hälften.

GRÖNSAKSBULJONG

Klyv en hel vitlök på mitten, tvärs över klyftorna. Tärna grönsakerna. Lägg dem och en av vitlökshal-

vorna i en rymlig kastrull och täck med kallt vatten.
Koka upp och skumma väl. Lägg i kryddorna och låt
sjuda i 30 minuter utan lock. Skumma då och då.
Sila buljongen och koka ihop den till hälften.

Till 1 liter färdig buljong

1/2 vitlök
2 morötter
2 gula lökar
2 tomater
2 selleristjälkar
100 g champinjoner (ca 10 st)
2 purjolökar
1 tsk torkad timjan
2 lagerblad
1 liten bit ingefära
1 litet knippe färsk dragon
eller 1 msk torkad
1 stjärnanis
1 tsk salt
10–12 vitpepparkorn

MUSSELBULJONG

Klyv en hel vitlök på mitten, tvärs över klyftorna.
Tärna grönsakerna. Lägg dem och en av vitlökshal-
vorna i en rymlig kastrull och täck med kallt vatten.
Koka upp och skumma väl. Lägg i kryddorna och låt
sjuda i 30 minuter utan lock. Skumma då och då.
Sila grönsaksbuljongen.

Skrubba musselskalen rena. Knacka de öppna
musslorna i bänken och släng de som inte sluter sig.
Släng även alla musslor med trasiga skal.

Kontrollera att musslorna inte är sandfyllda,
genom att lägga en mussla i taget i handen och försiktigt trycka skalhalvorna från varandra i sidled, ett

Till 1 liter färdig buljong

1 kg blåmusslor
1/2 vitlök
2 morötter
2 gula lökar
2 tomater
2 selleristjälkar
100 g champinjoner (ca 10 st)
2 purjolökar
1 tsk torkad timjan
2 lagerblad
1 stjärnanis
1 tsk salt
10–12 vitpepparkorn
1 msk matolja
4 dl torrt vitt vin

par milllimeter räcker. Är musslan dyfylld fjädrar inte skalen, utan innehållet rinner ut i handen. Är musslan frisk går skalhalvorna ihop igen, som ett självstängande gångjärn.

Hetta upp matolja i en kastrull. Lägg i musslorna och låt dem fräsa i någon minut. Tillsätt grönsaksbuljongen och vinet, lägg på ett lock och koka upp. Lyft upp musslorna när skalen har öppnat sig. Sila och koka ihop buljongen till hälften.

HUMMERFOND

Till 1 liter färdig fond

1 kg hummerskal
1/2 vitlök
1 morot
2 gula lökar
1 fänkålsstånd
2 msk olivolja
3 msk tomatpuré
1 knippe färsk dragon
eller 1 msk torkad
10–12 vitpepparkorn
2 lagerblad
1 tsk torkad timjan

Krossa hummerskalen. Klyv en hel vitlök på mitten, tvärs över klyftorna. Tärna grönsakerna. Fräs hummerskalen i olivolja i en rymlig kastrull. Tillsätt tomatpuré, en halv vitlök och grönsaker. Låt fräsa i någon minut. Täck med kallt vatten, koka upp och skumma väl. Lägg i kryddorna och låt sjuda i 20–30 minuter utan lock. Skumma då och då. Sila fonden och koka ihop den till hälften.

HUMMEROLJA

Krossa hummerskalen. Klyv en hel vitlök på mitten, tvärs över klyftorna. Tärna grönsakerna. Fräs hummerskalen i olivolja i en rymlig kastrull. Tillsätt tomatpuré, en halv vitlök och grönsaker. Låt fräsa i någon minut. Täck med olja och koka upp försiktigt. Lägg i kryddorna och låt dra på svag värme i 20–30 minuter utan lock. Sila oljan genom ett kaffefilter.

500 g hummerskal
1/2 vitlök
1/2 morot, tärnad
1 gul lök, hackad
1/2 fänkålsstånd, tärnat
2 msk olivolja
1 1/2 msk tomatpuré
5 dl neutral olja
1 knippe färsk dragon
eller 1 msk torkad
10–12 vitpepparkorn
1 lagerblad
1 tsk torkad timjan

ÖRTOLJA

Mixa örter, vitlök och olja. Låt dra i minst en timme. Sila örtoljan genom ett kaffefilter och smaksätt den med salt och peppar.

2 dl grovhackade färska örter
t ex basilika, dragon, persilja
1 vitlöksklyfta
2 dl olivolja
salt och vitpeppar

CURRYOLJA

Skala, kärna ur och tärna äpplet. Fräs äppeltärningarna och schalottenlöken i 1 msk olja i en kastrull. Tillsätt curry och fräs i ytterligare någon minut. Slå på resterande olja och koka upp försiktigt. Ta genast bort kastrullen från värmen och låt dra i minst en timme. Mixa blandningen och sila dem genom ett kaffefilter.

1/4 syrligt äpple
1 schalottenlök, hackad
2 dl matolja
2 msk Bombay Madras
curry powder

RÖDVINSSÅS

Till 2 dl färdig sås

1 liten bit morot, tärnad
1 röd lök, skivad
1 skiva bacon
1 msk matolja
1 tsk farinsocker
5 persiljekvistar
1 lagerblad
7 vitpepparkorn
4 dl rött vin
4 dl kalvsky, se recept s. 307
salt och vitpeppar
1/2 msk kallt smör

Fräs morot, lök och bacon i olja. Tillsätt farinsocker och kryddor. Tillsätt vin och koka ihop till hälften. Slå på kalvsky och koka ihop tills såsen har tjocknat.

Sila och smaksätt med salt, peppar och eventuellt mer farinsocker. Vispa ner smöret innan såsen ska serveras.

BEURRE MONTÉE

2 1/2 dl grönsaksbuljong,
se recept s. 309
2 1/2 dl rumstempererat smör

Koka upp buljongen och vispa ner smöret.

TOMATSÅS

6 mogna tomater, halverade,
urkärnade
3 schalottenlökar, finhackade
2 vitlöksklyftor, finhackade
1 msk olivolja
2 tsk tomatpuré
1 tsk grönpeppar
1 msk sherryvinäger
1 dl grönsaksbuljong,
se recept s. 308
1 krm strösocker
1 msk osaltat smör
salt och svartpeppar

Fräs schalottenlök och vitlök i olivolja utan att de får färg. Tillsätt tomater, tomatpuré och grönpeppar. Fräs i ytterligare någon minut. Slå på vinäger, buljong och strö över socker. Låt sjuda i 20 minuter. Mixa i smör och passera såsen genom en finmaskig sil. Smaksätt med salt och peppar.

TORKADE TOMATER

Skålla, skala, halvera och kärna ur tomaterna.

Gnid in en plåt med vitlök och olivolja. Salta och peppra plåten och lägg på tomathalvorna. Salta och peppra tomaterna och strö över örter samt florsocker. Torka dem i 75° ugn i cirka 3 timmar.

10 tomater
1 vitlöksklyfta
olivolja
salt och vitpeppar
1 msk finhackad timjan
och rosmarin
1 tsk florsocker

RISOTTOGRUND

Fräs schalottenlök, vitlök och lagerblad i olivolja. Tillsätt riset och låt fräsa i ytterligare någon minut. Slå på vinet och rör om tills det har kokat in. Sänk värmen och tillsätt buljongen, lite i taget, under omrörning. Koka tills riset är mjukt men fortfarande har en kärna kvar. Ta bort kastrullen från värmen. Vänd ner parmesanost och smör. Smaksätt risotton med salt och peppar.

4 schalottenlökar, finhackade
1 vitlöksklyfta, finhackad
1 lagerblad
1 msk olivolja
2 dl avorioris
1 dl vitt vin
5 dl kycklingbuljong,
se recept s.308
1 msk riven parmesanost
1 msk smör
salt och vitpeppar

KOKTA KRONÄRTSKOCKBOTTNAR

2 medelstora kronärtskockor
1 liter vatten
1 msk salt
1 dl olivolja
1/2 citron, juice
1 tsk askorbinsyra

Skär kronärtskocksbottnarna fria från blad och skägg. Koka bottnarna mjuka i saltat vatten, olivolja, citronjuice och askorbinsyra i 10–12 minuter.

GREMOLATA

1 citron
1 vitlöksklyfta, finhackad
1 msk finhackad bladpersilja
1 msk förstapressad olivolja

Tvätta citronen väl. Riv skalet på ett rivjärn. Pressa juicen från halva citronen. Blanda citronskal, citronjuice, vitlök, persilja och olivolja.

BOUQUET GARNI

1 gul lök
1/2 vitlök
2 purjolökar
1 morot
1 stjälk selleri
ett par timjankvistar

Halvera den oskalade löken. Lägg halvorna i en het och torr stekpanna med snittytorna ner. Låt dem få ordentligt med färg.

Klyv en hel vitlök på mitten, tvärs över klyftorna.

Snitta purjolökarna på längden och skölj dem. Skala moroten. Bind ihop allt utom löken och vitlöken till en bukett. Lägg i buketten, löken och vitlöken som smaksättning i alla ljusa köttbuljonger.

SALSA VERDE

Mixa örter, vitlök, kapris och sardellfiléer.

Blanda vinäger, senap och olja. Rör samman blandningarna och smaksätt salsan med peppar.

1 msk hackad bladpersilja
1 msk hackad basilika
5 myntablad
1 vitlöksklyfta
1 msk kapris
5 sardellfiléer
1/2 msk rödvinsvinäger
1 tsk dijonsenap
2 msk förstapressad olivolja
vitpeppar

PASTADEG

Blanda ingredienserna och arbeta väl till en smidig deg. Slå in degen i plastfilm och låt den vila i kylen i minst en timme.

500 g vetemjöl
4 ägg + 1 äggula
15 g salt

FLYTANDE KARAMELL

Koka ihop socker, 1½ dl vatten och vinäger eller citronjuice till en karamell i en tjockbottnad kastrull. Avbryt kokningen med resterande vatten. Ta bort stekpannan från värmen.

250 g strösocker
3 dl vatten
någon droppe vitvinsvinäger
eller citronjuice

CHOKLADFLARN

30–40 flarn

1/4 dl mjölk
1/2 dl matolja
130 g strösocker
4 ägg
40 g vetemjöl
20 g potatismjöl
180 g mörk choklad, smält

Koka upp mjölk, olja och socker.

Vispa ihop ägg, vetemjöl, potatismjöl och choklad.

Slå mjölken över äggblandningen och rör till en jämn smet. Stryk ut flarnsmeten tunt på silpatduk. Grädda i 200° ugn i cirka 7 minuter.

MADELEINEKAKOR

ca 50 kakor

100 g florsocker
40 g mandelmjöl
40 g vetemjöl
3 äggvitor
1 msk honung
100 g brynt smör

Sikta ner florsocker, mandelmjöl och vetemjöl i en bunke. Tillsätt äggvitor, honung och smör. Blanda väl. Fyll en spritspåse med smeten. Spritsa den i smorda madeleinekaksformar. Grädda kakorna i 175° ugn i 8–10 minuter.

CRÈME ANGLAISE (vaniljglassgrund)

6 äggulor
100 g strösocker
5 dl mjölk
1 vaniljstång, urskrapad

Vispa äggulor och socker vitt och pösigt.

Koka upp mjölk och vanilj i en kastrull.

Slå den varma mjölken över ägg- och socker-blandningen under vispning. Häll tillbaka den i kastrullen. Värm försiktigt under omrörning tills blandningen tjocknar. Gör ett rosenprov, se s. 247. Vaniljkrämen får inte koka. Ta bort kastrullen från värmen, sila och kyl snabbt.

CREME PÂTISSIÈRE (konditorkräm)

Vispa äggulor och socker vitt och pösigt. Sikta över maizenamjöl och blanda väl.

Koka upp mjölk och vanilj i en kastrull.

Slå den varma mjöken över äggblandningen under vispning. Häll tillbaka den i kastrullen och låt den koka på svag värme under kraftig vispning tills den tjocknar. Ta bort kastrullen från värmen, häll den i en bunke och täck med plastfilm. Låt svalna.

6 äggulor
120 g strösocker
35 g maizenamjöl
5 dl mjölk
1 vaniljstång, urskrapad

BRIOCHEBRÖD

Blanda mjöl, socker och salt.

Rör ut jästen i ljummen mjölk. Slå mjölken över mjölblandningen, tillsätt 3 ägg och blanda till en fast och smidig deg. Tillsätt resterande ägg, ett i taget, och arbeta degen under 10 minuter. Arbeta in smöret och låt degen vila i rumstemperatur i 3 timmar.

Fördela degen i två brödformar (cirka 1,8 liter). Låt jäsa i ytterligare 20 minuter.

Pensla briocherna med äggula. Grädda dem i 200° ugn i cirka 35 minuter.

Till 2 bröd

500 g vetemjöl
30 g strösocker
15 g salt
20 g jäst
1/2 dl mjölk
6 ägg
400 g osaltat smör, rumstempererat
1 äggula till pensling

VINAIGRETTE

1 tbsp balsamic vinegar
pinch of salt
4 tbsp olive oil
white pepper

Mix the vinegar and salt, then whisk in the oil little by little. Season with pepper.

TOMATO VINAIGRETTE

2 ripe tomatoes
1 tsp tomato purée
1 tsp sherry vinegar
1/2 shallot, chopped
1 small clove of garlic, chopped
100 ml olive oil
salt and black pepper

Cut the tomatoes in half and remove the seeds. In a food processor blend the tomato flesh with the tomato purée, vinegar, shallot and garlic, then whisk in the oil little by little. Strain and season with salt and pepper.

SAUCE VIÈRGE

1 lemon,
in segments with the skin removed
2 oranges,
in segments with the skin removed
10 basil leaves
1 tsp coriander seeds
200 ml extra virgin olive oil

In a food processor blend the lemon and orange segments with the basil, coriander seeds and olive oil.

TRUFFLE VINAIGRETTE

1 small fresh black truffle
50 ml truffle juice
juice of 1 lemon
1 tbsp sherry vinegar
salt and white pepper
250 ml rape seed oil
50 ml boiling water

In a food processor blend the truffle and the truffle juice. Add lemon juice, vinegar, salt and pepper. Whisk in the oil and boiling hot water little by little.

BROWN BUTTER VINAIGRETTE

Place the vinegar in a pan, bring to the boil and simmer to reduce by half.

Melt the butter in a pan and heat until turning light brown. Whisk the butter, the lemon juice and the olive oil into the vinegar and season with salt and pepper.

100 ml balsamic vinegar
1 tbsp unsalted butter
1 tsp freshly squeezed lemon juice
1 tbsp extra virgin olive oil
salt and white pepper

VEAL STOCK

Roast the veal bones in a roasting pan in a 225°C oven for about 30 minutes. Spread the tomato purée over the bones towards the end of the cooking time. Pour away the fat from the roasting pan and place the bones in a large stock pot. Cover with cold water. Bring up to a boil and skim well.

Brown the carrots, onion, celariac and garlic in oil in a hot pan, then place in the stock pot with the bones. Add the leeks, bay leaf and peppercorns. Simmer for 6–8 hours without a lid. Skim from time to time. Add more water if required so the bones are always covered. Strain the stock, return it to the heat and reduce by half.

For 1 litre of finished stock

1 kg veal bones
3 tbsp tomato purée
1 carrot, chopped
2 onions, chopped
200 g celariac
1/2 garlic bulb with skin on, cut across the bulb
1 tbsp oil
1 leek, chopped
1 tsp dried thyme
2 bay leaves
10–12 white peppercorns

LIGHT VEAL STOCK

For 1 litre of finished stock

1 kg veal bones
1 tsp salt
1 bouquet garni (p. 326)
2 bay leaves
10–12 white peppercorns
couple of sprigs of parsley

Put the veal bones in a large stock pot and cover with cold water. Bring to the boil, add salt and skim well.

Add bouquet garni, bay leaves, peppercorns and parsley. Simmer for 4–5 hours without a lid. Skim from time to time. Add more water if required so the bones are always covered. Strain the stock, return it to the heat and reduce by half.

CHICKEN STOCK

For 1 litre of finished stock

2 chicken carcasses
1 tsp salt
1 bouquet garni (p. 326)
2 bay leaves
10–12 white peppercorns
couple of parsley sprigs
1 sprig of rosemary

Rinse the carcasses well. Place in a large saucepan and cover with cold water. Bring to the boil, add salt and skim well.

Add bouquet garni, bay leaves, peppercorns and herbs. Simmer for 4–5 hours without a lid. Skim from time to time. Add more water if required so the carcasses are always covered. Strain the stock, return it to the heat and reduce by half.

VEGETABLE STOCK

Dice all the vegetables. Place in a large stock pot and cover with cold water. Bring to the boil and skim well. Add the garlic, herbs, bay leaves, ginger, spices and peppercorns and simmer for 30 minutes without a lid. Skim from time to time. Strain the stock, return to the heat and reduce by half.

For 1 litre of finished stock

2 carrots
2 onions
2 tomatoes
2 celery stalks
100 g white mushrooms
(around 10)
2 leeks
1/2 garlic bulb with skin on,
cut across the bulb
1 tsp dried thyme
2 bay leaves
1 small piece of ginger
1 small bunch of fresh tarragon or 1 tbsp dried
1 star anise
1 tsp salt
10-12 white peppercorns

MUSSEL STOCK

Dice all the vegetables. Place in a large stock pot and cover with cold water. Bring to the boil and skim well. Add the garlic, thyme, bay leaves, star anise, salt and peppercorns, simmer for 30 minutes without a lid. Skim from time to time. Strain the stock.

Clean the mussels well under running water. Throw away any mussels which do not close when tapped gently and also discard any with broken shells. Ensure they are not filled with sand.

For 1 litre of finished stock

1 kg mussels
2 carrots
2 onions
2 tomatoes
2 celery stalks
100 g white mushrooms
(around 10)
2 leeks
1/2 garlic bulb with skin on,
cut across the bulb
1 tsp dried thyme
2 bay leaves

1 star anise
1 tsp salt
10–12 white peppercorns
1 tbsp oil
400 ml dry white wine

Heat the oil in a saucepan, add the mussels and fry for one minute. Add the vegetable stock and the wine, cover and bring up to boil. Lift out the mussels when all the shells are open. Strain the stock and reduce by half.

LOBSTER STOCK

For 1 litre of finished stock

1 kg lobster shells
2 tbsp olive oil
1 carrot
2 onions
1 bulb of fennel
1/2 garlic bulb with skin on,
cut across the bulb
3 tbsp tomato purée
1 bunch of fresh tarragon
or 1 tbsp dried
2 bay leaves
1 tsp dried thyme
10–12 white peppercorns

Crush the lobster shells. Fry them in olive oil in a large saucepan. Dice the vegetables. Add them, the garlic and the tomato purée to the pan and fry for one minute more. Cover with cold water and bring to the boil and skim well.

Add the garlic, tarragon, bay leaves, thyme and peppercorns and simmer for 30 minutes without a lid. Skim from time to time. Strain the stock, return to the heat and reduce by half.

LOBSTER OIL

500 g lobster shells
2 tbsp olive oil
1/2 carrot
1 onion
1/2 fennel bulb
1/2 garlic bulb with skin on,
cut across the bulb
1 1/2 tbsp tomato purée

Crush the lobster shells. Fry them in olive oil in a large saucepan. Dice the vegetables. Add them, the garlic and the tomato purée to the pan and fry for one minute more. Cover with oil and bring up to the boil slowly.

Add the tarragon, thyme, bay leaf and pepper-corns and leave on a very low heat for 20–30 minutes without a lid. Strain the oil through a coffee filter.

500 ml plain oil
1 bunch of fresh tarragon
or 1 tbsp dried
1 tsp dried thyme
1 bay leaf
10–12 white peppercorns

HERB OIL

In a food processor blend the herbs, garlic and oil. Leave to infuse for at least one hour. Strain the oil through a coffee filter and season it with salt and pepper.

200 ml coarsely chopped
fresh herbs,
eg basil, tarragon, parsley
1 clove of garlic
200 ml olive oil
salt and white pepper

CURRY OIL

Peel, deseed and dice the apple. Sweat the apple and shallot in 1 tbsp of oil which has been heated in a saucepan. Stir in the curry powder and sweat for another minute. Add the rest of the oil and slowly bring up to the boil. Remove the saucepan from the heat and leave to infuse for at least one hour. In a food processor blend the curry oil mixture and strain through a coffee filter.

1/4 slightly tart apple
1 shallot, chopped
200 ml plain oil
2 tbsp Bombay Madras
Curry powder

RED WINE SAUCE

For 200 ml sauce

1 small piece of carrot, diced
1 red onion, sliced
1 slice of bacon
1 tbsp oil
1 tsp brown sugar
5 parsley stalks
1 bay leaf
7 white peppercorns
400 ml red wine
400 ml veal stock, (p.320)
salt and white pepper
1/2 tbsp cold butter

Sweat the vegetables and the bacon in the oil. Add brown sugar, bay leaf and peppercorns. Pour in the wine and reduce by half. Add the veal stock and reduce until thick.

Strain and season with salt, pepper and if necessary some more brown sugar to taste. Whisk in the cold butter before serving.

BEURRE MONTÉE

250 ml vegetable stock (p.321)
250 ml butter
at room temperature

Bring the vegetable stock up to boil and whisk in the butter.

TOMATO SAUCE

6 ripe tomatoes,
halved and deseeded
3 finely chopped shallots
2 cloves of garlic,
finely chopped
1 tbsp olive oil
2 tsp tomato purée
1 tsp green peppercorns
1 tbsp sherry vinegar
100 ml vegetable stock (p.321)
1 pinch of sugar
1 tbsp unsalted butter
salt and black pepper

Sweat the shallots and garlic in olive oil. Add tomatoes, tomato purée and green pepper. Sweat for another minute. Add the vinegar and stock and sprinkle with sugar. Simmer for 20 minutes. Place the mixture in a food processor, add the butter and blend. Strain through a fine sieve. Season with salt and pepper.

DRIED TOMATOES

Blanch the tomatoes for 10 seconds in boiling water then drop into iced water. Remove the skin, cut in half and remove the seeds.

Rub an oven tray with garlic and olive oil, then sprinkle with salt and pepper. Place the tomato halves on the tray and sprinkle with salt, pepper, herbs and sugar. Place in a 75°C oven for approximately 3 hours or until the tomatoes are thoroughly dried.

10 tomatoes
1 clove of garlic
olive oil
salt and white pepper
1 tbsp finely chopped fresh thyme and rosemary
1 tsp icing sugar

BASIC RECIPE FOR RISOTTO

Sweat the shallots, garlic and bay leaf in olive oil. Add the rice and sweat for another minute, then add the wine and stir on a high heat until the wine has evaporated. Lower the temperature and add the stock, a ladle at a time, stirring constantly. When all the stock has been added and the rice is soft but still has a slight bite to it remove from heat. Gently stir in the parmesan cheese and the butter. Season the risotto with salt and pepper.

4 shallots, finely chopped
1 clove of garlic, finely chopped
1 bay leaf
1 tbsp olive oil
200 ml avorio rice
500 ml chicken stock (p.320)
100 ml white wine
1 tbsp grated parmesan cheese
1 tbsp butter
salt and white pepper

BOILED ARTICHOKE HEARTS

2 mid-sized artichokes
1 litre water
1 tbsp salt
100 ml olive oil
juice of 1/2 lemon
pinch of bicarbonate of soda

Remove the hearts from the artichokes. Bring the water to the boil, add salt, olive oil, lemon juice and bicarbonate. Add the artichokes and boil until soft, approximately 10 –12 minutes.

GREMOLATA

grated rind of 1 washed lemon
juice of 1/2 lemon
1 clove of garlic, finely chopped
1 tbsp finely chopped
flat leaf parsley
1 tbsp extra virgin olive oil

Mix the lemon rind, juice, garlic, parsley and olive oil together.

BOUQUET GARNI

1 onion
1/2 garlic bulb with skin,
cut across the bulb
2 leeks
1 carrot
1 celery stalk
few sprigs of thyme

Cut the unpeeled onion in half. Place them in a hot, dry pan cut-side down and brown well.

Cut the leeks lengthwise and rinse. Peel the carrot. Tie everything except the onion and the garlic together to form a bouquet. Use the bouquet, cara-melised onion and garlic to enhance the flavour of light meat and vegetable stocks.

SALSA VERDE

In a food processor blend together the herbs, garlic, capers and anchovies.

In a separate bowl mix the vinegar, mustard and oil. Add the two mixtures together and season with pepper.

1 tbsp chopped
flat leaf parsley
1 tbsp chopped basil
5 leaves of mint
1 clove of garlic
1 tbsp capers
5 anchovy fillets
1/2 tbsp red wine vinegar
1 tsp Dijon mustard
2 tbsp extra virgin olive oil
white pepper

PASTA DOUGH

Mix the ingredients together and knead until a smooth dough is formed. Wrap the dough in cling-film and leave to rest in the fridge for at least an hour before using.

500 g flour
4 eggs + 1 egg yolk
15 g salt

LIQUID CARAMEL

In a thick based sauce pan placed over a high heat boil the sugar, 150 ml of the water and wine vinegar together until a caramel is formed. Stop the process by adding the rest of the water. Remove from the heat.

250 g caster sugar
300 ml water
a dash of white wine vinegar
or lemon juice

CHOCOLATE BISCUIT (thin)

For 30–40 biscuits

25 ml milk
50 g plain oil
130 g caster sugar
4 eggs
40 g flour
20 g potato flour
180 g dark chocolate, melted

Bring the milk, oil and sugar to the boil.

Whisk the eggs, flour, potato flour and chocolate together. Pour the milk over the egg mixture and stir until smooth. On a non-stick baking mat, place small spoonfuls of the batter to form round biscuits, or shape as desired. Bake in a preheated oven 200°C for approximately 7 minutes.

MADELEINE COOKIES

around 50 cookies

100 g icing sugar
40 g ground almonds
40 g flour
3 egg whites
1 tbsp honey
100 g brown butter

Sieve the icing sugar, almonds and flour into a bowl. Add the egg whites, honey and butter. Mix well. Fill a piping bag with the mixture and pipe into buttered madeleine moulds. Bake at 175°C for 8–10 minutes.

CRÈME ANGLAISE
(base recipe for vanilla ice cream)

6 egg yolks
100 g caster sugar
500 ml milk
seeds from 1 vanilla pod

Whisk egg yolks and sugar together until white and fluffy .

Add the vanilla seeds to the milk and bring to the boil. Pour the hot milk over the egg and sugar mixture whisking constantly. Place the cream back in the saucepan and over a low heat, stir constantly until the mixture thickens and coats the back of a spoon. It must not boil. Remove the saucepan from the heat, strain and cool quickly.

CREME PÂTISSIÈRE

Whisk the egg yolks and sugar together until white and fluffy. Sieve the corn flour over and stir well.

Add the vanilla seeds to the milk and bring to the boil.

Pour the hot milk slowly over the egg mixture whisking constantly. Place the cream back in the saucepan over a low heat, simmer, whisking thoroughly until thick. Remove the saucepan from the heat, pour it into a bowl and cover with clingfilm. Leave to cool.

6 egg yolks
120 g caster sugar
35 g cornflour
500 ml milk
seeds from 1 vanilla pod

BRIOCHE

Mix flour, sugar and salt together.

Dissolve the yeast in the lukewarm milk. Pour the milk and yeast into the flour mixture, add three eggs and mix until a firm and smooth dough is formed. Add the rest of the eggs, one by one and knead the dough for 10 minutes. Knead in the butter and let the dough rest, covered at room temperature for 3 hours.

Place the dough into two bread moulds (approximately 1.8 litre). Leave to rise for another 20 minutes.

Brush the top of the brioche with egg yolk. Bake at 200°C oven for approximately 35 minutes.

500 g flour
30 g caster sugar
15 g salt
20 g fresh yeast
150 ml lukewarm milk
6 eggs
400 g unsalted butter
at room temperature
1 egg yolk

INDEX
index

INDEX MED DRYCKESFÖRSLAG

KALLA

VARMA

SÖTA

INDEX A–Ö

INDEX WITH SUGGESTIONS FOR DRINKS

COLD

POTATO PANCAKES WITH BLEAK ROE   40
Beer and vodka or champagne – the choice of drink
depends on how festive the occasion is.

VEAL AND CHANTERELLE TERRINE WITH   44
MADEIRA VINAIGRETTE
The Pinot grape goes well with this. Choose a wine from
the New World, as these wines are more reasonably priced
than, say, a Burgundy.

PEPPER MOUSSE WITH ROASTED PEPPER,   48
OLIVES AND DEEP-FRIED ONION RINGS
Choose a Chardonnay without too much oak character
to go with the fresh taste of this dish.

GOATS' CHEESE MOUSSE WITH BEETROOT   52
AND BASIL
Enjoy this with a white wine from the Loire, such as a
Sancerre or Pouilly Fumé.

MACKEREL TERRINE WITH MUSTARD SAUCE   56
AND SPINACH SALAD
Try a Chardonnay with a hint of oak; a wine from South
Africa, Chile or Argentina is recommended.

TARTAR OF SALMON WITH SCALLOPS AND CURRY   60
This needs a fresh, medium-bodied wine to suit the
curry flavour, for example, a Riesling from Alsace.

GRAVAD BALTIC HERRING X 3   63
Why complicate things? Serve beer and aquavit,
preferably a spiced variety.

CHICKEN SALAD WITH MANGO AND CHILLI   69
A good accompaniment to this is a white wine with a
little more taste, without being too powerful, such as
a fresh Chardonnay.

WARM

SWEET

INDEX

CAPPUCCINO ICE CREAM WITH ALMOND FOAM 242
AND MADELEINE COOKIES
Try serving a glass of Vin Santo or Recioto di Soave
with the ice cream.

CLAFOUTIS 246
A Tokaji or a Late Harvest from Chile or Australia will
give the right sweetness. The last two in particular are
very good value for money.

SAFFRON PANCAKE FROM GOTLAND WITH 250
BLACKBERRIES
Setubal from Portugal or a light fruity port are pleasing
accompaniments to the pancake.

RED BERRIES IN CHAMPAGNE JELLY 255
A medium-sweet or sweet sparkling wine makes a good
match for the red berries.

CHOCOLATE TRUFFLE 258
Perhaps the best way to bring out the chocolate taste is
with a good cup of freshly made coffee.

POOR KNIGHTS WITH SPICY BOILED PEARS 262
AND SPICY ICE CREAM
Madeira of Bual or Malmsey character goes well with
the rich tastes.

MILLE-FEUILLES WITH CARAMEL PEARS AND 266
CARDAMOM CREAM
This calls for a sweet, aromatic white wine with a lot of taste,
for example, a Recioto de Soave or a Vin Santo from Italy.

WARM CHOCOLATE MOUSSE 270
Enjoy the chocolate with a medium-sweet to sweet sherry
or a madeira of Bual or Malmsey character.

WAYS TO BE THANKFUL

LISA M. GERRY

NATIONAL GEOGRAPHIC KiDS

WASHINGTON, D.C.

Being **thankful** means **paying attention and acknowledging** the things **going right in our lives** instead of dwelling on what's going wrong. It sounds simple, right? **And it is, really.**

But it's also **LIFE-CHANGING.**

Practicing gratitude is like putting on a pair of **what's good goggles. It's making the decision to look for all the little and big things that are awesome**—or even just A-OK—**throughout your day.**

By taking the time to notice and tune in to all the awesome things— like the taste of your morning muffin, the smell of honeysuckle on your walk to school, the incredible constellation of freckles on your face, your cat's cute little nose, or your best friend's laugh—you'll begin to see **even more awesome things start to happen.** It's like the **GOOD** starts to **MULTIPLY.**

When you make the decision to sit with those good gratitude feelings, **it can transform the way you feel on a daily basis.** Researchers have found that people who practice gratitude may notice a **lift in their mood, kinder feelings toward others, and a greater sense of peace.** Um, yes please!

Adopting an attitude of gratitude is like developing a **superpower.** While you might not be able to fly or see through brick buildings with x-ray vision, you will be able to find little bits of good sprinkled throughout the toughest of times. **This practice is a muscle and when you exercise it, you will become stronger and it will become easier.**

And research has found that **people who are thankful tend to do good stuff for other people, making other people's lives—and the world—better.** A recent study showed that when people do good stuff for other people, it actually changes their brains! **Gratitude is some powerful stuff!**

This book is filled with ways to strengthen those gratitude muscles. **There are crafts and projects, challenges and fun quizzes— all to help you notice and feel more thankful for the amazingness in your life.**

We all have the **power to focus on and appreciate the positive in our lives and in the world.** So, read on and get ready to **be inspired,** get **motivated,** and learn new ways to say—and **give**—thanks!

Oh, and thank YOU
for reading!

5

Make Time for
Belly Laughs.

1

Laughter is like joy bubbling out of your body. It's the song your soul sings when it's happy. Whether you've got a goofy giggle, a cheeky chortle, or a loud LOL, take a second to experience how good it feels to laugh. Then go ahead and laugh some more.

LAUGHING MATTERS

Not only does laughing *feel* great, it's actually healthy for you! Laughing decreases the stress hormones in your body, improves your immune system, and boosts endorphins, which are happy-making chemicals that your brain releases.

NEED A LITTLE INSPIRATION?
Check out these five
knee-slappers from Nat Geo's
Just Joking book series.

Q What do you call a sneezing train?

A Ah-choo-choo.

Q What is it called when two dinosaurs bump into each other?

A A Tyrannosaurus wreck.

Q What do you call a chicken staring at a head of lettuce?

A Chicken sees-a salad.

Q When do mice like to relax?

A The squeak-end.

Q Where do tigers exercise?

A Jungle gyms.

Date : / /

Subject :

Date

2

Keep a
Gratitude
Journal.

If you're in the market for more happiness (and who isn't?), this is for you. Gratitude is appreciation for what's good and meaningful to you in your life. Studies have found that thinking about things that you're grateful for can make you happier, help you sleep better, improve your health, benefit your relationships, ease aggression, raise your self-esteem, reduce stress, and more.

One **powerful way** to put gratitude into practice is by keeping a **GRATITUDE JOURNAL.**

STEP ONE. Throughout your day, be on the lookout for anything good. Pay attention to happy feelings, positive thoughts, fun, love, and laughter. All of these are sure to point you toward things to be thankful for.

STEP TWO. At the end of every day, write down three things that you're grateful for. Be specific.

You might be grateful for your **sweet grandma,** or that your cold finally went away. Perhaps you're grateful that your friend **saved you a seat on the bus,** or for the **warm, chewy brownie** you ate last night. You could be grateful for the **big oak tree** you pass on the way to school, or that you were voted class president. **Big, small,** and everything in between—**GRATITUDE comes in all shapes and sizes.**

3

Use Your IMAGINATION.

How cool is it that you can create any kind of world you want inside your head? There, you can be a brave astronaut befriending aliens, a powerful hero saving the world, or a fearless explorer on the hunt for lost treasures. The possibilities are endless! To show your appreciation for your amazing, magical mind, exercise your creativity like you would a muscle. Spend time every day letting your imagination run wild.

GIVE IT A
▶▶GO!

Take out a piece of paper, choose one of these writing prompts, and for 10 minutes, write about **whatever** comes to mind. **The more wacky and wild the better!**

Writing Prompt 1:
Imagine you are on a walk in your neighborhood, when all of a sudden, you notice a little golden door on the sidewalk. This door has never been there before. It's much smaller than a regular door, but just big enough for you to squeeze through, and there is a bright light beaming through the cracks all around it. You walk over to the door and open it. Whoa! You can't believe your eyes. What do you see? What happens next?

Writing Prompt 2:
You've just won one million dollars in the lottery! How do you celebrate? How do you spend your money? How does your life change?

Writing Prompt 3:
Imagine you could choose any superpower for one day. What superpower would you choose? What would you spend the day doing? Where would you go? Who would you visit? What would be the top three things you'd want to experience using this superpower?

13

Appreciate All the **Amazing** Things Your **Body** Can Do.

It's **easy to get caught up** thinking about what your **body cannot do.** For instance, you might **not** be able to **slam-dunk,** you might **not** be able to **run a mile,** and hey, you still might **not** be **tall enough** to ride on that awesome new roller coaster with five full loop-the-loops. Your body might **not** be able to **spontaneously sprout the kind of hair you wish you had,** you might not be able to **sing a lick,** and you may be hopeless when it comes to **hula hooping.**

The truth is, there will **always, always** be things you **wish** your body could do **better, faster,** or even at all. But, if you spend your time thinking about those things, you will miss out on the chance to be **super-duper happy in the body you have.** So, whenever you start to think about the things you **can't do,** picture a **stop sign in your mind.** Then, switch to thinking about the things your **body can do.** Even when you're **feeling down** and it doesn't seem like your body can do much, **start small and make a list.**

14

Can you **walk** to the mailbox? Can you **bend down** to tie your shoes?

When your **favorite song** comes on the radio, can you **move your body** to the beat?

Can you hold **someone's hand** when they're scared? Can you give your mom and dad **a hug?**

Can you **feel** the sun or the wind or the rain **on your skin?**

If you answered **yes** to any of these, then your **body** is **already amazing.**

15

16

Take Care of Your **Body.**

Now that you've **made a list** of all the amazing things your body can do (#4), put your **appreciation** into action by keeping it **healthy** and **happy.**

 Get enough sleep. Most doctors recommend that kids ages 6 to 12 should regularly get 9 to 12 hours a day for optimal health.

 Find ways to relax. Stress can hurt your health, so find some ways to unwind, like reading a book, listening to music, meditating, walking, painting, or hanging out with friends.

 Exercise. Experts also recommend kids and teens do 60 minutes or more of physical activity each day. That could be skateboarding, break dancing, playing soccer, or even pogo-sticking (uh, that's a word, right?). The important thing is to just get your body moving!

 Eat fruits and vegetables. Try to eat fewer sweets and salty snacks and instead eat more things that grow from trees and sprout from the soil.

 Protect your noggin. Wear a helmet when you ride your bike, skateboard, or roller skates.

 Wear your seatbelt.

6

DO WHAT YOU CAN TO MAKE THE WORLD A BETTER PLACE.

When Corinne Hindes was 11 years old, she noticed a homeless man on the side of the road near where she lived in California, U.S.A. "He didn't have a single bag or a change of clothes," says Corinne. "All he had was a T-shirt and ratty, ripped up jeans." Instead of turning away or going on with her day, Corinne decided she wanted to do something to help. "I felt like I couldn't continue to look at him and not do anything. I was part of his community, and I had to help him. I finally turned to my mom and said, **'Mom, we *have* to do something.'**"

CORINNE HINDES

And do something she did. Corinne, who was an avid ski racer, spent a lot of time at ski resorts. During one of her frequent visits to the lost and found to find her runaway hat, she had an idea. **She could collect the bags of winter clothes left behind at ski resorts** (which previously were given to secondhand shops like Goodwill) **and donate them to homeless shelters.**

Six years later, Warm Winters has grown into a successful nonprofit. **"We're in 13 states now, 33 ski resorts, and we've helped more than 33,000 people,"** says Corinne. "It's been an amazing journey." And the man she saw on the side of the road? "His name is Billy," she says. "I was able to get clothes to him for many years. **He has a job now, an apartment, a car, and a dog. He's doing really well!"**

On the next page, Corinne talks about how she's making the world better by helping others. Read on to learn more, get inspired, then be on the lookout for opportunities for you to do good, too!

6 DO WHAT YOU CAN TO MAKE THE WORLD A BETTER PLACE.

Q: How did you know how to start a nonprofit when you were just 11 years old?

A: When we first started, we would do it all ourselves: pick up the lost and found at the ski resort, load it into our car, take it home, sort through everything, and then take it either to the homeless shelter or pass items out face-to-face on the street. Then, in 2013, we partnered with The Jefferson Awards and got our official nonprofit status. My mother has been a great mentor to me. She's taught me so much about what it means to run an organization and a business.

Q: What made you want to keep going and expand Warm Winters?

A: Honestly, the gratification I got from passing out the clothes face-to-face kept me going. I would sit and talk to these people for hours. I would listen to their stories and make friends with them. So often, people living on the streets are ignored, and no one even looks at them. I could feel the joy they felt having someone show interest in what they had to say. It was the most powerful thing for me.

20

Q It sounds like the fact that you treated these people with dignity was as meaningful to them as the warm clothes you gave them.

A Absolutely. Something that I've learned is the value of face-to-face interaction. The number one thing that I encourage my volunteers to do is to go to the streets and talk with someone. [Note: We encourage our volunteers to have a buddy with them and always have a parent present if they are under 15.] These are people who aren't asked those questions—ones that we get asked on a daily basis—because people tend not to pay attention to them. Learn their name, find out where they were born. Ask how they got to the streets and what their passions are.

Q What's next for you?

A I am headed to college to study business management and leadership, and will hopefully continue to grow Warm Winters. I want to continue to build a movement, create change, and help people.

Q What advice would you give other young people who want to make the world a better place?

A You can't change the whole world in a day, but you can take a small step to change one person's whole world in a day. It's the little things that really add up to create movements and help people. It can be something as simple as a conversation. Anything that you have to give is worth something, so nothing is too small.

Q How does being thankful play a role in doing good for other people?

A Taking care of the community, embracing the people around you, giving each other love and anything else that you can; it's just a healing process, and gratitude itself is a form of healing.

Q When do you feel grateful when you're working with Warm Winters?

A I feel most grateful when I'm talking to people who are homeless, when I'm able to hear their stories and have them confide in me. I'm most grateful in those moments, because someone who has never met me before suddenly has the trust in me to share a story and tell me a little bit about themselves. I think that is incredible.

TAKE GOOD CARE OF YOUR PETS!

Pets. Are. The. BEST! They're sweet snuggle monsters, super funny, and crazy cute, and they bring us so much happiness. The best way to show your pets you're thankful for them is to take great care of them. To do that, take them on walks, feed them healthy foods, brush them, give them a safe space to live and play, and take them for regular vet visits.

Stand by for cuteness!
Three *National Geographic Kids* readers
introduce us to their precious pets.

Henry, 14, and his dog, Maisy, 8

Maisy's Favorite Toy: Maisy's "baby" is an off-white, fleece star.

Maisy's Best Trick: Catching popcorn and treats in her mouth midair!

Henry's Favorite Thing About Maisy: Her kind personality and her fluffiness— she's so soft to pet!

Sayla, 15, and her dog, Max, 8

Max's Favorite Toy: His squeaky snowman.

The Cutest Thing About Max: His ears!!

Sayla's Favorite Thing About Max: No matter what emotion you're feeling, he's always there for you!

24

Teagan, 10, and her cat, Basil, 2

Basil's Favorite Toy:
Absolutely anything with a feather!

Basil's Best Trick:
He can jump up on surfaces on command.

Teagan's Favorite Thing to Do With Basil:
Taking him for walks outside on a leash. Basil will let anyone pick him up. He's very gentle and never uses his claws.

APPRECIATION STATION

If you're desperate for a dog, but one's not in the cards for you right now, don't worry—there are other ways to have a playdate with a pup. You can volunteer at a local animal shelter, and there are now apps, like Wag!, that will match a dog lover in need of some furry-friend time with someone who needs a dog walker—or even with a dog living in a shelter that needs to be walked. Of course, ask your parents first!

8

Show Your Family You LOVE THEM

(even though they sometimes drive you crazy!).

Sure, it's **embarrassing** when your mom licks her finger to get something off your cheek, and yes, it's **super annoying** when your brother puts his retainer on the side of his plate at dinner. But this **wild bunch is still your family**, and sometimes, they're even pretty great.

9 Take stock of what you **do** have.

Like a roof over your head.

There are two ways to compare— comparing UP or comparing DOWN.

Comparing UP

means that you are comparing YOURSELF, YOUR LIFE, or your CIRCUMSTANCES to someone who you THINK has it BETTER THAN YOU. For example, you might think, "My friend Beatrice has her own bedroom and her own bathroom. My house is tiny. I don't even have my own room!"

This type of comparison and thinking about WHAT YOU DON'T HAVE or what you have LESS OF often leads people to FEEL ANXIOUS AND SAD.

Comparing DOWN

means that you are looking at what you do have with the understanding that SO MANY people throughout the world HAVE MUCH LESS. So you might say, "Wow, there are people in this world who don't have homes of their own. Even though I share my bedroom, I am SO LUCKY to have a warm place to sleep at night with soft sheets and a comfy pillow."

This type of comparison, which includes COMPASSION FOR OTHER PEOPLE and their struggles, is a GREAT WAY TO PRACTICE GRATITUDE.

10

Have a Party for Pizza!

Sure, pizza is a big (and delicious) part of most parties, but why not switch it up a bit and throw a party for pizza? If ever there was something to celebrate, it's pizza!

Five Fun Facts About Pizza:

1. Pepperoni is the most popular topping in the United States and the United Kingdom.

2. Pizza was invented in Naples, Italy, in the 1800s, when people began adding tomatoes to flat focaccia bread.

3. Different countries like all sorts of different pizza toppings. In Japan, popular toppings include mayonnaise and squid. In Brazil, you might find green peas, raisins, or hardboiled eggs atop your pie.

4. The average American is thought to eat about 23 pounds (10 kg) of pizza a year.

5. The world record holder for largest pizza was made in Rome, Italy, in 2012 and had a total surface area of 13,580.28 square feet (1,261.65 m²). And bonus, it was gluten free!

PAY ATTENTION TO YOUR BREATH.

The **first step** to being thankful is **being present.** Being present helps you **stop** thinking about the past or **worrying about the future** so that you can **appreciate this very moment,** just as it is. Sometimes, it can be **hard** to be present when there's a lot going on inside your head. One way to **slooowwww down** and center yourself in the here and now is to **pay attention to your breath.**

There are lots of **cool breathing exercises** you can try. Here are two to get you started.

SLOW DOWN, GET CENTERED, EXERCISE *1*

1. Start by sitting or lying down in a comfortable place.
2. Place your right hand on your stomach and your left hand on your chest. As you breathe, notice the way your stomach and your chest rise and fall.

3. Close your mouth and gently breathe in through your nose for the count of four.
4. Hold your breath and count to three or four, whichever is most comfortable for you.
5. Then slowly exhale deeply through your mouth until it feels like no air remains in your lungs.
6. Repeat this five times, or until you feel calmer and more centered.

BREATHE YOUR WAY TO CALM, EXERCISE 2

1. Sit comfortably with your back straight and tall and your head held high.

2. Place the pointer and middle fingers of your right hand between your eyes.

3. Take a few gentle breaths.

4. Use your thumb to close your right nostril and inhale through your left nostril.

5. Use your ring finger to close your left nostril and hold your breath for three counts.

6. Open your right nostril and exhale slowly through it, then pause for a moment.

7. Inhale slowly through the right nostril now.

8. Close both nostrils and hold your breath for three counts.

9. Then open the left nostril and exhale slowly through it, pausing for a moment.

10. Now inhale slowly through the left nostril. Close both nostrils and hold your breath for three counts.

11. Repeat this cycle five to seven times, or until you feel calmer and more centered.

Be Aware of Your Impact on the Planet.

12

WHEN SOMETHING IS REALLY IMPORTANT TO YOU, IT MAKES SENSE THAT YOU WOULD WANT TO TAKE GOOD CARE OF IT, RIGHT?

Well, that same idea can be applied to more than just your new scooter or game console. Take, for instance, our oceans. Sure, oceans are crazy fun—you can snorkel in them, cruise in boats, and jump in their waves. And did you know that Earth's oceans are home to more than 700,000 species? And more than half of the oxygen we breathe comes from plants in the ocean. (It's produced as a by-product of photosynthesis by marine plants like plankton and kelp.)

So, yeah, oceans are pretty great.

(12) BE AWARE OF YOUR IMPACT ON THE PLANET.

Here are five ways you can help protect oceans:

1. Organize a beach cleanup with friends and family and spend a few hours picking up all of the trash you see.

2. Encourage your family to eat only sustainable seafood.

3. Recycle all plastic bags and bottles, because when thrown in the trash, they can end up in the ocean.

4. Learn about climate change and how not to contribute to it. Rising temperatures have a big impact on oceans, making the water warmer and more acidic, which disrupts the ecosystem.

5. When you're done building sandcastles and playing at the beach, fill in any holes so that newly hatched turtles heading to the ocean don't fall in (and then have trouble climbing back out).

38

Grace C. Young is an ocean engineer and a National Geographic Emerging Explorer. She recently spent 15 days living 66 feet (20 m) below the ocean in Aquarius, the world's only underwater laboratory. Aquarius, which is located off the Florida Keys, measures 43 x 20 x 16.5 feet (13 x 6 x 5 m) and weighs approximately 81 tons (74 t). It has six bunk beds, hot water, a mini-kitchen, climate control, computers, and wireless internet. Grace works to create technologies that help us better understand and manage the oceans. Right now, she builds cameras that help us see underwater in 3D. She uses them to study the ecosystem's health. So cool!

39

LOVE SOMETHING? 13
LEARN MORE
ABOUT ITS HISTORY!

Picture this: You strap on a cool helmet (maybe it has a unicorn horn or a faux spiky hairdo), put your schoolbooks in your basket, hop on your bike, and start peddling. The wind is on your face, your cheeks are flapping, and you ring your bell just because, why not? Right now, on this bike, life is good.

But did you know that bikes also have a really cool bikestory, er, backstory? Yep, that's right. Your precious peddler actually helped pave the way for women's rights.

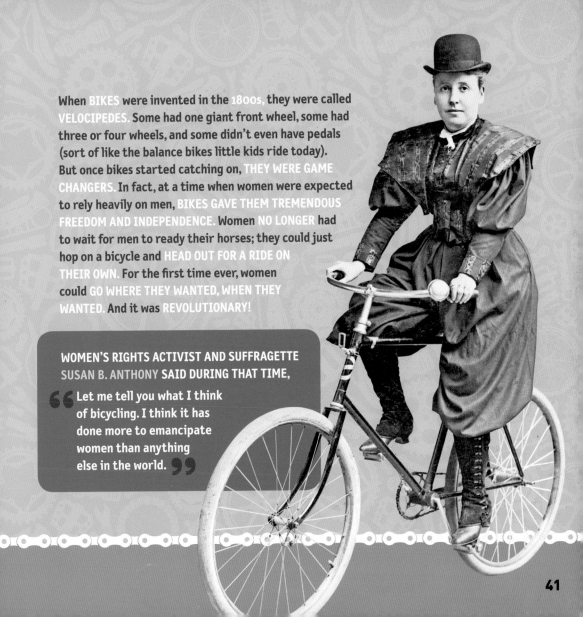

When BIKES were invented in the 1800s, they were called VELOCIPEDES. Some had one giant front wheel, some had three or four wheels, and some didn't even have pedals (sort of like the balance bikes little kids ride today). But once bikes started catching on, THEY WERE GAME CHANGERS. In fact, at a time when women were expected to rely heavily on men, BIKES GAVE THEM TREMENDOUS FREEDOM AND INDEPENDENCE. Women NO LONGER had to wait for men to ready their horses; they could just hop on a bicycle and HEAD OUT FOR A RIDE ON THEIR OWN. For the first time ever, women could GO WHERE THEY WANTED, WHEN THEY WANTED. And it was REVOLUTIONARY!

WOMEN'S RIGHTS ACTIVIST AND SUFFRAGETTE SUSAN B. ANTHONY SAID DURING THAT TIME,

" Let me tell you what I think of bicycling. I think it has done more to emancipate women than anything else in the world. "

HONOR YOUR WILD: IDEAS.

Sure, your ideas might be a little out-there, but many of the best ones are! Don't count 'em out just because they're kooky, and don't let naysayers discourage you from seeing your ideas through. Creativity requires that you think about things in new and interesting ways. Write down your ideas, share them with friends and family, come up with plans for how you could make your ideas a reality, and take a second to thank your brain for being so imaginative and unique.

15

a dog with an underbite

Take
Pleasure
in *Little Things*
(no matter how weird).

44

catching *snowflakes* on your tongue

bubble wrap

peeling a clementine in one long strip

Go ahead, be **delighted** in **little things** like brand-new school supplies, **bubble wrap,** folded chips, the smell of a library book, a **dog** with an **underbite,** pizza bubbles, or the sound of rain on the window.

GIVE IT A GO

Make a list of **five to 10 little things** that make **YOU** smile.

16 Marvel at RAINBOWS.

The word "marvel" means "to be filled with wonder and astonishment." Letting yourself be amazed by something is a great way to give thanks for things that might otherwise be taken for granted. Things like rainbows, for instance. Because, well, rainbows are awesome!

HOW DO RAINBOWS WORK?

You've probably already noticed that the prime time to spot a rainbow is when the sun begins to shine right after a rainstorm. That's because rainbows appear when light from the sun passes through raindrops. The light from the sun is called white light. And though it appears white to us, it is actually made up of seven different colors: RED, ORANGE, YELLOW, GREEN, BLUE, INDIGO, and VIOLET. But, when the white light passes through a raindrop, it scatters into the seven individual colors, which is called refraction. Then, the light—now separated into the seven different colors—bounces out of the raindrop, which is called reflection, making a rainbow!

APPRECIATION ★ STATION ★

When Ella Tryon was six years old, she was admitted to the hospital for a severe food allergy. To lift her spirits, she decided to color a picture of a rainbow, but soon found out that the hospital's playroom didn't have all the colors she needed. So, Ella started the nonprofit Help Me Color A Rainbow to make sure other kids in hospitals had access to their own boxes of crayons. Since then, she has donated more than 30,000 boxes of crayons to children's hospitals in the United States. Go, Ella, go!

17

Treasure Friends Who Just *Get* You.

They'll join in on your **silly dances**, **talk with you for hours** about the characters in your favorite books, and **laugh their heads off** at jokes only you guys understand. There's no explanation needed when you're together— you're like **peas in a pod**.

18

And Treasure Friends Who *Challenge* You.

They **encourage you** to think about things in new ways, **introduce you to foods** you've never tried, and **teach you stuff** you never knew you didn't know. These **mind-opening buds** help you **see new perspectives**, **respect different opinions**, and have a broader understanding of the world.

19 Thank
YOUR LUCKY STARS FOR
Cute Things.

A fluffy, roly-poly puppy.
A baby panda. A tiny turtle.
A sleepy sloth.

When we see adorable animals, both in pictures and IRL, our brains release a chemical that makes us feel happy, loving feelings. Sometimes, we feel such a rush of big feelings, we may even grit our teeth and feel like we want to squeeze something (ahem, cheek-pinching grandmas). There's even a term for it: CUTE AGGRESSION.

In the Filipino language Tagalog, the word "GIGIL" means just that. It's "an uncontrollable feeling, when one is overwhelmed by an emotion, typically used in reference to something cute such as a baby or a puppy."

The next time you see something *aww*-inducingly cute, remember to appreciate the warm, happy feelings it gives you.

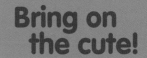

Bring on the cute!

Want to up the cute quotient in your life? Ask a parent if you can check out an animal live cam. Some zoos, national parks, and animal rescue nonprofits have found a way to share the cute by setting up cameras that stream live video of adorable animals to viewers around the world. You can spend hours watching brown bears fish for salmon on the Katmai National Park and Preserve website, pandas rolling and munching leaves on the Smithsonian's National Zoo Panda Cam, or even the soothing sight of sea nettles swimming on the Vancouver Aquarium's Jelly Cam.

53

ERIKA
SKOGG

JUMP (20)
at the chance
to TRAVEL.

ERIKA SKOGG is a WORLD TRAVELER and a self-proclaimed TRAVEL LOVER! She teaches photography workshops and leads groups on National Geographic Expeditions in places like MOROCCO, CUBA, and THE GALÁPAGOS.

Q **When did you discover your passion for travel?**

A In college, I signed up for a study abroad semester in Italy to study photography. It was the first time I ever traveled alone, especially in a new country where I didn't speak the language. I was so nervous to leave home and do something by myself, but I quickly learned that it was incredibly easy to maneuver my way through Italy using trains and buses, by asking for help, and simply following the signs.

I had so much fun learning how to read guidebooks and exploring places all by myself, and from there I was inspired to spend an entire year in Taiwan teaching English. I spent the weekends traveling the country by scooter, and during my time in Asia, I even took a trip to Thailand and Cambodia by myself. I kept meeting friendly people from all over the world and never once ended up eating a meal alone.

Q Why do you think travel can be such a transformative experience for people?

A Travel gives us the opportunity to meet people from other countries who have had different life experiences than us, and who, therefore, have different points of view. It's very easy to feel that the differences between "us" and "them" can be intimidating or scary, but travel allows us the opportunity to form ideas for ourselves, instead of listening to the news or other people's opinions.

Q How does gratitude play a role in your travels?

A I have always felt most grateful to the complete strangers who make my trips not only memorable but possible! I rely a lot on the people who live in the places I travel to help me find my way or allow me to take a photograph of them.

Also, traveling abroad has made me incredibly grateful for everything I was given growing up in the United States, which I wasn't truly aware of until I started traveling. I feel most grateful for the simple things now: access to clean water and a warm, comfortable place to sleep at night ... things I just assumed everyone else had as well.

Q What's one way that you like to express your gratitude?

A I like to print photographs I take of people during my travels. I either ask for their address so I can mail them a printed copy, or if I return to the country, I go out of my way to find them again and hand them back in person. Some people I give photos to have never had their photograph taken, let alone had a printed copy. Instead of just taking photographs, I like to give them back to say "Thank you."

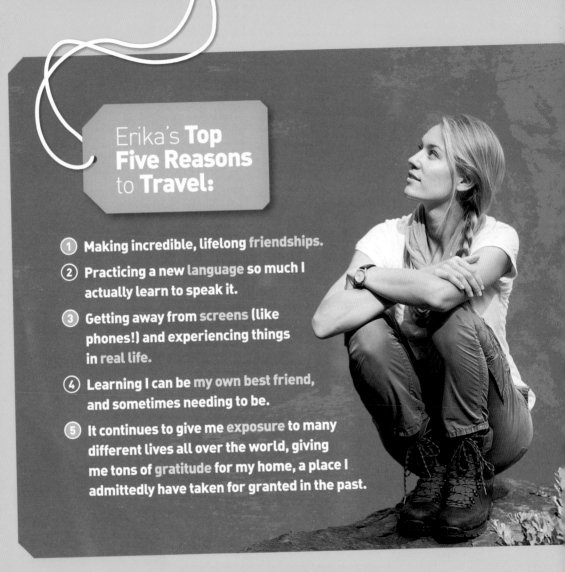

Erika's **Top Five Reasons** to **Travel:**

1. Making incredible, lifelong friendships.
2. Practicing a new language so much I actually learn to speak it.
3. Getting away from screens (like phones!) and experiencing things in real life.
4. Learning I can be my own best friend, and sometimes needing to be.
5. It continues to give me exposure to many different lives all over the world, giving me tons of gratitude for my home, a place I admittedly have taken for granted in the past.

CURB THE
COMPLAINING.

Just like how exercising regularly makes it easier to run and jump and play, studies have found that by **THINKING NEGATIVE THOUGHTS REGULARLY,** you can actually **REWIRE YOUR BRAIN** in a way that makes negative thinking your default. Also, just being around people who complain a lot can really bring your mood and happiness level down. So, to keep yourself from becoming a **NEGATIVE NANCY** or a **DANNY DOWNER,** try not to dwell on things that you don't like and, instead, look on the bright side. **THEN PICK PALS WHO DO THE SAME.**

GIVE IT A ▶▶▶ GO!

Try not to complain for **one week.** Catch yourself when you do and switch gears to **find something going right.** So, sure, it might be raining and the bus might be late, but it's also **pizza day** at school and you're wearing a supercomfy new shirt. **TA-DA!**

You've **turned negative feelings** into **positive ones** all with the **power of your mind.**

22 THANK SOMEONE FROM YOUR PAST.

A quick way to boost positive feelings—both in you and someone else—is by telling someone how much they mean to you. One superspecial way to do this is by thinking of someone from your past who you may not have thanked way back when and writing them a letter.

Maybe it's someone who was welcoming when you started a new school, or a teacher who made you feel better when you were going through a hard time, or a soccer coach who stayed after practice to teach you how to juggle the ball.

Be specific, be sincere, and let them know how their actions made you feel. Then take a minute to think about how it would feel to receive a letter like that. Now pop it in the mail. You'll feel great and so will they!

23

Think of SOMETHING You're Looking FORWARD TO.

TURN UP the Music!

Music can **pump you up** when you need a boost, **keep you company when you're feeling glum,** and **give you all the feels** when you've got a crush. Here are five more reasons to give thanks to terrific tunes:

1.
Playing a musical instrument has been found to **improve memory.**

2.
Humans aren't the only ones who like to **dance—parrots** and **elephants** can get down and **boogie,** too!

MIN   MAX

4.
Musical instruments are works of art! Take the violin, for example. A single violin is made from more than **70 individual pieces of wood!**

3.
Music can help **calm you down** when you're nervous.

5.
Our brains release **happy-making chemicals** when we listen to music we like.

65

Be still. 25

When your **mind** is **busy** or things around you feel **chaotic**, it's very easy to get caught up and to forget what's really important. You may even feel nervous, overwhelmed, or **stressed out.** But, when you recognize that happening, there's something you can do. **You can slow down, get quiet, and BE STILL.**

25 BE STILL.

Turn off all your electronics and find a quiet place to sit or lie down.

If it helps you to listen to soft, soothing music, do that. Maybe you'd like to look at a **calming picture** from somewhere beautiful in nature—like a field of flowers or an underwater coral reef. Try watching the rain, leaves rustling on the trees, or birds **outside your window.**

Let yourself just be

still for a few minutes.

When your mind starts to drift to worries or things you need to do, **bring the focus back to your breath.**

GIVE IT A GO!

Do you need some stillness in your life but can't sit or lie down? No problem! Stillness and quiet are always within your reach. Even in the middle of a busy hallway or a crowded gym, you can stop, take a few deep breaths, and gently remind yourself to SLOW DOWN.

26

Think about the **BEST PART** of your **day.**

Then **share it** with your **family.**

27 Marvel at SCIENCE.

Isn't science amazing? Through experimentation and observation, scientists are able to better understand the physical and natural worlds. Then they can apply what they've learned to invent new things to make our lives—and the world around us—better. Every once in a while, take a minute to think about, and appreciate, just how we benefit from the brainstorms and brilliance, discoveries and determination of scientists.

Turn the page for three scientific inventions to be super thankful for.

1. EYEGLASSES

The FIRST EYEGLASSES were invented in the 1200S IN ITALY. They were worn by monks and scholars and either held up in front of their faces or balanced on their noses. After the printing press was invented in the 1400S, AND MORE PEOPLE BEGAN LEARNING TO READ, the demand for glasses grew. Today, it's estimated that 75 PERCENT OF ADULTS IN THE UNITED STATES use either glasses or contacts.

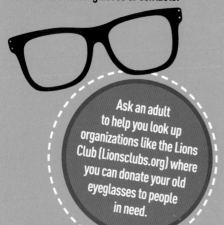

Ask an adult to help you look up organizations like the Lions Club (Lionsclubs.org) where you can donate your old eyeglasses to people in need.

2. PENICILLIN

Before the discovery of penicillin, doctors didn't have a way to fight patients' infectious diseases. PEOPLE DIED from what are now completely CURABLE DISEASES, like strep throat, and wounded soldiers often died from INFECTION rather than from their wounds. IN 1928, Alexander Fleming found some MOLD GROWING IN AN UNCOVERED PETRI DISH that contained *staphylococcal* bacteria. When he examined the Petri dish under a microscope, he saw that the bacteria close to the mold were DYING! Fleming was able to then identify the mold and, upon further inspection, he realized that it was the "juice" from the mold that was killing the bacteria. He called his DISEASE-FIGHTING MOLD JUICE "penicillin." TODAY, we still use penicillin to treat bacterial infections like ear and sinus infections.

3. WI-FI

It's hard to imagine life without WIRELESS COMMUNICATION. It's such an IMPORTANT part of how we send and receive information now. The SCIENCE BEHIND IT can be traced back to an invention by Hollywood actress Hedy Lamarr and her friend, composer George Antheil, who in the 1940s invented a SECRET COMMUNICATION SYSTEM to fight the Nazis in World War II. By switching radio frequencies in a preprogrammed pattern, their technology made it possible for CLASSIFIED MESSAGES to be sent by the government WITHOUT BEING INTERCEPTED by the enemy.

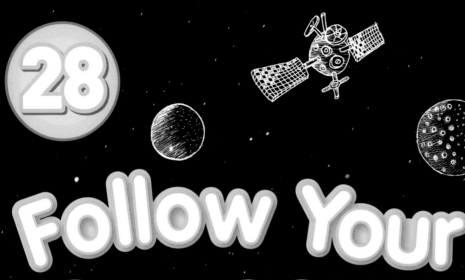

28
Follow Your CURIOSITY.

CURIOSITY is the desire to want to know or learn more about something. INVESTIGATING something you're interested in—whether it be comedy, cooking, or the cosmos—is a GREAT WAY TO PUT YOUR APPRECIATION FOR IT INTO ACTION. RESEARCH, READ, TRY NEW THINGS, ASK LOTS OF QUESTIONS, and HAVE AN OPEN MIND. Enjoy the process of DISCOVERING more about the things you find FASCINATING.

29

LEARN to

SAVOR.

Sometimes happy moments can feel like they're over in a flash. Savoring is a way to make the most out of happy, good feelings and make those feelings last longer. Here's how to let the good times grow:

PAY ATTENTION. One way to savor is to be present and to recognize the positive feelings you're experiencing in the moment. For example, if you're about to eat a delicious cookie, instead of gobbling it, Cookie Monster—style, slow down as you're eating it. Don't rush through your treat, give yourself plenty of time to make the most of it. Put away your phone, turn off the TV, and appreciate each bite that you take, paying close attention to all of the delicious flavors that you're tasting.

REMINISCE. Even though your vacation is over, your happy feelings about it don't have to be. Tell people about your fun adventures, share stories with people who were there, look through pictures and videos you took of your trip, and let your happy thoughts linger.

PASS IT ON. A great way to pump up positive feelings about something you love is to share it. Then, not only do you get to experience it, you'll feel great helping someone else experience it, too! So, the next time you hear a funny joke, tell other people! Or, if you read the best book, let a friend borrow it, so you can talk about it together. If you learn a new skill, teach someone else! If you discover a cool new candy, split some with a friend.

EXCHANGE
INFORMATIO
ACCOMMODAT
EXCURSIO
OUVENIRS / P
CHANG
RATE

30 MAKE A GRATITUDE PLEDGE.

Gratitude, or being thankful for what's good in your life, is a mind-set. And it's a choice. You have to choose to look at all that's going right instead of dwelling on what's wrong.

GIVE IT A GO!

Write a **gratitude pledge** on a piece of paper, tape it somewhere that you'll **see it every day** (like your bathroom mirror), **and recite it to yourself each morning.** This pledge will serve as a **great reminder** to notice warm feelings, as well as **situations to be thankful for.**

Your pledge could be something like **"I pledge to notice good things,"** or **"I pledge to count my blessings,"** or **"I pledge to look on the bright side when things aren't going my way."**

82

31 GET COZY

There is nothing better than feeling warm and relaxed, so[ft] and snuggly. There is even a Danish word, *hygge* (pronou[nced] hoo-guh), that means the happiness and feeling of well-b[eing] that comes from simple, cozy pleasures.

Some things that might enhance the hygge in your life in[clude] thick, warm socks ... drinking hot chocolate while watchin[g] snow fall ... lighting candles to create a soft glow ... a big[,] comfy sweater ... a crackling fire in the fireplace ... throw[s] blankets ... even your favorite pair of sweatpants (which Danes call *hyygebuskers*). Practicing hygge means findin[g] great joy and comfort in small, simple pleasures.

GIVE IT A ≫ GO!

Make a list of five things that bring **hygge** into your life.

32

Smile.

When something GOOD happens, SMILING is one of the ways your body says "THANK YOU." And, even if YOU DON'T FEEL LIKE SMILING at anyone, just SMILING BY YOURSELF CAN HAVE SOME RADICAL RIPPLE EFFECTS. When you smile, chemicals like dopamine, endorphins, and serotonin are released in your brain. These help you RELAX, make you FEEL HAPPIER, and can even LOWER YOUR BLOOD PRESSURE AND DECREASE PAIN.

Now that's something to smile about.

"Sometimes your joy is the source of your smile, but sometimes your smile can be the source of your joy."
—Thich Nhat Hanh, spiritual leader and peace activist

33

TREASURE AWESOME TEACHERS.

Oh, what a difference a great teacher makes! Great teachers make learning fun, happily go the extra mile to make sure you understand, and make their students feel special. If you have a great teacher (or you've had one in the past), let them know!

"Let us *REMEMBER:* One **BOOK,** one pen, *ONE CHILD,* and **one teacher** can **change** the **world.**"

—Malala Yousafzai, activist

(see page 193)

34 GO ON ADVENTURES.

Imagine flying in a helicopter along the coastline of Hawaii with your two best friends. To your right are majestic, mossy green sea cliffs and below you, there's nothing but a thousand feet of air and then the Pacific Ocean. Your mission today? To find a rare plant species on a remote island.

Pretty cool, right?

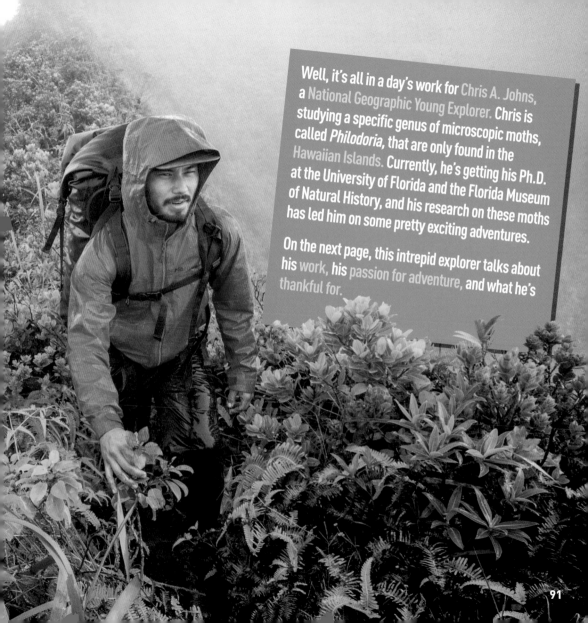

Well, it's all in a day's work for Chris A. Johns, a National Geographic Young Explorer. Chris is studying a specific genus of microscopic moths, called *Philodoria*, that are only found in the Hawaiian Islands. Currently, he's getting his Ph.D. at the University of Florida and the Florida Museum of Natural History, and his research on these moths has led him on some pretty exciting adventures.

On the next page, this intrepid explorer talks about his work, his passion for adventure, and what he's thankful for.

91

34 GO ON ADVENTURES.

Q HOW DID YOU DECIDE THIS IS SOMETHING YOU WANTED TO DO?

A I started doing environmental conservation work because I wanted to be outside. It was pretty simple: I like being outside with my friends. But over the course of training to be a scientist, I gained a much deeper appreciation of the natural world.

Q SO, HOW WOULD YOU DEFINE ADVENTURE?

A I would say that adventure is exploring something unknown. Personally, I like adventure when it's about 30 to 40 percent uncomfortable, and when it's with my good friends. I think adventures help you to continue developing who you are and your understanding of your place in the world.

Q HOW DOES ADVENTURE PLAY A ROLE IN THE WORK THAT YOU DO?

A It's all been an adventure. As of about 40 years ago, only two people had ever worked on this genus of micromoths, and only a handful of people even knew about them. So, the entire process of discovering more about this organism and exploring its biology has been an adventure in itself. I came into this project not knowing anything about insects, and now, I'm, like, the world expert on this one very tiny little moth.

Q WHAT IS ONE OF YOUR FAVORITE ADVENTURES THAT YOU'VE BEEN ON?

A My favorite field excursion for this project was to some cliffsides on the island of Molokai in Hawaii. They're some of the tallest sea cliffs in the world. Some of the best natural ecosystems often occur in these really steep areas, because the pigs and deer and goats that like to eat the native plants can't get to them. We wanted to go there to look for this super-rare, critically endangered plant that is in the sunflower family. The moth that I study specializes a lot on members of the sunflower family. So, two of my best friends and I got in a helicopter early one morning and flew along, right next to the sea cliffs. The helicopter pilot just put the very front of the skids down on the side of the cliff, and we delicately crawled out. We spent two days looking for the plant, and we actually found it! It hadn't been seen on that island for 30 years. We think we may have seen signs of a micromoth, *and* we also found a snail species that hadn't been seen in more than 50 years, which is pretty crazy.

Q WHAT ARE YOUR ADVENTURE MUST-HAVES?

A My tent, my sleeping mat, a rain jacket, a long-sleeve shirt, a headlamp, and I always end up bringing far more camera gear than I need.

A They're about the size of a small eyelash in length and width. They have these beautiful, long antennae that stretch back the whole length of their body. The coolest part, I think, is that they have these crazy color patterns of oranges, blues, and these metallic, silvery colors spaced in between. If you were to see one on your finger, you wouldn't be able to tell, but once you look at them up close, they're pretty crazy looking.

Q HOW DO YOU THINK BEING THANKFUL PLAYS A ROLE IN THE ADVENTURES THAT YOU GO ON?

A The nice thing about being a biologist is that everyone in this field agrees that we don't know everything. It's wonderful. So, through adventure, through the research that a biologist does, through exploring the unknown, I get a better sense of where I fit into the entire picture—it's definitely something that I end up feeling grateful for all the time.

Q HOW DO YOU LIKE TO EXPRESS YOUR GRATITUDE?

A I like passing it on to other people. Gratitude is a really powerful tool to feel within yourself and to exercise in the world. I think it often gets expressed by being nice to other human beings and giving them the space and time to be who they are, and reflecting good things back to them.

35

CELEBRATE ALL THE WAYS YOU'RE UniQuE!

That funny patch of freckles on your hand. Your wild hair. Your distinctive voice. Thank goodness we are not all the same! The things about us that are different are the things that make us special.

36

Look UP and Admire the Sky.

When you're **RUSHING** to get to practice, **WAITING** at the bus stop, or **LOOKING DOWN** at a book or a game, you might not notice what's right above you. But today, **STOP WHAT YOU'RE DOING AND LOOK UP.** Do you see a butterfly? Clouds? Planes? Where you live, do you see just a sliver of the sky peeking out between buildings? Or endless blue as far as you can see?

LOOKING AT THE SKY, with no other goal than to observe it, is a **GREAT REMINDER** that no matter what else is happening, there is **BEAUTY AND WONDER AROUND US ALL THE TIME,** and it's **PRETTY AMAZING TO BE ALIVE.**

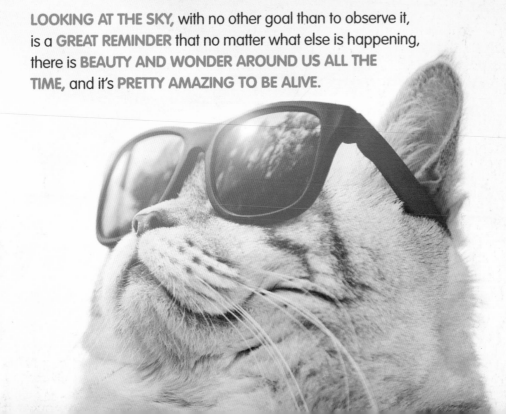

37

Find FUN in NOT-SO-FUN tasks.

It may be tough to muster up good feelings when you're taking out the trash or doing your homework or cleaning your room—but it's not impossible!

Instead of thinking about what else you wish you were doing, **try being present** as you complete the task. For example, as you walk the trash outside, feel the air on your skin and listen for any animals that might be nearby, like a bunny or a chipmunk. Imagine your muscles moving and your lungs filling with fresh air. Not up for whistling while you work? **Then just try a little smile (or at the very least, not a frown).**

Next try to frame the not-so-fun task in a way that **acknowledges your good fortune.** Think about how taking out the trash keeps your house a clean and comfortable place to live. Is the garbage in your neighborhood picked up by trash collectors? If so, think about how **fortunate you are** to have access to sanitation services like that when there are people in the world who don't.

Lastly, think of a way to **make it fun!** Can you skip the garbage all the way outside? Only hop on one foot? Try not to step on any cracks on the way out? Be silly! Make it a game!

INTRODUCE YOURSELF to NEW KIDS at SCHOOL.

38

It can be hard moving to a new place where you might not know your way around, have any friends, or even speak the language. You can make a huge difference to a new student at your school just by saying "Hi." Invite them to sit with you at lunch, be your partner in science class, or hang out after school. You might just make a new friend, and it feels great being able to help someone have a happier day!

39

TUNE IN to Your SENSES.

Take a walk today, or find a comfy spot to sit, and tune in to one of your five senses. What do you hear, taste, feel, smell, or see?

Make the Most of This Moment.

40

When things get hectic, it can be tough not to get lost in thought about what's to come, like next week's test, tomorrow's soccer practice, or even what's for dinner.

It can also be a challenge not to think about the past, like that time you tripped in the lunchroom, missed a shot in basketball, or what someone said to you earlier in the day.

You can think and think, but the future hasn't come yet, and the past has already happened, so there's nothing you can do to change it.

BUT, that doesn't mean you're powerless. Quite the opposite in fact. There's a lot you can do in this very moment.

Don't miss out on all the fun you can have *right now* by worrying too much about the past or fretting about the future. Get busy doing something that makes you happy—like reaching out to a friend, doing a craft, or reading a book—or something that helps prepare you for the future, like studying, practicing, or even just relaxing.

"Yesterday's the past, tomorrow's the future, but today is a gift. That's why it's called the present."
—Bil Keane, cartoonist

105

Practice RANDOM ACTS of *Kindness.*

41

Has anyone ever done something **out of the blue** that **brightened** your day? Maybe your **parents** put a note in your lunch bag, **someone you don't know** very well told you they like your new shoes, or a **friend** brought an extra snack to share with you at lunch.

Feels pretty great, right? You can pass that feeling on by practicing your own **random acts of kindness.**

"Throw kindness around like confetti." —Unknown

Enjoy!

10 Random Acts of Kindness

1 Sit with **someone** who is eating alone.

2 **Hold the door open** for someone.

3 Put a sticky note on the bathroom mirror in a public place with **a positive message** like "You look great!" or "I hope your day is as **amazing** as you are!"

4 Do your brother's or sister's **chores** for them.

5 If you see someone taking a picture of a group, **offer to take it** so that they can get in the photo.

7 Help a **neighbor** shovel snow or rake their leaves.

6 Need a certain **school supply** for one of your classes? **Bring an extra** in case someone **forgets** theirs.

8 Offer to **put someone else's cart back** at the grocery store.

10 If someone needs a day off from **walking their dog,** offer to do it for them.

9 Pay someone a **genuine** compliment.

42 Say "Hello"

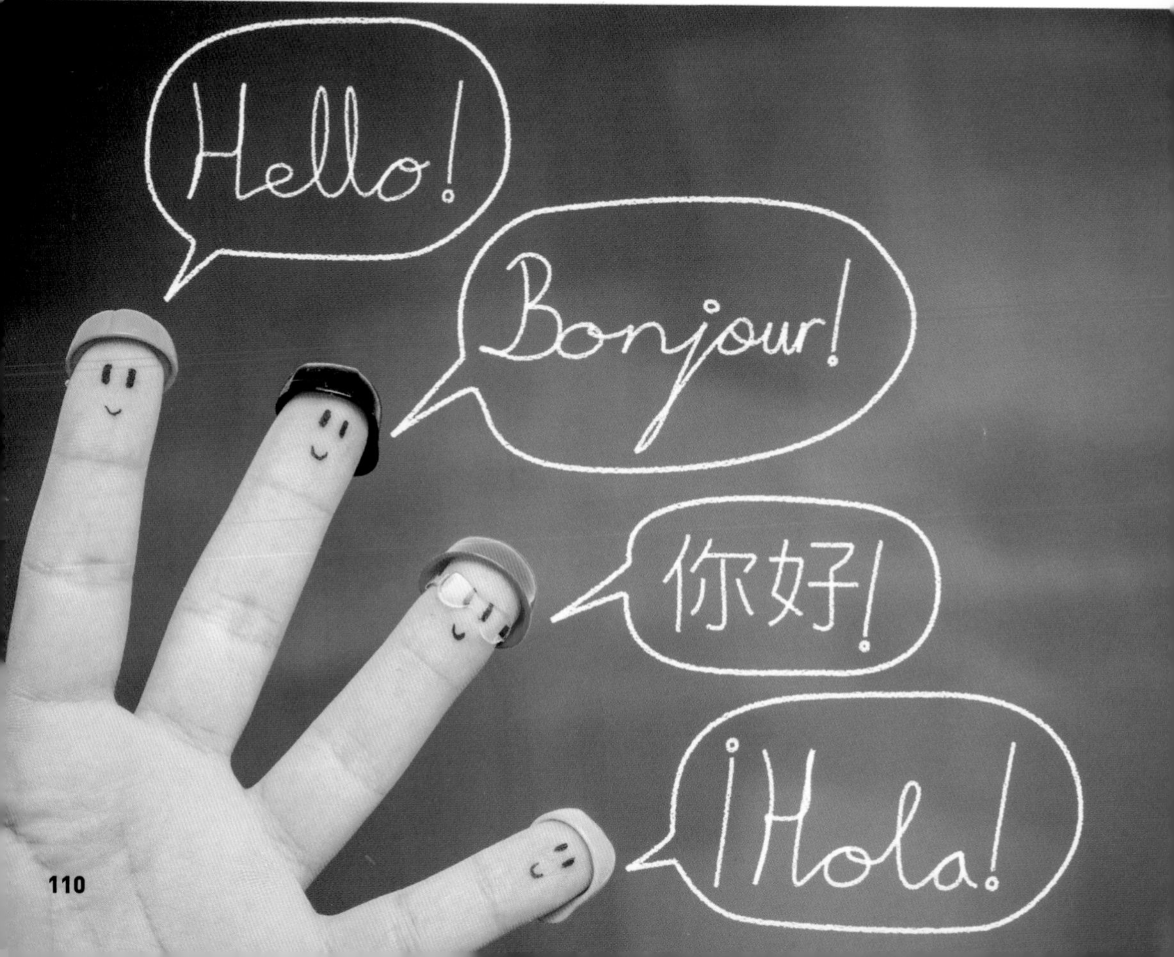

and "Goodbye."

A great way to **SHOW APPRECIATION** for the people in your life is by enthusiastically **ACKNOWLEDGING THEIR PRESENCE.** That means that when they are arriving or leaving, **LOOK UP, MAKE EYE CONTACT, SAY "HI" OR "GOODBYE," AND EVEN CHAT FOR A FEW SECONDS.** Let it be known that you **see them** and it **matters to you** that they're there. They will feel more **valued,** and you'll both feel more **connected to one another.** Win-win!

43
DO A VICTORY DANCE!

What's **difficult** for one person might be **easy-peasy** for another. You might be more nervous about getting a shot at the doctor's office, whereas your friend might not like speaking in front of a crowd. But when you do something that's hard for you—however small it may seem to other people—CELEBRATE! Be proud of your personal victories. Revel in those **good feelings** and what it is you accomplished.

113

MAKE *the* MOST *of Your* WEEKENDS.

44

Ahhh, weekends! **Two whole days** to do with what you please. It might be tempting to veg out in front of the TV for hours at a time, **but instead,** try to think of something you could do that would be more **meaningful** and **maximize the fun.**

GIVE IT A ≫GO!

Here are five ideas to get the **brainstorm ball** rolling:

1. Look into visiting a local **museum.**
2. Organize a **big scavenger hunt** for a friend or family member. Leave clues around your house or neighborhood leading to a fun prize!
3. Pack a picnic and spend the afternoon at a park.
4. Sign up for a **run** or **walk** that **benefits a charity** you admire.
5. Take a **hike** with your **family** on a local nature trail.

Stop and smell

the roses, and the **cookies,** and the fresh-cut grass.

What's a **smell** that makes you **happy?** What's your **favorite food smell?** What do the **different seasons** smell like to you? What scent do you associate with your **favorite holiday?** Different scents can **energize** us, **calm** us, make us **hungry,** or bring **back memories.**

Lemon VANILLA Bacon the ocean Honeysuckle Clean laundry

Pizza RAIN Coconut PEPPERMINT Barbecue POPCORN coffee ORANGE

Lemon VANILLA Bacon the ocean Honeysuckle

Coconut PEPPERMINT Barbecue POPCORN coff

VANILLA Bacon th

PERMINT Barbecue

Honeysuckle

coffee ORAN

A fire in the firep

LAVENDER Cookies B

PINE TREES Ro

GIVE IT A GO!

Now try making a **list** of your **five favorite smells.**

117

46

LOVE

Love is the ultimate expression of gratitude. So, worry less about whether it's cool, and let yourself be enthusiastic about how much you love something or someone. And let yourself be loved in return!

Cherish the Changing of the SEASONS.

47

Depending on where you live in the world, you might get **snow that covers the ground** in a crunchy blanket during the winter months, or **leaves bursting with color** in the fall. But no matter where your hometown resides, each of the seasons—**summer, fall, winter, and spring**—brings lots to be thankful for.

WHAT CREATES SEASONS?

Earth rotates around the sun, and it takes one year for it to make one lap. As Earth rotates, it sometimes tilts toward the sun. Other times, it tilts away from the sun. Different parts of the planet experience the different seasons at different times—it all depends on where on Earth you live.

If it's summer where you live, then the part of Earth where you are is tilting toward the sun. The sun's rays are hitting that part of Earth more directly than they do at any other time of the year. So the days are warmer and longer. When it's winter where you are, the part of Earth where you live is tilted away from the sun. So the days are colder and shorter.

47. CHERISH THE CHANGING OF THE SEASONS.

Here are just a few of the many reasons to celebrate the seasons:

SPRING

1. **Shedding** a few layers (ahem, big winter coat!)
2. **Flowers**
3. **Longer days**
4. Plants turning **green** again and leaves returning
5. Lots of baby **animals** everywhere

SUMMER

1. **Watermelon**
2. Playing in the **sprinkler**
3. Eating **ice-cream cones** outside
4. **Summer break**
5. **Picnics**

FALL

1. Changing **leaves**
2. **Cooler** temperatures for playing outside
3. **Halloween**
4. New school **supplies**
5. Apple **pie**
   Apple **doughnuts**
   Apple **cider**

WINTER

1. **Snow** days
2. **Snuggling** up with a book
3. Fuzzy socks, **mittens,** and hats
4. Hot **chocolate**
5. Warm bubble **baths**

123

Make a
Gratitude
Jar.  (48)

Just by **PAYING ATTENTION** to what's **GOOD IN YOUR LIFE** and in your day—your blessings, your successes, your gifts and talents—you can **BECOME EVEN HAPPIER.** Pretty cool, right? Here's one way to do just that.

STEP 1:
Find an empty jar.

STEP 2:
Every time something happens that you're THANKFUL FOR (you got a good grade on a test, your dad made your favorite dinner, or your drama teacher said your monologue gave her goose bumps), WRITE IT DOWN on a little slip of paper, fold it, and PUT IT IN THE JAR.

STEP 3:
On days when you're feeling GRUMPY or SAD or like you need a pick-me-up, reach into the jar and read a few (or all!) of the papers you put in. Remember that on any day, in any situation, there is always something to be thankful for.

49

Get Out Into Nature.

Nature is amazing. If you ever feel overwhelmed with what's going on in the news, your school, or even your house, go outside and sit still. Wait long enough, and you're sure to see something that reminds you that we are just one small part of life on Earth. While we stress about spelling tests and soccer tryouts and whether so-and-so likes so-and-so, squirrels are still scurrying busily, looking for nuts, fish are swimming in the streams, and little seedlings are sprouting into big, strong oak trees.

There are so many ways to express appreciation for the natural world— you can protect it, photograph it, paint it, write poems about it, teach others about it, and also, get out there and enjoy it!

127

49 GET OUT INTO NATURE.

Here are a few ways to **experience** the magic that is **Mother Earth:**

2. Put out a bird feeder and try to identify the birds that come to it.

3. Go for a nature walk.

1. Visit an orchard and pick fruit.

APPRECIATION STATION ★

When Christian Thomas was five years old he became the youngest person to hike the entire length of the Appalachian Trail. He and his parents hiked the 2,189-mile (3,523-km) trail in eight months. Christian, who was given the trail nickname "Buddy Backpacker," then set his sights on the 2,660-mile (4,281-km) Pacific Crest Trail, which he completed in less than a year, and the 3,100-mile (4,989-km) Continental Divide Trail, which he just completed last year. At nine years old, he is the youngest person ever to complete all three of the United States' longest hiking trails, a feat called the Triple Crown. One way that Buddy likes to pass the time while hiking? By listening to music and podcasts on his headphones!

50 Take care of your things.

A great way to show that you care about your belongings is by doing your best to keep them in good condition. Accidents happen—it's easy to leave things on the bus, forget them out in the rain, or have them wind up in the hands of a younger sibling.

But, there are things you can do to keep your favorite stuff feeling fresh. For example:

- If you have a fishing pole that you love to use, make sure to rinse it with freshwater after each use, rinse your lures, and oil your gears if you're not going to use your pole for a while.

Just by doing a little research, you can become an almost-expert on how to keep the stuff you love in tip-top shape.

- If you notice a button's fallen off of your favorite coat, look up a how-to video online and sew it back on!

- If you have a bike you love, clean it so it doesn't get rusty, keep the tires inflated, and replace your brake pads when they get worn.

131

PRACTICE 51
Mindfulness.

MINDFULNESS is paying attention to the present moment, without judging it, on purpose.

To practice mindfulness, you bring your **awareness** to what's happening in this **very moment.** One way to do this is by tapping into one of your **five senses.** Another way to practice mindfulness is to pay attention to the **sensations in your body:** Is your stomach growling? How does the table feel beneath your palms? How warm and cozy do your feet feel in your socks?

Instead of thinking about what you did **five minutes ago,** or starting to plan what you'll be doing **five minutes from now,** being mindful means focusing on what's happening RIGHT HERE, RIGHT NOW.

Practicing mindfulness is a really important part of being thankful. When we practice mindfulness, we are **more likely** to notice and pay attention to **what's good** and **what's beautiful** in the **present moment.**

GIVE IT A GO!

Go for a **"thankful walk"** around your neighborhood or around a nearby park. While you walk, **pay careful attention** to what you feel, see, hear, and smell. Take notice of all the things you encounter that you're **thankful for.**

The way the air feels on your skin ... beautiful flowers ... the smell of grass ... chirping birds ... white fluffy clouds. If your **mind wanders,** gently bring it back to what you're experiencing on the walk and continue to take note of things that make **you feel grateful.**

133

Rejoice in SNOW DAYs!

52

Snowball fights, sledding, snow angels, hot chocolate, cozy movie marathons, mittens—and NO school!

Snow days = The. Best. Days. Ever!

(And if you live somewhere where you don't get snow, you can be thankful your swim practice won't be canceled, your shoes won't get soggy from slush, and you won't get stuck shoveling snow!)

The 2016 winner of the International Snow Sculpture Championships in Breckenridge, Colorado, U.S.A., was a piece called "Rhonda and Her Recycling Robo-Octopus." The sculpture, which was created by Team USA–Vermont, portrayed a fictional 14-year-old scientist named Rhonda, riding in her own invention, a Robo-Octopus that cleans the ocean floor. Fun fact: Each of the 16 teams starts with a 12-foot (3.7-m)-tall, 50,000-pound (22,680-kg) block of snow and has 65 hours to complete a sculpture.

53

CATCH (and release) FIREFLIES.

These sparkly little insects can make a normal night feel magical. Fireflies, or lightning bugs, are one of the surefire signs summer has arrived. Their little glowing bodies light up backyards, baseball fields, forests, and big open meadows. Chase them, catch (and release) them, or just sit back and watch their twinkly light show.

WHY DO FIREFLIES GLOW?

Fireflies, a type of beetle, emerge at night and only live for about two months in the summertime. They prefer warm environments and moisture. You'll often see them in humid climates or near bodies of water. They have an organ near their stomach that takes in oxygen. The oxygen then mixes with a substance called luciferin, which is already present in their systems, to create light.

PLaY.

Sure, you may not be into the same toys you played with when you were little. Maybe you don't even play with toys at all. **BUT YOU ARE NEVER TOO OLD TO PLAY.**

So what is play, exactly?
Play is something you do for
no other reason than to have fun.

And while your goal might be just to have a great time
(AND YOU WILL!), research has shown that some of
the BEST learning can come from playing. Play teaches
you HOW TO THINK OUTSIDE THE BOX, be more CREATIVE, keep
going when things get tough, WORK AS A TEAM, bond with others, be
present, and HAVE FUN!

Here Are **10** Ways to Infuse Your Day With a Little More PLaY.

1 Dust off your old coloring books, sharpen some crayons or colored pencils, and spend time trying to stay inside the lines.

2 Get some friends and neighbors together for a big group game like charades, flashlight tag, or Frisbee.

3 Bust out some Play-Doh or clay. Try making animals, shapes, or figures. Bonus points for sculpting a self-portrait.

4 Institute family game nights.

5 Check out a play script from the library, get a group of friends together, and act it out.

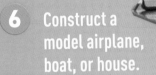

6 Construct a model airplane, boat, or house.

7 Put together a jigsaw puzzle with your friends or family.

8 Decorate cookies or a cake, just because. No special occasion necessary.

9 Go bowling, play laser tag, or check out an arcade.

10 Make a goofy video with your friends—act out skits, pretend to be talk show hosts, or make a cooking tutorial.

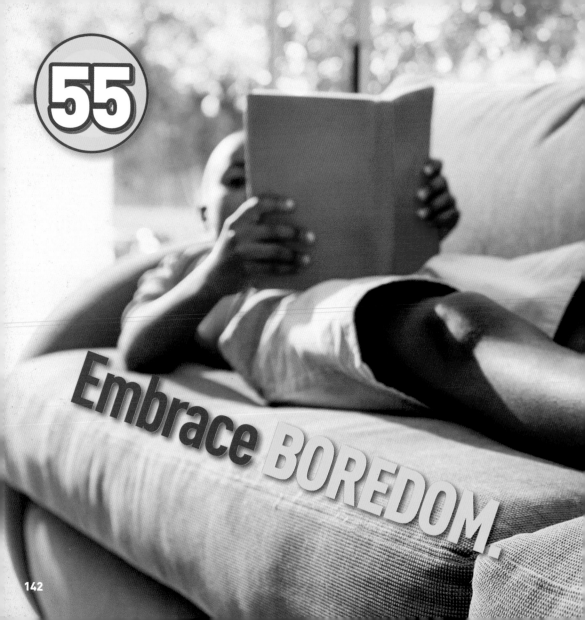

55

Embrace BOREDOM.

DO YOU REMEMBER TWO WEEKS AGO WHEN YOU WERE SUPER STRESSED? You had chores you had to do, two tests to study for, and a big project due the next day. Well, now you are actually bored. With, like, nothing to do.

BUT INSTEAD OF WHINING AND COMPLAINING, JUST BE BORED. BLISSFULLY.

Downtime—for both your body and your mind—is important and healthy. Next time you feel boredom settling in, be thankful that you have a moment when there's nowhere you need to be and nothing you need to be doing. Let your mind wander, read a book, come up with creative ways to entertain yourself, or just lie in the grass and watch the clouds pass overhead.

143

56

LOOK IN THE MIRROR AND FIND SOMETHING YOU LIKE.

The way your hair looks today. The gap between your front teeth. Your freckles. Your eyes (which look just like your mom's). Your smile. Your long legs. Your short legs. Your ears (that you just learned how to wiggle).

It can be anything. But, every day, find something.

Sit Down for Breakfast.

57

Instead of rushing out the door with a bagel or a cereal bar, wake up a few minutes earlier so that you can actually enjoy your breakfast. Try this for one week and see how it feels: Sit down with your breakfast, think about what you'd like to accomplish today, and enjoy the food that's providing your body with the nourishment and energy you need to reach your goals.

Check out these dishes you might see on breakfast menus around the world.

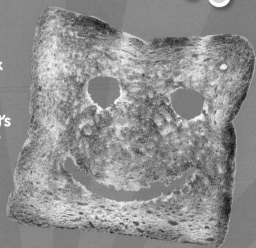

Where: **Honduras**

Breakfast Fave:
Fried eggs, refried beans, tangy sour cream, cheese, avocado, sweet fried plantains, and tortillas

Where: **Japan**

Breakfast Fave: Miso soup and pickled vegetables

Where: **Morocco**

Breakfast Fave: A dish called *khlea* made from small strips of dried beef mixed with fried eggs

Where: **England**

Breakfast Fave: Eggs, grilled tomatoes, sausage, and baked beans

Where: **China**

Breakfast Fave: Rice porridge

147

58

TREASURE the STORIES Your FAMILY TELLS AGAIN and AGAIN.

Be Part of the Solution.

59

There will be many times in your life when you notice things that aren't right or that could be better. In these moments, look for opportunities to help. Look for ways to be part of the solution.

That's exactly what **Gitanjali Rao,** winner of the **2017 Discovery Education 3M Young Scientist Challenge,** did! When she was just 11 years old, she learned about the water crisis happening in **Flint, Michigan, U.S.A.** The water crisis began in 2014, when it was discovered that there were high levels of lead in the drinking water, which can make people very, very sick. The people of Flint still can't drink the water that comes from their faucets and have been told they may not be able to until 2020. "I did some research, and I realized it wasn't only in Flint—there are more than 5,000 water systems in the U.S. with lead contamination," says Gitanjali. "That's when it kind of sank in that it's a pretty big problem."

So, Gitanjali put her love of science to work and invented a device, called **Tethys,** that can quickly detect lead in water.

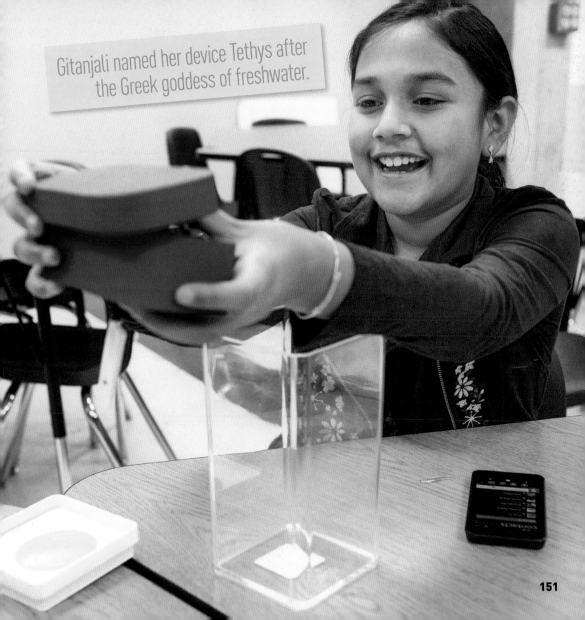

Gitanjali named her device Tethys after the Greek goddess of freshwater.

151

59 BE PART OF THE SOLUTION.

Q: What inspired you to create Tethys?

A: I had originally been introduced to the Flint water crisis through my STEM (science, technology, engineering, and mathematics) lab. But I didn't think about creating a device until I saw my parents testing for lead in our water, which made a real-world connection for me. I thought [that] if it's taking this long to test for lead in our house, then imagine how long it would take to test in schools or places like Flint, Michigan, and every household. So that's when I developed my idea for my device.

Q: How did you come up with the ideas for the technical parts?

A: I follow the MIT Department of Materials Science and Engineering research page to see the latest developments in technology. That's where I found out that there is a way to use carbon nanotube sensors in order to detect hazardous gases. And I realized that if we can use carbon nanotubes to detect hazardous gases, why not extend it to a liquid medium and use them to detect lead in water? So, I did two months of planning, and then I was picked as one of the top 10 finalists for the Discovery Education 3M Young Scientist Challenge. When I met my 3M mentor, she helped me take the idea and turn it into real life.

Q: What advice would you give to other young people who want to be a part of the solution, too?

A: In the beginning of the process, I didn't know if I really wanted to try because it required complex equipment, and I didn't know for sure that I could actually accomplish it other than proposing my idea. My instant reaction was that if I didn't accomplish it, I would feel really bad about myself, so I thought about skipping it and trying something simpler. But then I decided to go for it! If I didn't understand something, it was OK. I had a mentor who guided me, or I asked for help. The worst response I could have gotten was a "no", but if I didn't try, I never would have known if it worked. I'd like to tell other people who have an idea but who are hesitant to execute it to not be afraid to try. Failure is just another step to success. There are people who are ready to help. All we need to do is ask!

Q: What are you working on now? What's next for you?

A: I'm working on scale testing on Tethys, in partnership with Denver Water. I recently changed my sensor design for better usability. I have also enhanced it to allow data upload and analysis to potentially create a heat map that shows locations with more or less lead levels. This may help people take action. In parallel, I am researching advances in genetic engineering and potential solutions to the problem of adolescent depression. I call this my "Happiness Detector."

What do you like to do when you're NOT studying and practicing science?

- I play two sports—I fence and I swim.
- I like to go for walks around my neighborhood; we've got a nice trail in my backyard.
- I go for bike rides with my friends.
- My family's a big baking family. We don't bake cakes or pies—instead, we make desserts from all around the world, like macaroons, baklava, and marzipan.

60
Be a bookworm.

Congrats! You picked up the book in your hands, so you're off to a good start!

There is so much to be thankful for when it comes to books, including ...

- Snuggling up on a rainy day with **nothing else to do but read.**
- The **anticipation** of waiting for a **new book** to come out in your **favorite series.**
- Knowing that no matter where you are in the world, you can learn more about **new people** and **places** and **ideas,** just by reading a book!
- Learning all sorts of awesome **new vocabulary words.**
- Knowing that even when you're going through something tough, you can probably find a book about someone who has **experienced something similar.**
- Cool **bookmarks!**
- The **suspense!** The **tears!** The *awws!* The **laughs!**

Jake Marcionette is the youngest author to ever have a book on the *New York Times* Best Seller list. Jake wrote and published his first book when he was only 12 years old! The book, *Just Jake,* is a funny adventure about a sixth grader whose life gets upended when he moves to a new state and school. Jake started his writing career during summer breaks from school, when his mom had him and his sister write every day, from breakfast until lunch. What started as sort of a pain eventually turned into a passion, and now Jake has written three books in the Just Jake series and even has plans for a new line of books.

Learn More About Your Family's History

61

Give thanks for your ancestors by learning more about where you came from.

Ask your parents and grandparents to help you fill out a family tree. When you add a new name, ask around to see if people in your family know any stories or information about that person.

Also, ask your parents and grandparents about what life was like when they were little.

You can ask BIG questions:

What were some of the greatest advancements and inventions that happened when you were growing up?

What were your hopes and dreams as kids?

Ask simpler questions to get a sense of what their lives were like and how things have changed:

What was your favorite treat to buy at the store?

What was your favorite toy or game to play when you were my age?

62

LOOK FOR A LESSON IN STRUGGLES.

You might be saying, "C'MON, NOT EVERYTHING HAS A SILVER LINING." And you're right, **NOT EVERYTHING DOES.** Some things just plain stink. But most difficult situations come **JAM-PACKED WITH LESSONS.** In fact, **WE LEARN THE MOST ABOUT OURSELVES,** and others, as we **NAVIGATE TOUGH TIMES.** Challenges, failures, mistakes, disagreements, heartbreak, jealousy, fear—they all offer **OPPORTUNITIES** to become a **BETTER PERSON, OPEN YOUR HEART, BE MORE COMPASSIONATE, COMMUNICATE BETTER,** and more.

GIVE IT A ▶▶GO!

The **next time** you encounter a difficult person or a challenging situation, **ask yourself:**

- What can I learn from this?
- What can I do to be better suited for a similar situation in the future?
- What can I take from this that might help me become a better me?

Celebrate today.

63

YOU CAN'T DO **anything** ABOUT WHAT HAPPENED **yesterday.** YOU **can't** DO ANYTHING ABOUT WHAT'S **going to happen** TOMORROW. BUT THERE IS **one day** THAT'S WITHIN YOUR **control—today.** SO GO AHEAD AND **create a great one.**

64

And Celebrate That Tomorrow Is a New Day.

MAYBE TODAY WAS HARD. MAYBE IT WAS really hard. BUT, GUESS WHAT? TOMORROW YOU GET TO start all over again. CLEAN SLATE. FRESH START. New day.

65

Bask in Bubble Baths.

Baths are a great way to have some alone time to soak in the day's events, ease muscle tension, and reflect and enjoy the moment. Studies have even found that baths can help improve your mood.

Add bubbles to the equation, and you get all of the great benefits of a bath plus bubble beards and bubble wigs. Score!

Be a WILD ANIMAL Advocate.

66

LIONS AND TIGERS AND BEARS—OH, MY! IT'S PRETTY AWESOME THAT WE GET TO ROAM THE SAME EARTH AS THESE MAJESTIC CREATURES.

All wild animals deserve to live healthy, happy, wild lives. Unfortunately, there are many species around the globe in danger of going extinct. So, to honor them and to show our gratitude for their existence, it's up to us to do the best we can to make sure our actions don't have a harmful impact on them.

Even though you might not come in contact with many giraffes, gorillas, whales, rhinos, or elephants, there are things you can do in your everyday life to protect wild animals.

66 BE A WILD ANIMAL ADVOCATE.

Here are just a few ways you can help:

Do your research.

Do a quick search on an animal you're interested in. Find out more about its habitat, the food it eats, and any threats to its well-being.

Support organizations that protect wildlife.

Hold a car wash, bake sale, or neighborhood-wide garage sale to raise money and awareness.

Recycle.

Recycling can reduce the need to cut down more trees, which protects forests and the animals that live in them.

Don't litter.

Never throw trash on the ground and also pick up any that you see. Wild animals, like birds and turtles, can mistake trash for food, which can cause them to get sick or even choke. Plastic trash or wire can get wrapped around an animal's beak, leg, or body, and, if eaten, can clog the digestive tract. Even spit-out gum can get stuck in an animal's fur or on its wings.

Don't buy products that harm animals.

These include clothes or jewelry that use endangered animal furs, ivory, rhinoceros horn, tortoise shell, or crocodile skins.

Encourage your family not to use harmful chemicals on your lawn.

Pesticides and herbicides can hurt pets and honeybees, and when it rains, these chemicals get washed into bodies of water, which isn't healthy for the animals living there.

Buy cruelty-free toiletries.

These are products that were not tested on animals.

Write to your members of Congress.

Let them know that it's important to you that they support laws and legislation that protect wild animals.

Biodiversity is the variety of life on Earth, or within a particular ecosystem. Each living thing affects the health and existence of other living things. For example, who knew that we have bats to thank every time we eat corn on the cob? It's true! Bats eat pests, like earworm larvae, that harm corn crops. That's just one example, but all life is connected, which is why each and every species is important and in need of our protection.

67 Always say

Here are a few folks who probably deserve a "Thanks!" today:

Whoever refills your water or brings you food at a restaurant

Coaches, teachers, or instructors who inspire or motivate you

The people who serve food in your cafeteria

Write a Fan Letter.

68

Think of someone in the public eye who INSPIRES you, ENTERTAINS you, or just plain MAKES YOU HAPPY. Then, LET THEM KNOW! It could be an ATHLETE, a POLITICIAN, an ACTOR, a SINGER, a COMEDIAN, an AUTHOR, an ACTIVIST, or anyone else.

Ask an adult to help you find an address where you can send them a token of your APPRECIATION. You could WRITE A NOTE or a POEM, PAINT A PICTURE, or MAKE A VIDEO of you singing a song.

However you choose to communicate it, the most IMPORTANT thing is that you let them know WHAT THEY MEAN TO YOU and that you're THANKFUL for them!

69

Savor a Scoop
(or two or three) of
Ice Cream.

Whether creamy or crunchy, wild and wacky, or sweet and simple, ice cream is always awesome. And whatever form it takes—an ice-cream sundae, ice-cream float, ice-cream cake, or a sweet, drippy cone—it is bound to be delicious. Next time you eat ice cream, slow down and celebrate each bite.

The two founders of Ben & Jerry's Ice Cream, Ben Cohen and Jerry Greenfield, met when they were in the seventh grade. Years later, as adults, they decided to try starting a business together. They landed on the idea of an ice-cream shop after they discovered that the equipment needed for their first business idea—a bagel shop—was too expensive. Ben and Jerry, who are still best friends to this day, were the inventors of chocolate chip cookie dough ice cream, which is still their most popular flavor worldwide. But, beyond the deliciousness they'd put out into the world, Ben and Jerry were determined to do good. In 1985, they started the Ben & Jerry's Foundation, committing 7.5 percent of the company's profits to philanthropy efforts that support social justice, protect the environment, and support sustainable food systems.

10 WILD AND WACKY ICE-CREAM FLAVORS

1. Sweet corn
2. Huckleberry
3. Goat cheese
4. Cereal milk
5. Garlic
6. Mustard
7. Avocado
8. Cinnamon toast
9. Lobster
10. Bacon

175

Learn MORE About Other PEOPLE... and CELEBRATE What Makes Us DIFFERENT and the SAME.

One powerful way to practice gratitude for humans around the world, including the ways that we are different and the ways that we are similar, is to learn about other people, the richness of different cultures, and the wild range of human experiences.

Meet **National Geographic Young Explorer Asha Stuart.** She has made it her life's work to do just that. As a **documentary filmmaker** she observes what life is like for people around the world and then she creates a record of it that can be shared with others.

Q What is a project that you've worked on that you've felt particularly proud of?

A I recently finished a documentary called *The Lost Tribe of Africa*. It's about the Siddi tribe in India, which many people don't know exists. Sometime between the 15th and 19th centuries, they were forcibly taken from their homes in Africa and brought to India where they were made slaves. Today the Siddi people continue to struggle to find their own identity in a country that never wanted them there.

Q Do you remember one of the first documentary films you saw that had an impact on you?

A *Nanook of the North* is the first documentary I remember seeing. It's about the ways of life of some ancient Inuit tribes. It was the first time that I had ever seen indigenous people on film. For some reason, that this ancient tribal culture could come alive for the modern viewer was pure magic to me. The documentary allowed me to get a glimpse of their real, raw lives and of that time in history.

Inuit are indigenous people of northern Canada and parts of Greenland and Alaska.

Q What is it that you love about learning about other people, places, cultures, and customs?

A Learning about other places that are completely different from my own reminds me that there is something fundamental about the human experience that binds us all together. Everyone wants things like basic respect, a decent life, and good relationships, and although it may look different in my country than it does in yours, at the core we want the same things.

Q What about your work most excites you?

A It might sound cliché, but it's true: Meeting new people all around the world is what most excites me about my work. I feel like as a documentarian I've been granted access to many places that others would never have access to, and for me that feels like such a privilege.

Q What qualities does one need to be a great documentary filmmaker?

A Listening, listening, listening. We conduct such in-depth interviews about people's communities and their lives, and typically when we go on assignment, we're dealing with something we don't know much about before we get there. So listening becomes essential to the task itself, as well as being a critical aspect of mutual respect and becoming part of the communities we work with.

Q When do you feel most grateful when you're creating your work?

A When the work brings visibility about a subject, people, or a place that would otherwise go relatively unnoticed. I feel especially thankful when that visibility gains traction into something actionable that brings about much needed change in a community.

Q How do you think learning about other people and the way they experience life relates to practicing gratitude?

A I feel very grateful that people trust me enough to open up and share their intimate lives and thoughts and feelings. I think that the differences between cultures and people is what makes the world such a rich and exciting place. And for that I think many of us are extremely grateful.

71

Get to know your unique point of view.

**Your Life EXPERIENCES +
Your THOUGHTS + Your FEELINGS
= Your POINT OF VIEW**

Knowing what you think and feel, and why, is a great way to APPRECIATE what makes you uniquely YOU.

72

And get to know the unique point of view of others.

ALL AROUND THE WORLD, HUMANS HAVE SUCH DIFFERENT DAY-TO-DAY EXPERIENCES. WE SPEAK DIFFERENT LANGUAGES, EAT DIFFERENT FOODS, PLAY DIFFERENT GAMES, AND CELEBRATE DIFFERENT HOLIDAYS.

But, when you sit down with someone and talk to them, you will find that there's much about us that's the same. Most folks love their families and want to be healthy and happy and safe, have fun, and have access to opportunities to help them live their best lives.

Learning about how other people think and feel is a GREAT WAY to show thanks for how diverse people are.

73 GET LOST IN SPACE.

Sometimes, it's IMPORTANT to get a little **perspective** about our place in the UNIVERSE. So let's start here:

EARTH, the planet where we LIVE, is one of eight planets that rotate around our sun, MAKING OUR SOLAR SYSTEM. This solar system is just ONE SMALL part of a much LARGER galaxy called the MILKY WAY. In the whole universe—which includes all existing matter and space—there are more stars than grains of sand on all the beaches on Earth. That's at least a BILLION TRILLION STARS!

We are just little specks in what is an almost UNIMAGINABLY GINORMOUS universe.

Milky Way galaxy

YOU ARE HERE

Next time you go outside at night, take a few minutes to look up at the sky. THINK about how, in the big scheme of things, each one of us is so very small and *SO VERY PRECIOUS.*

That we **exist**—right here, right now— is AMAZING.

74 VOLUNTEER.

10 Awesome Ways to VOLUNTEER

1. **Walk dogs** at a local animal shelter.
2. **Help sort** and **box food** at a food pantry.
3. **Visit** or **play games** with older folks at a **retirement home.**
4. **Serve meals** at a homeless shelter.
5. Hold a **bake sale** for your favorite **charity.**
6. Help out with **after-school events** at the **library** in your town.
7. Participate in a **trash cleanup** with an environmental organization.
8. **Donate** your old clothes, toys, and sports equipment to a **local shelter** or **Goodwill.**
9. **Tutor** younger kids in reading.
10. Participate in a **run** or **walk** to raise money and awareness for a cause you care about.

A huge way to give thanks for your own blessings, gifts, and good fortune is to help other people. Be on the lookout for opportunities in your neighborhood, community, or school to lend a helping hand. Then, consider volunteering your time and energy with a local organization that could use your help.

75

Train yourself to see

beauty everywhere.

It's there if you look for it.

76

Be Amazed by Your Brain (and Your Ability to Change It!).

The HUMAN BRAIN is INCREDIBLE. This THREE-POUND (1.4-kg) POWERHOUSE contains BILLIONS of nerve cells that receive information, process it, then relay messages throughout the body in SPLIT SECONDS. Your brain is the CONTROL CENTER FOR EVERYTHING happening in your body—the way your MUSCLES MOVE, your FEELINGS and MOODS, even HOW FAST YOUR HEART BEATS.

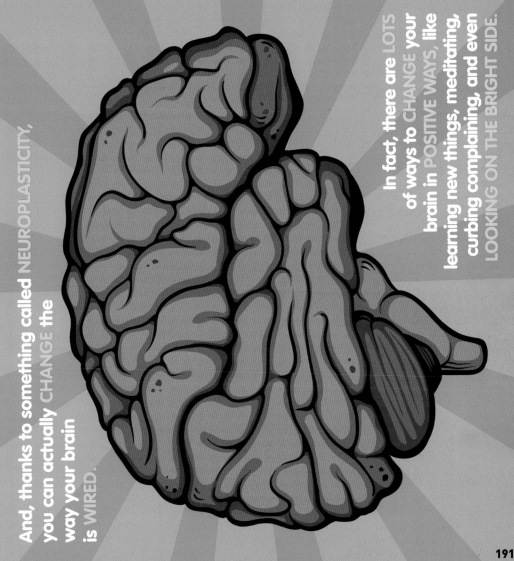

And, thanks to something called NEUROPLASTICITY, you can actually CHANGE the way your brain is WIRED.

In fact, there are LOTS of ways to CHANGE your brain in POSITIVE WAYS, like learning new things, meditating, curbing complaining, and even LOOKING ON THE BRIGHT SIDE.

191

Find **Awesome**

When you're looking to be inspired, motivated, or challenged to be better, find someone to look up to. This could be a teacher, a sibling, a politician, a parent, an athlete, or an actor. They might be someone you know or someone you've only ever seen on TV or read about in history books.

Once you've found someone you think is pretty great, do some research. Read interviews the person has given, check out a biography from the library, or ask the person to meet so you can pick their brain.

The idea isn't to try to be just like them, but instead to find little nuggets of wisdom, pieces of advice, or tips of the trade that can educate and inspire you on your own personal journey to greatness, and to ultimately being the best YOU.

ROLE Models.  **77**

Four **Awesome** Folks to **Look Up To:**

Who they are:
Malala Yousafzai

What they do:
Activist/Author/Oxford University student

A couple reasons they're awesome:
When she was 15 years old, Malala was shot by the Taliban in Pakistan for advocating for girls' education. She is the youngest winner of the Nobel Peace Prize, and with her father, she founded the Malala Fund, which aims to give all girls access to education.

Who they are: Lin-Manuel Miranda

What they do: Composer/Lyricist/Actor

A couple reasons they're awesome: By creating the hit musical *Hamilton*, he taught loads of fans about Alexander Hamilton, one of America's Founding Fathers. He's also raised millions of dollars for the Hispanic Federation, which supports Hispanic families and Latino institutions and has provided tremendous support to Puerto Rico after Hurricane Maria.

Who they are: Emma Watson

What they do: Actress/UN Women Goodwill Ambassador

A couple reasons they're awesome: Not only did she star as Hermione in the awesome Harry Potter movies, she is an advocate for girls' education and women's rights around the world. As a UN Women Goodwill Ambassador, she's spoken on behalf of the organization HeForShe, which asks men to speak out about gender equality, and she also started a feminist book club on Goodreads called Our Shared Shelf that anyone can join.

Who they are: LeBron James

What they do: Professional basketball player/Community leader/Education advocate/Philanthropist

A couple reasons they're awesome:
Not only is he one of the greatest basketball players of all time, LeBron cares deeply about helping others and giving back to the community. Recently, with his nonprofit, the LeBron James Family Foundation, he created the I Promise School, in Akron, Ohio, U.S.A., where he grew up. The aim of this innovative school is to help students who are at risk of falling behind their peers and who would benefit from some extra help. In addition to a top-notch education, students at the I Promise School will receive additional types of assistance to help them succeed, like free meals and snacks, a bicycle and helmet, and college tuition.

195

78

Admire Art.

Great art has the power to stir up big, even unexpected feelings. Great art is **a window** into **another world;** it can give you a glimpse into how someone else experiences life. A piece of art can make you **mad,** it can make you **sad,** it can **inspire you,** or help you **feel less alone.**

TO ADMIRE ART IS TO APPRECIATE IT.

Going to a **museum** and **doing a full tour** is GREAT, but consider, as an alternative, doing a **deep dive** into **ONE ARTIST** or even **ONE WORK OF ART.** Read about the **artist's life** and **work,** the **techniques** and **tools** he or she used, how their **style evolved over time,** what **inspired** them, and what was going on in the world when your **FAVORITE** work was created.

197

BE A GOOD

A great way to show thanks to someone in your life is by being a good listener when they speak. Put away any distractions (like electronics or toys), don't interrupt, and ask thoughtful follow-up questions to make sure you understand what they're saying.

80 Try Your BEST NOT TO WASTE.

You know the feeling: When you're eating a crazy-good cookie, you don't want to drop a single crumb. If you only have one hour to play at the park, you don't want to spend a single minute dillydallying. And, if you've worked hard to save money, you don't want to blow it on something silly that you don't really want.

Wasting something, or using it up carelessly, is the opposite of really appreciating it. So, here are a few easy ways to conserve precious resources:

→ Turn off lights and electronics when you leave a room.
→ Take shorter showers and turn off the faucet while you brush your teeth.
→ Walk or ride your bike instead of taking a car.
→ Cook only as much food as you're going to eat or save leftovers to eat later.
→ Learn how to fix things instead of throwing them away.
→ Use reusable grocery and lunch bags.
→ Put down your electronics.

APPRECIATION STATION

Americans produce an estimated 4.5 pounds (2 kg) of garbage A DAY, and much of that is food packaging. Think about it: water bottles, wrappers, straws, cardboard boxes, plastic containers—not to mention plastic grocery bags, which take years to decompose in landfills. So, waste-free stores are now opening around the world that do away with packaging altogether. Customers bring their own reusable containers, like canning jars, cloth bags, or canisters, and then fill them with loose foods—everything from beans and cereal to spices and candy. Ta-ta for now, trash!

01

Celebrate Sunshine.

82

And REVEL in the RAIN.

Make Someone a HOMEMADE Gift.

If you want to **thank someone** for something they did, or just show them that **you're thankful for them in your life**, give them a **superspecial** token of your appreciation, by **making it yourself**.

FIVE HANDMADE Thank-You GIFT IDEAS:

1. A personalized greeting card

2. A knit plush or pillow

3. Homemade cookies

4. A clay bowl, figurine, or jewelry

5. A homemade picture frame (see the next page for instructions)

207

GIVE IT A >>GO! Here's how to make a **homemade picture frame.**

YOU WILL NEED:
- Four large craft sticks
- Glue
- Beads, buttons, pom-poms, shells, or any other decorations you like
- Paint (and paint pens and glitter if you'd like)
- Ruler
- A photo to frame

DIRECTIONS:

STEP 1: Paint the craft sticks however you'd like and let them dry.

Step 2: Glue the craft sticks in a square. Let the glue dry completely.

Step 3: Then, decorate your frame. Use shells, pom-poms, buttons, glitter, stickers—anything you like!

Step 4: Using a ruler, measure the frame opening.

Step 5: Carefully cut the photo to fit the opening in your frame.

Step 6: Glue the photo to the back of the frame so that the picture shows from the front.

Voilà! You've made a superspecial and heartfelt homemade gift.

84

"Never be afraid to raise your voice for honesty and truth and compassion against injustice and lying and greed. If people all over the world ... would do this, it would change the earth." —William Faulkner

SPEAK UP
FOR THOSE IN NEED.

Show gratitude for your voice and your ability to speak out by talking about issues and people that need help and attention. You have the power to create positive change, and it all starts with the simple act of talking about the things that need to be better.

- When you see someone being bullied → Tell a teacher or a trusted adult.
- When you see an injustice happening in your community → Talk about it with friends and family, reach out to your mayor or governor, call your representatives in Congress to voice your concern, or write a letter to your local newspaper.
- When you see animals in need → Bring attention to the cause by telling others, posting photos, or holding a fund-raiser.
- When you learn about something happening in the country or in the world that needs attention → Ask questions about it in class, post about it on your social media, bring it up at the dinner table, and brainstorm ways you can make a difference.

85

When You Have More Than You Need—

SHARE.

Whatever it may be—
food, pencils, quarters
for the vending
machine—give a little
when you can.

86 Celebrate

Being thankful extends beyond just what is happening in your own life. Think about someone you care about who is doing well and be thankful that good things are happening for them. Then, let them know you're excited for them. Consider writing them a note of congratulations, picking them a flower, or bringing them a cookie. They'll feel great, and so will you!

214

other people's achievements.

215

Seek out—then share—stuff that makes you smile. 87

Be on the lookout for good news, funny jokes, inspiring stories, or aww-inducing cuteness. Then, pass on that positivity by sharing it with friends and family. A photo of a porcupine and a bulldog who became BFFs? Sure! An inspiring story about a local hero? Yes, please! A five-year-old geography expert? You betcha! Making someone else smile is sometimes just a newspaper clipping or a mouse click away!

Give Thanks to Unsung Heroes! Like Bees!

88

When you don't see all of the hard work being done to make something, it can be easy to take it for granted. This is true for lots of things—like birthday parties, school projects, or choir recitals. Sure, you may really enjoy the final product, but you might not fully appreciate the sweat, tears, and hours of work that went into creating it.

Take for example—**bees.** While we are going about our days, bees are busy work, work, working away. Some people even think of bees as a bother and wish they'd just buzz off.

But bees are actually **tiny, winged superheroes.**

Not only do bees produce **delicious honey,** more than **one-third** of the **world's crops** and more than **90 percent of wild plants** are dependent on bee pollination. Bees pollinate by transferring pollen and seeds from one flower to another, which **fertilizes** the plant so that it can grow the things that we later eat—like apples, oranges, mangoes, broccoli, cucumbers, and pumpkins (to name a few).

219

In recent years, lots of bees have disappeared, which worries scientists and farmers. They think there are a number of factors contributing to the decrease, including climate change, pesticide use, and habitat loss.

More Bees, Please! Five Fun Facts About Bees!

1. There are more than 20,000 species of bees in the world.

2. Bees aren't the only pollinating species—in fact, there are more than 200,000 different species around the world that act as pollinators, including moths, butterflies, birds, bats, and even some small mammals (like some monkeys!).

3. In places around the world where bee populations have dwindled, like some parts of China, farmers pollinate their flowers and crops by hand.

4. The average worker bee lives for just five to six weeks. During this time, she'll produce around a twelfth of a teaspoon of honey.

5. Honeybees have six legs, four wings, and five eyes (two large compound eyes on either side of their head as well as three simple light-detecting eyes in the center).

GIVE IT A
>> GO!
If you want to help out the bee population, plant flowers or plants in your yard that are native to your area and are a variety of shapes and colors. Make sure there are plants blooming during each season, so there's always nectar and pollen for the bees to eat, and only use natural pesticides.

89
Have Empathy.

You practice empathy **when you put yourself in someone else's shoes,** when you think about how it would feel to be them and **experience what they're experiencing.**

You can **practice empathy during happy times**—how would it feel to win the class presidential election?—**and hard times**—how would it feel to be left out of a game at recess?

If someone in your life is going through a hard time, **think about what it might feel like** to be them right now. If you were going through something similar, **what might brighten your spirits or make you feel less alone?**

Even **animals** appear to be capable of **feeling** and **expressing empathy for one another.** In fact, a recent study done at Emory University in the United States found that when one prairie vole was **exposed to stress,** another prairie vole would often **comfort** and **console** them by grooming them. Aww!

223

Share your skills.

90

EVERYONE'S good at *something.*

What's your *special skill?*
KNITTING?
SINGING?
TELLING JOKES?

Think of ways to USE YOUR SKILLS and TALENTS to *help other people,* or at the very least *bring a smile to their face.*

91
Celebrate
EVERYTHING.

Celebrate holidays, celebrate birthdays, celebrate days of the week that end in "y." Celebrate little things, celebrate big things, and celebrate everything in between.

"The more you celebrate your life, the more there is in life to celebrate." —Oprah Winfrey

Don't SWEAT the SMALL STUFF.

92

Hey, stuff happens. It's **absolutely OK** to feel sad or mad or frustrated when it seems things **aren't going your way.**

But, **even when times are tough,** it's still possible to **feel thankful.**

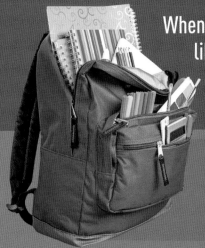

When something happens that gets you feeling like, *Woe is me!*, **think about how things could be worse,** then **be grateful they're not.** For example:

- You forgot your homework at home. → **It could be worse!** → Your teacher **could have said** you'd receive a 0, **but** instead you get to bring it in tomorrow for partial credit.

- You got mud all over your new shoes. → **It could be worse!** → You **could have** slipped in the mud and been covered head to toe (**plus**, you can probably wash the shoes).

- You broke your brother's fidget spinner. → **It could be worse!** → You **could have** broken his computer or his game console, which would have been **a lot** more expensive to fix.

Take a minute to be **thankful** that things **aren't worse.**
Things are **looking up** already!

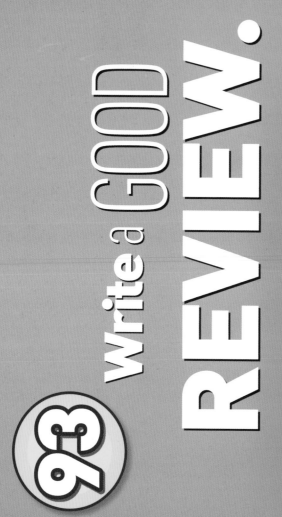

93

Write a GOOD REVIEW.

If you've had a great experience somewhere, like at a restaurant, store, or a cool museum, tell the owners, managers, or staff about your positive experience. Write a nice note on a comment card, send them an e-mail, or even ask your parents to help you write an online review.

231

DAYDREAM.

94

232

233

95

ORGANIZE A TRASH
CLEANUP.

SHOW YOUR **APPRECIATION** FOR THE PLACES YOU **ENJOY** BY GATHERING A GROUP AND **PICKING UP TRASH** THERE. (DON'T FORGET TO **WEAR GLOVES!**)

96

Appreciate Life's Many Surprises.

LIFE has a way of *KEEPING YOU ON YOUR TOES.*

You NEVER KNOW what's around the **next corner.**

It might be a **wild adventure,** a *FUN* new *FRIENDSHIP,*

or a **life-changing** *OPPORTUNITY. EVERY* new day has the

POTENTIAL for all sorts of **surprising** *TWISTS* and *TURNS.*

236

Be DAZZLED by BEAUTIFUL

Whether they're the as-big-as-your-head roses growing in your neighbor's garden, a rainbow patch of wildflowers brightening the side of the highway, or one lone dandelion growing up from a crack in the sidewalk, take a moment to stop and appreciate little bits of beautiful wherever they may be.

And, while you're at it, check out these three kooky blooms.

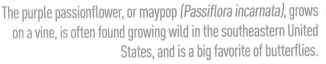

The purple passionflower, or maypop *(Passiflora incarnata)*, grows on a vine, is often found growing wild in the southeastern United States, and is a big favorite of butterflies.

The monkey face orchid *(Dracula simia)* is found in the forests of Ecuador and smells like oranges.

The happy alien flower *(Calceolaria uniflora)*, also known as Darwin's slipper, is found in South America and was discovered by Charles Darwin.

239

98

BE IN AWE.

The world is breathtaking. Life is incredible. Your capacity to do amazing things is big and real and awesome. Don't forget to sit still every once in a while and wonder at it all.

99 PAY IT

One **COOL WAY** to show your **GRATITUDE** for a good deed someone does for you is by **PAYING IT FORWARD**, or performing the same, or a similar, good deed for **SOMEONE ELSE**.

FORWARD.

For example, if someone loans you a pencil in class, to PAY IT FORWARD, you would bring an extra pencil the next day to loan to someone who doesn't have one. Or, if someone teaches you how to beat a level on your video game or how to jump double Dutch, to PAY IT FORWARD, you would teach someone else.

PAYING IT FORWARD *is a great way to keep the* GOOD GRATITUDE VIBES *flowing.*

100

Take This
Thankful
QUIZ.

If ever you're having trouble coming up with reasons to be thankful, hopefully this quiz will prompt some new ideas. Just grab a piece of paper and jot down your answers.

1.
Something **silly**
I'm grateful for is
_____.

5.
Someone I am
grateful for at school
is _____.

9.
I am **getting
better** at
_____.

13.
My favorite
smell is
_____.

17.
I **feel my best**
when I
_____.

2. _____ and _____ make me feel **cozy.**	**3.** I get **so happy** when I see _____.	**4.** The **best part** of my day today was _____.
6. My **favorite subject** to study is _____.	**7.** I really want to **know more** about _____.	**8.** One part of my **body** that is working well is _____.
10. I am **proud** that I _____.	**11.** I love **spending** **time** with _____.	**12.** _____ makes me **laugh.**
14. My **favorite** **food** is _____.	**15.** I am **looking** **forward** to _____.	**16.** My **favorite spot** in (or outside of) my house is _____.
18. I would like to **visit** _____.	**19.** My favorite **family** **tradition** is _____.	**20.** Something I love about this **season** is _____.

We asked **National Geographic Kids** readers what they were **THANKFUL FOR,** and here are just a **few** of the many responses:

"I am thankful that people are aware of global warming and endangered animals, and want to do something about it."

"I'm thankful for clean water, because I know others don't always have it."

"I am thankful to live in a country that supports different views and opinions and gives the people a voice."

"FOOOOOODDD!"

246

247

WAYS TO BE THANKFUL

Give it up for all the great things in your life! There's so much to appreciate and celebrate. Check out this list of 100 ways you can put thankfulness into practice. Which one do you like doing the most? Can you think of any others?

1. Make time for belly laughs.
2. Keep a gratitude journal.
3. Use your imagination.
4. Appreciate all the amazing things your body can do.
5. Take care of your body.
6. Do what you can to make the world a better place.
7. Take good care of your pets!
8. Show your family you love them.
9. Take stock of what you do have.
10. Have a party for pizza!
11. Pay attention to your breath.
12. Be aware of your impact on the planet.
13. Love something? Learn more about its history.
14. Honor your wild ideas.
15. Take pleasure in little things.
16. Marvel at rainbows.
17. Treasure friends who just get you.
18. And treasure friends who challenge you.
19. Thank your lucky stars for cute things.
20. Jump at the chance to travel.
21. Curb the complaining.
22. Thank someone from your past.
23. Think of something you're looking forward to.
24. Turn up the music!
25. Be still.
26. Think about the best part of your day. Then share it with your family.
27. Marvel at science.
28. Follow your curiosity.
29. Learn to savor.
30. Make a gratitude pledge.
31. Get cozy.
32. Smile.
33. Treasure awesome teachers.
34. Go on adventures.
35. Celebrate all the ways you're unique!
36. Look up and admire the sky.
37. Find fun in not-so-fun tasks.
38. Introduce yourself to new kids at school.
39. Tune in to your senses.
40. Make the most of this moment.
41. Practice random acts of kindness.
42. Say "Hello" and "Goodbye."
43. Do a victory dance!
44. Make the most of your weekends.

45. Stop and smell the roses, and the cookies, and the fresh-cut grass.
46. Love.
47. Cherish the changing of the seasons.
48. Make a gratitude jar.
49. Get out into nature.
50. Take care of your things.
51. Practice mindfulness.
52. Rejoice in snow days!
53. Catch (and release) fireflies.
54. Play.
55. Embrace boredom.
56. Look in the mirror and find something you like.
57. Sit down for breakfast.
58. Treasure the stories your family tells again and again.
59. Be part of the solution.
60. Be a bookworm.
61. Learn more about your family's history.
62. Look for a lesson in struggles.
63. Celebrate today.
64. And celebrate that tomorrow is a new day.
65. Bask in bubble baths.
66. Be a wild animal advocate.
67. Always say "Thank you."
68. Write a fan letter.
69. Savor a scoop (or two or three) of ice cream.
70. Learn more about other people and celebrate what makes us different and the same.
71. Get to know your unique point of view.
72. And get to know the unique point of view of others.
73. Get lost in space.
74. Volunteer.
75. Train yourself to see beauty everywhere.
76. Be amazed by your brain (and your ability to change it).
77. Find awesome role models.
78. Admire art.
79. Be a good listener.
80. Try your best not to waste.
81. Celebrate sunshine.
82. And revel in the rain.
83. Make someone a homemade gift.
84. Speak up for those in need.
85. When you have more than you need—share.
86. Celebrate other people's achievements.
87. Seek out—then share—stuff that makes you smile.
88. Give thanks to unsung heroes! Like bees!
89. Have empathy.
90. Share your skills.
91. Celebrate everything.
92. Don't sweat the small stuff.
93. Write a good review.
94. Daydream.
95. Organize a trash cleanup.
96. Appreciate life's many surprises.
97. Be dazzled by beautiful flowers.
98. Be in awe.
99. Pay it forward.
100. Take this thankful quiz.

INDEX

Boldface indicates illustrations. If illustrations are included within a page span, the entire span is **boldface**.

Find Out More

Grab a parent and visit these websites for more information!

1. natgeokids.com
2. HispanicFederation.org
3. HeForShe.org
4. LeBronJamesFamilyFoundation.org
5. Malala.org

PHOTO CREDITS

**For my best friend and sister, Alison, for
who I am so very thankful. —L.M.G.**

Since 1888, the National Geographic Society has funded more
than 12,000 research, exploration, and preservation projects
around the world. The Society receives funds from National
Geographic Partners, LLC, funded in part by your purchase.
A portion of the proceeds from this book supports this vital
work. To learn more, visit natgeo.com/info.

For more information, visit nationalgeographic.com, call
1-800-647-5463, or write to the following address:

National Geographic Partners
1145 17th Street N.W.
Washington, D.C. 20036-4688 U.S.A.

Visit us online at nationalgeographic.com/books

For librarians and teachers: ngchildrensbooks.org

More for kids from National Geographic: natgeokids.com

National Geographic Kids magazine inspires children to explore
their world with fun yet educational articles on animals, science, nature, and more. Using fresh storytelling and amazing
photography, *Nat Geo Kids* shows kids ages 6 to 14 the fascinating truth about the world—and why they should care.
kids.nationalgeographic.com/subscribe

For information about special discounts for bulk purchases,
please contact National Geographic Books Special Sales:
specialsales@natgeo.com

For rights or permissions inquiries, please contact
National Geographic Books Subsidiary Rights:
bookrights@natgeo.com

Designed by Rose Gowsell-Pattison

The publisher would like to thank the team who helped make
this book possible: Ariane Szu-Tu, editor; Lori Epstein, photo
director; Callie Broaddus, art director; Molly Reid, production
editor; and Gus Tello and Anne LeongSon, design production
assistants.

Library of Congress Cataloging-in-Publication Data
Names: Gerry, Lisa, author.
Title: 100 ways to be thankful / Lisa M. Gerry.
Other titles: One hundred ways to be thankful
Description: Washington, DC : National Geographic Kids, 2019.
| Audience: Age: 8-12. | Audience: Grade 4 to 6.
Identifiers: LCCN 2018036047| ISBN 9781426332753
    (paperback) | ISBN 9781426332760 (hardcover)
Subjects: LCSH: Gratitude--Juvenile literature. | BISAC:
    JUVENILE NONFICTION / Social Issues / Values & Virtues. |
    JUVENILE NONFICTION / Social Issues / Manners &
    Etiquette. | JUVENILE NONFICTION / Body, Mind & Spirit.
Classification: LCC BF575.G68 G47 2019 | DDC 179.9--dc23
LC record available at https://lccn.loc.gov/2018036047

Printed in China
18/PPS/1